Contents

THE PRACTICE OF CRITICAL DISCOURSE ANALYSIS

AN INTRODUCTION

Meriel Bloor & Thomas Bloor

Hodder Arnold

A MEMBER OF THE HODDER HEADLINE GROUP

First published in Great Britain in 2007 by
Hodder Education, a member of the Hodder Headline Group,
338 Euston Road, London NW1 3BH

www.hoddereducation.co.uk

Distributed in the United States of America by
Oxford University Press Inc.
198 Madison Avenue, New York, NY10016

British Library Cataloguing in Publication Data
A catalogue record for this book is available from the British Library

Library of Congress Cataloging-in-Publication Data
A catalog record for this book is available from the Library of Congress

ISBN-10: 0 340 91237 5
ISBN-13: 978 0 340 91237 9

1 2 3 4 5 6 7 8 9 10

Typeset in 10/12 pts Berling Roman by Charon Tec Ltd (A Macmillan Company), Chennai, India
www.charontec.com
Printed and bound in Malta

What do you think about this book? Or any other Hodder
Education title? Please send your comments to the feedback
section on www.hoddereducation.com.

Acknowledgements

We are indebted to Teun van Dijk for generous support in the initial and interme-diate stages and for advice and practical assistance; also to Malcolm Coulthard for substantial help with Chapter 10. Our thanks also go to Imogen Bloor for medical expertise and critical input to Chapter 9; to Helen Basturkmen for permission to use her research data; to Penny Vevers for sharing her knowledge of the news media; and to Hilary Nesi and Tim Kelly for access to the BASE corpus (and Hilary for additional help). We are grateful to Carmen Caldas-Coulthard, Ian Duffield, Sheena Gardner, Keith Richards, and Ben Mills for valuable information and to anonymous reviewers of our initial proposal for sound advice. We are, of course, responsible for surviving faults. We would also like to thank our supportive desk editor, Bianca Knights, and our indefatigable copy editor, Susan Dunsmore.

1 Background and theory

Social action and discourse are inextricably linked.

(Scollon 2001)

1.1 This book and how to use it

This book is designed to provide a general introduction to the study of discourse and the practice of Critical Discourse Analysis (CDA). It introduces the social concerns of the discipline, and gradually introduces a range of techniques that are available to the critical discourse analyst. It seeks to develop readers' awareness of language and ideology and provides practice in analytic skills applied to various types of discourse. We hope that those who read this book will become more sensitive to the role of discourse as a controlling force in society and have a deeper understanding of the way language is used to persuade and manipulate both individuals and social groups. We hope that readers of this book will feel more able to question their own roles as participants in conventional discourses and thus to engage effectively in discourses that work towards social justice.

In this first chapter, we give an overview of the field in general, introduce some technical terms, and give some indication of the development of the field.

Each chapter focuses on a different aspect of critical discourse analysis. Most chapters include an introduction to social issues of interest to discourse analysts, some examples of analysis, and some discussion of theory. Each chapter presupposes an understanding of what has come in earlier in the book, so students may prefer to read each chapter in sequence.

Towards the end of each chapter there are *Activities*, with suggestions for discussions, and practice in analysis. Finally, there is a section called *Further study* with suggestions for extra reading. To make the book easier to follow, we do not normally give references to other CDA work in the chapters themselves. Where we discuss other people's research or use examples from it, we refer the readers to the sources in notes or in the *Further study* section.

Most technical terms are explained and illustrated as they are introduced. However, in case a technical term is not clear, a *glossary* and a short grammatical *appendix* at the end of the book have been provided.

1.2 The multidisciplinary nature of CDA

The word *discourse* itself has a number of complex uses, which are introduced later in this chapter, but for now we will use it to mean symbolic human interaction in its many forms, whether directly through spoken or written language or via gesture, pictures, diagrams, films, or music. In this book, the focus is on language with occasional references to gesture and pictures, but that is not because we see other types of discourse as less significant.

Where critical analysis has focused on the linguistic aspects of discourse, it has also been known as Critical Linguistics or Critical Linguistic Analysis (see Fowler et al, 1979). Because of the wide range of influences from different areas of study – not simply linguistic – the field is also known as Critical Discourse Studies. In this book, we make use of close analysis of texts, including functional linguistic analysis in some cases, but in addition we consider broader issues such as the social context of discourse, the role of discourse in social practices, and the function of specific texts. For these reasons, we have chosen to refer to the field, in the main, as CDA.

The branch of linguistics we use from time to time in this book is known as Systemic Functional Linguistics (SFL). This branch of grammar stresses the importance of social context (the context of culture and the context of situation) in the production and development of language, both historically and in terms of meaning in individual discourse events. In addition, functional linguistics, unlike some branches of linguistics, has always been concerned not only with words and sentences, but also with longer texts and collections of texts (corpora) above the level of the sentence.

However, linguistic methods are not the only methods used in CDA and we recognize the strengths that can come from a multidisciplinary approach. The aims and objectives of linguistics differ from the aims of CDA. Linguists, in general, are concerned with the way in which language or discourse 'works', and their interest is in language for its own sake. Critical discourse analysts, on the other hand, are interested in the way in which language and discourse are used to achieve social goals and in the part this use plays in social maintenance and change.

This means that CDA shares interests – and sometimes methods – with disciplines that study social groups and social structures, such as anthropology, sociology, ethnography and ethnomethodology, and with disciplines that are concerned with human cognition and behaviour, such as cognitive and social psychology. In its methods, CDA also draws heavily on literary theory, and the philosophy of language and communication, particularly on work on speech acts and conversational maxims, which we return to later. Sociolinguistics has been influential in CDA, and many of those currently working in CDA are (or have been) sociolinguists.

These methods include: (1) context analysis (see Chapter 2); (2) observational techniques, such as ways of recording and transcribing natural language; (3) participant observation where the researcher has (or takes up) a role in the target discourse community in order to study the discourse processes; and (4) the use of informants, such as experts in particular fields, to explain or interpret what is happening in the target community with respect to its discourse practices.

In recent years, professionals from a variety of backgrounds have become interested in discourse issues. Historians, business institutions, lawyers, politicians and medical professionals, to name but a few, have used discourse analysis to investigate social problems relating to their work. Van Dijk (1997a), who prefers the term Critical Discourse Studies (CDS) for this reason, described it as 'A new cross-discipline that comprises the analysis of text and talk in virtually all disciplines of the humanities and social sciences.'

A frequently reported example is the analysis of doctor–patient discourse; another is forensic linguistics, which investigates legal and police discourse. CDA examines practices and customs in society both to discover and describe how they work and also to provide a critique of those practices. To do this, it is necessary to try to understand, from one's analysis: (1) what is going on in an event; and (2) whether it maintains the existing social structure or is likely to change or revise it. CD analysts identify and study specific areas of injustice, danger, suffering, prejudice, and so on, even though the identification of such areas can be contentious. While it is now widely accepted that many social problems arise from the injudicious use of language or other forms of communication, it is an open question how far beneficial effects can result from intervention in discourses alone. In this book, however, we take the view that CDA can help to raise awareness and point people in the direction of change.

1.3 Some examples of CDA practice

As a simple illustration, it is commonly recognized that we can be influenced, and sometimes misled, by persuasive language in the form of advertising or persistent marketing, much of which may distort the truth in subtle ways. The study of such texts is a legitimate and common area for CDA to engage in. Some of this work has focused on visual representation, some on written or spoken discourse and some on the complementary nature of the visual and the verbal. Awareness of the means used by advertisers can empower individuals to resist pressure to buy goods they may not need or even want. We return to this topic in Chapter 9.

Another set of social problems that we all recognize concerns issues in criminality. These include the identification of criminals, police interviewing techniques, confessions, and cross-examination in court. Forensic linguistics, as it is known, is an established branch of CDA. Work in forensic linguistics, which has involved the co-operation of police, lawyers, and others involved in the legal process, has been productive in establishing justice in specific cases and fairer practices in general. We return to this topic in Chapter 10.

It is worth noting that some social problems are particularly difficult to analyse and are better investigated by teams in which a discourse analyst works co-operatively with other professionals and the subjects of the study. For example, we can observe, often in our own homes, that families can develop aggressive speech styles, which then become habitual. These can be transmitted to the children who then use aggressive speech styles in a wider social context, such as a school playground. This can make it difficult for them to form viable friendships and can result in bullying either by others or by themselves. A critical discourse analyst would need to study such a family in some depth in order to reach any conclusions about how the situation could be improved. This could involve observation to identify the situations in the home where aggression is displayed, recordings of the conversations that ensue, further studies of the children outside the home, and so on. CDA could discover a great deal about what was going on in such a situation, but, in order to enact change, other professionals would need to be involved – perhaps child psychologists, social workers and certainly, of course, the teachers. For this reason, there is great scope for CDA as part of team research.

Which method or combination of methods is chosen depends on the choice of research question. This, in turn, depends partly on the nature of the social problem and partly on the disciplinary background of the analyst. Both these factors will influence the choice or combination of methods.

In this book, we refer to different types of analysis, ranging from the analysis of context, to the analysis of attitudes, stance and opinion and to the ways in which messages are carried and meaning is constructed in context. We see the immediate social context as inextricably linked to the discourse and the meaning as inextricably linked to the wording.

1.4 Matters of principle

In recent years there has been considerable discussion to establish the principles of CDA and to propose research goals for the discipline. Here we mention just a few of the principles that have been proposed.

Discourse analysts, in fact, all social researchers, are themselves tied to the discourse group they are investigating, either as members of the same social group or as observers of it. Often, the researcher holds similar beliefs and attitudes to the participants in the discourse that is under analysis. For this reason, they need to be highly critical of their own roles in the social structure and be prepared to make clear their own position with respect to the topic of research. The critical discourse analyst does not attempt the type of objectivity that is sometimes claimed by scientists or linguists, but recognizes that such objectivity is likely to be impossible because of the nature of their experience. Instead, they are critical of and open about their own position.

Ethical practice is essential. Observation and recording of social behaviour can be an extremely sensitive matter. Proper permission must be sought, and issues regarding the privacy of individuals or named institutions must be carefully considered. This is particularly so in cases where publication is involved.

Most critical discourse analysts tolerate varied approaches. The discipline is relatively new and, as we have suggested above, contributions both to theory and practice come from an indefinite number of sources. What is more, it is a truly *international* project with contributions from many countries and many cultures. For this reason, it is difficult at the present time to define the boundaries of CDA as a discipline.

Some have identified crucial areas of social change where CDA can play a part. For example, Teun van Dijk's research focuses on racism, Norman Fairclough is working on issues relating to global capitalism (or 'new capitalism'), and Robert de Beaugrande is presently largely concerned with ecological issues.[1]

Central to CDA is the understanding that discourse is an integral aspect of power and control. Power is held by both institutions and individuals in contemporary society and any challenge to the status quo challenges those who hold power. Thus a commitment to 'social equality, fairness and justice' is itself a challenge to those who are responsible for maintaining the inequalities, unfairness and injustice in contemporary society and must be of major concern to those who challenge the status quo.

The word 'critical' can sometimes be misleading. In its popular use, it is often used for a negative evaluation as in 'The chair of the governors is really critical of the head teacher', meaning that the chair thinks the head is not successfully running the school. In CDA, it is used more with the sense of *critique*, meaning that analysis may, on occasion, be directed towards a positive outcome, such as investigations of successful resistance texts (like those written during the anti-racial discrimination movements in the USA in the 1960s).

1.5 Language and institutions

Much social practice in complex modern society is institutionalized. Business, government, education, the law, for example, are essentially verbal. Sometimes, of course, communication in institutions also depends on pictorial, iconic or diagrammatic representation, and any face-to-face interaction involves facial expression, gesture and reference to the non-verbal, such as pointing to objects or pictures.

When we look at the highly structured organizations that hold most power and that control the way we live and influence the way we think, we can see that language is an integral part of that control. In some cases, it may be the very existence of certain types of social practice or the existence – or non-existence – of certain texts (say, for example, immigration regulations) that is of interest to critical discourse analysts.

If we try to think critically about how we use the languages we know, either in intimate social events or in larger structures, it is useful to have training in what some scholars have called 'making strange'. That is to say, in being able to observe what is going on in a way that an alien studying our planet might do. Often we are so familiar with a custom that we find it unremarkable until we contrast it with customs from other places and other times. We say that it has become *normalized*.

Take the case of weddings or funerals. These are relatively straightforward institutional practices that are well established and may date back in their present form for hundreds of years. Almost all cultures have some kind of ritualistic ceremony for such major life events as birth or naming, marriage and death. These may or not involve a religious aspect. Those ceremonies with which we are familiar seem normal while others seem odd – or even disgusting – unless we can see them, as it were, through the eyes of those who practise them.

Yet sometimes even old-established practices change. These may happen because we are enabled to look at our own ceremonies as though we were strangers or it may happen because other social changes lead us to question the status quo. An example can be given from the traditional marriage ceremony of the Church of England. For hundreds of years, English brides made a promise that differed from the one made by the bridegroom. The man was required to agree that he would marry the woman and live with her. He also had to promise 'to love her, comfort her, honour and keep her in sickness and in health'. The woman was required to make the same promises but *in addition* she had to promise 'to obey him and serve him'. Interestingly, these promises were also made in many secular marriages conducted in registry offices by marrying couples who were not necessarily of the same faith or indeed of any faith.

Gradually, in the second half of the twentieth century, many women became aware of the enormity of this inequality, which had been enshrined in the written version of the marriage ceremony dating back hundreds of years, and they refused to make the extra promise to obey and serve their husbands. This led to much more flexibility in the wording of the ceremony, first in secular marriages and more recently even in church weddings. Whether you consider this change to be an improvement depends on your social position, but overall most couples seem to agree that it was a change for the better. No doubt there are a few traditionalists who still cling to the original wording.

Something which has become normalized can be changed – for better or worse – which is why this principle of 'making strange' is important to discourse analysts in all aspects of their work.

Another example relates not just to the use of a particular wording but to the grammar itself. From the middle of the nineteenth century until relatively recently, it was considered 'correct' practice in English to use 'he' and 'him' as singular pronouns to stand in place of sex-indefinite nouns. So, if we were talking or writing about an author, artist, doctor, teacher, director, or bank manager and we did not know whether the person in question was a man or a woman, we would refer to that person with the pronoun 'he' or 'him'. This usage was taught in schools and expounded by grammarians. But, even at that time, the use of 'they' as a singular gender-free pronoun was fairly common in spoken English, but published written English followed the grammarian's prescriptive code.[2] The only exceptions were when the job or activity involved was one that at that time was normally done only by a woman, such as *nurse*. For some women's jobs, even the nouns were marked for gender as in *maid, waitress, actress*. Although it was often observed by grammarians that 'he' was gender-free in cases such as this (whimsically expressed as 'male embraces female'), the pronoun system reflected a social situation where most of the powerful and creative jobs were done by men. For a long time some women objected to this pronoun use, but it was only as more and more women held jobs traditionally done by men, and vice versa, that there was a sufficiently large group of objectors for the situation to begin to change. Now, it has become generally acceptable for the gender-free 'they' to be used as a singular as well as a plural pronoun, or as an alternative to the use of 'he or she'.

1.6 Some basic terms and tools

Discourse

The word *discourse* has come to be used with a number of different senses. Through lack of other terms, we have to use the word with quite a few senses. Unfortunately, this is unavoidable in a book of this type. Probably the best method of grasping the differences between them is just to read on and get used to the ways in which the word is used. Here, though, we give some indication of the main uses of the word:

1. In its broadest sense, 'discourse' refers to all the phenomena of symbolic interaction and communication between people, usually through spoken or written language or visual representation. Thus, we can talk about *human discourse*, the *study of discourse*, and so on.

2. The term has been used to indicate simply *spoken* interaction. This meaning of the term has a long history; *The Shorter Oxford English Dictionary* refers to its use in 1559 to mean 'communication of thought by speech, talk, conversation'.

Nowadays, we normally use the term in the more general sense to include written discourse. Of course, where necessary, we can specify *spoken discourse* as distinct from *written discourse.*

3. 'Discourse' is sometimes used in contrast with 'text', where 'text' refers to actual written or spoken data, and 'discourse' refers to the whole act of communication involving production *and* comprehension, not necessarily entirely verbal. (Text is discussed further below.) The study of discourse, then, can involve matters like context, background information or knowledge shared between a speaker and hearer.

4. 'Discourse' is frequently used to refer to the general communication that takes place in specific institutional contexts. For example, we can talk about *the discourse of science, legal discourse*, and so on. This is useful shorthand, but, of course, it is an abstract concept that does not bear much relationship to individual communicative events since each of these discourses is realized in different ways depending on the situations involved. Thus the discourse of science includes many types of interaction, including lectures, research reports, theoretical discussions, to name but a few. Similarly, legal discourse embraces actual written laws, statutes, contracts, wills, conventional courtroom exchanges, cross-examination, and so on.

5. 'Discourse' is sometimes used (*a discourse*) to mean a particular text (written or spoken), usually a fairly long treatment of a subject, such as a lecture, sermon or treatise, as in *a discourse on ethics.* You will not find this meaning of the term in this book although it is still current in some academic contexts.

6. *Multi-modal discourse* refers to discourse which relies on more than one mode of communication. A great deal of discourse relies on multi-modal resources, particularly as modern technology enables us to access visual information so easily. For example, a magazine might make use of words, photographs and drawings; a science textbook might incorporate written text with diagrams; a film uses both pictures, words and music to transmit its messages.

Text

Text is a product of discourse. It is normally used to describe a linguistic record ('a text') of a communicative event. This may be an electronic recording or a written text, which may or may not incorporate visual materials or, in the case of an electronic text, music. Beaugrande and Dressler (1981) proposed that a text as a meaningful speech event will meet seven standards of textuality: *cohesion* (the ways the words are connected in sequence); *coherence* (the outcome of cognitive relations, such as mutual knowledge – discussed below – between the participants in the discourse); *acceptability* (the form of the text in terms of appropriateness to the cultural setting and the way in which it is received by those taking part); *intentionality* (the text producers' discourse purpose, goals or plan); *informativity* (how far the degree of information transmitted is more or less suitable for the receivers in the circumstances); *situationality* or relevance (the factors which make a text relevant to the situation in which it occurs); and *intertextuality* (the way in which a text relies on previous texts for its form and references and the ways in which it may incorporate other texts).

Domain

'Discourse domain' is the term for a socially recognized context within which the discourse takes place. If we talk of scientific discourse, 'science' is the domain. However, this is a very broad domain, which may not be much use at the actual level of analysis. A domain may have a narrower focus and embrace, say, the social setting in which the discourse takes place. Thus offices, universities, and places of worship along with their recognized structures may be seen as domains. The media may be seen as a domain, but the critical discourse analyst is more likely to be concerned with discourse from a more specific domain such as the BBC or *The New York Herald*. Within a domain there are certain recognized social practices and conventional *genres*.

Social practice

People within specific domains engage in *social practices*. Technically, these people are often referred to as *actors*. Social practices are human behaviours which involve following certain socially established conventions (some might say 'rules') within which the actors have some degree of individual freedom and opportunities for unique behaviour. Examples of social practices include *business meetings, religious services, birthday parties*, and so on. Most social practices involve knowledge of linguistic and discoursal conventions in whole or in part. For example, in a religious service, one may need to know where to stand, kneel or sit as well as something of the verbal conventions (prayers, for example). The knowledge and skills required to engage in social practices are part of socially shared knowledge. They may have been 'picked up' through experience or contact with other actors or they may have been learned via specific instruction within the home environment or as part of education or training. Although social practices are often well established and persistent within a particular culture, they are rarely 'frozen' and unchanging. One instance of a social practice is a *social event*, which when language-based (such as a committee meeting) is also known as a *speech event*.

Genre

'Genre' is the term used for a specific product of a social practice. It is a form of discourse, culturally recognized, which, more or less, obeys socially agreed structures. The term is well known in literary and film studies, from which it has been borrowed by discourse analysts. Examples of literary and linguistic genres are novels, poems, university lectures, biology lab reports, letters, theatre reviews. Genres can be classified crudely or more delicately – so the genre *letter* could be sub-categorized into, say, *business correspondence, letter to the editor, friendly letter, love letter*, each having its own format and stylistic characteristics. The genre of *poem* could be sub-categorized into *sonnet, ballad, epic*, and so on. 'Genre' is also sometimes used as a term for social events that use regular linguistic and discoursal patterns, such as *committee meeting*, and thus, to some extent, can overlap with the term *social practice*. Genres can also be seen from the point of view of the institutions within which they evolved. Thus *minutes of meetings, annual reports, business correspondence* are associated with business institutions; *lectures, seminars, tutorials, textbooks, notes, essays*, and *examination papers* are associated with educational institutions. Swales (1990: Chapter 3) described *genre* as a socially recognized, recurrent, culturally defined speech event. Genres have their own formal characteristics which can be identified, described, and taught.

Speech community and discourse community

The term *speech community* has been used in different ways by linguists and anthropologists, and is not without its problems. It is generally used to refer to a group of speakers who share common features of language because they frequently interact with each other. An example might be the people of a certain geographical region or social group that share a common dialect of a language. Thus, in Britain we find that most people born and brought up in Newcastle upon Tyne and the surrounding area tend to speak with a particular regional dialect known popularly as Geordie, although for any individual this might be modified by many social or individual factors. However, the term *speech community* has also been used for all speakers of a language, such as English or Japanese, regardless of where they were born or live. Most people in the world today are members of more than one social group and switch speech styles and even languages at different times depending on who they are with or what they are engaged in. These factors have led to some uncertainty in the use of the term. We cannot resolve the conflicting uses of this term, except to say that anyone using the term should make clear precisely how they are using it.

Children who attend a certain school might share a particular style of speech – perhaps including certain slang expressions, but, in their own homes with their family, they may use a different style of speech or even a different language.

The boundaries of social groups are often debatable. Someone may claim the existence of a social group where another would deny that it exists, either because it has too few members or because its boundaries cannot be defined. As far as a speech community is concerned, it would be necessary to establish that the members of the group shared not only certain characteristic behaviours and social constraints, but also speech styles. Thus, while some might, rightly or wrongly, recognize a specific ethnic or gender group as a social community, it would not necessarily be the case that they would form a speech community (and still less a discourse community).

The term *discourse community* is an extension of this idea to refer to communities where the people concerned may meet frequently or rarely or sometimes not at all, but still communicate and develop specific discourses. Traditionally, these have often been professional, business or academic communities, such as medical researchers, scientists, or managers of multinational companies, who read the same reports or journals, publish in the same journals, write letters to each other, and so on. There are also communities of people who share the same hobbies or interests. With the development of technology, we now have internet communities (or *virtual communities*) such as on-line chat groups, fan clubs, and so on. As well as being members of a speech community, many of us are additionally members of discourse communities.

One major difference between a discourse community and a speech community is the degree of conscious participation that takes place. We usually become members of a speech community as an accident of where we were born or happened to find ourselves. With a discourse community, on the other hand, we may choose to become members by application or invitation, often because we have had a certain type of education, qualification or training. Another difference is that members of a discourse community broadly agree about their common goals or interests and about their means of interaction. This results in the development of specialist genres within that community.

Speech acts

Speech act theory originated in the work of the philosopher Austin in the 1950s (published 1972). He observed that, in certain contexts, utterances can perform 'illocutionary acts', not simply report on facts or give information. We can use language to make a promise, give an instruction, name a ship, marry someone, or make a bet, and so on. A speech act may be interpreted by the listener as a different act from that intended by the speaker, but usually we understand from our knowledge of a social situation what act is taking place. For example, if you are sitting near to an open window and a friend says, 'It's freezing in here', you might well not interpret this as a simple comment on the weather but rather as an intended instruction to close the window. Philosophy has also provided us with answers to the question of how we 'pick up' culturally on the meaning of a speech act, which may appear to an outsider to say something completely different. This is further discussed in Chapter 2.

Participants and social roles

The *participants*[3] are those persons who are engaged in a specific act of discourse. These may be *speakers*, *listeners*, *readers*, *writers* and each will be playing a social role. The term *role* is used much as it is in drama where an actor plays a role in a film or dramatic production. Most of us are called on to play many roles in our normal everyday life. For example, take a man named Ahmed. At home, he is a husband and father but, during his working day, he is an architect. He is also the accountant of the local tennis club where, on Saturday mornings, he acts as an umpire. In each of these roles he is engaged in different social practices, is likely to use different genres and the language associated with those practices and genres. When he is being a dad, he behaves like a dad and sounds like a dad, when he is being an umpire, he looks like an umpire and sounds like an umpire, and so on in every role. And yet, at the same time, he is always himself.

Ideology

We can gloss *ideology* as a set of beliefs or attitudes shared by members of a particular social group. As critical discourse analysts, it is important to be aware that most discourse used by members of a group tends to be ideologically based. However, the beliefs or attitudes that stem from ideology may not always be held consciously by individuals. They can be so deeply ingrained in our thought patterns and language that we take them for granted as self-evident. Where a belief is held consciously, it is possible to consciously question what it means or even to stand out against it as an individual. However, where it has become a socially imbued unconscious attitude, it is much more difficult to question – even to oneself – and extremely hard to challenge openly in the social arena.

An aspect of ideology can be carried, sometimes inaccurately, by a single word. In many countries in the world today, a shared belief is in *democracy*. It is then easy to make the assumption that *democracy* is the preferred system of government in all places at all times. However, there is more than one kind of democracy and there is at least the possibility of other desirable systems of government. Prime Minister Tony Blair, in a speech to his political party (2005) defending the war in Iraq, said:

> The way to stop the innocent dying is not to retreat, to withdraw, to hand these people over to the religious fanatics, . . . but to stand up for their right to decide their government in the democratic way the British people do.

Blair, here, makes the assumption that British democracy is the most highly valued model for everyone, a view that a British listener might accept without thinking but which does not stand up to close examination when we look at other nations that call themselves 'democratic'. If someone then writes, say, about the breakdown of democracy in a certain state, we are inclined to automatically think that this is a bad thing without questioning what exactly is meant in that particular case.

An ideological position can also be hidden (or at least screened) by the use of words, such as when an act of war is termed 'peacekeeping'. The critical discourse analyst must always be on the lookout for hidden ideological positions since one of the main ways in which CDA achieves its aims is by making explicit those aspects of ideology that underpin social interaction. The process of investigating meaning by breaking it down into its component parts is known as *deconstruction*. We can engage in this process in various ways, but one way is to analyse the grammar and choice of words in a text to reveal the undercurrents of association and implication.

Frames

Frame is a word used to describe a cognitive model that links together separate entities in our mind. Lakoff (2004) defined frames as 'mental structures that shape the way we see the world' and that are triggered by words. They are part of the unconscious mind and operate automatically to help us make sense of the world. A classic example[4] is based on the game of cricket. The expressions *cricket pitch*, *cricket ball*, *cricket bat* are each mentally associated with each other. Anyone who is familiar with the game has a concept ('frame') of how these are related. Any account of the game will use the words *pitch*, *ball* and *bat*. Along with words like *umpire*, *wicket* and *crease* (not preceded by the word 'cricket'), they form a category of things that are related. Cricket, like most cognitive models, is culture specific – baseball players fit *ball* and *bat* into a different frame. Similarly, there are cognitive frames associated with the word *democracy*, which are established in different ways across nations and political parties. Framing is important in CDA because the way we view the world carries cultural messages that become normalized and accepted as everyday common sense. Yet, frames, like values, vary from culture to culture, and they affect the way we view authority, social groups and identity.

The set of frames that is handed down in a culture and that is held in common by members of a group is known as the *archive*. The archive facilitates communication within that group, but makes it more difficult to communicate across groups.

1.7 What makes CDA 'critical'?

As we have said, much of the discourse analysis of the twentieth century was essentially *non-critical*, which is to say that it did not present a critique of social practices. It had three main purposes: (1) to identify and describe how people use language to communicate; (2) to develop methods of analysis that help to reveal the categories (or varieties) of discourse and the essential features of each; and (3) to build theories about how communication takes place.

Although these questions are important, there have always been some discourse analysts with a broader agenda, and gradually their number has increased. They see discourse both as a product of society and also as a dynamic and changing force that is constantly influencing and re-constructing social practices and values, either positively or negatively. In order to approach this broader agenda, they need to address and analyse discourse practices in critical ways, questioning the texts and processes that they study. This requires commitment to social concerns.

Critical discourse analysis has much in common with critical social research, which has been concerned with seeking out the origins of social problems and finding ways to analyse them productively. Many of those involved with CDA see themselves as part of this movement.

It can be quite difficult to extract the aims of CDA as we have done for mainstream discourse analysis. The problems addressed by critical discourse analysts range from those of major international importance (macro issues) to relatively small-scale ones concerning individuals (micro issues). The macro and micro are significantly interrelated and both are equally valid as subjects for analysis. Thus, critical analysis may address general issues such as the verbal representation of ethnic issues or, at the other extreme, the tragedy of a single innocent person who may be unfairly convicted of a crime. Those working in the field differ according to their specific concerns, but are agreed about certain major principles. Moreover, since CDA is a rapidly developing field, new objectives may well arise.

Briefly – and tentatively – then, we propose that the main objectives of *critical discourse analysis* are:

○ to analyse discourse practices that reflect or construct social problems;
○ to investigate how ideologies can become frozen in language and find ways to break the ice;
○ to increase awareness of how to apply these objectives to specific cases of injustice, prejudice, and misuse of power.

To these practical objectives, we can add the more theoretical aims that have been proposed for the subject:

○ to demonstrate the significance of language in the social relations of power;
○ to investigate how meaning is created in context;

❍ to investigate the role of speaker/writer *purpose* and authorial *stance* in the construction of discourse.

Activities

1. Make a list of genres that are associated with the practice of medicine. Remember to include both spoken and written speech events that are socially recognized as taking place regularly.

2. Working, if possible, within a small group, identify the speech communities to which each of you belongs and the discourse communities of which each of you is a member. Which of these do you share with other members of the group?

3. Discuss the meaning of the quotation from Roger Scollon (2001), which was given at the beginning of this chapter: 'Social action and discourse are inextricably linked'. Consider how far action and discourse are linked in a social setting of your choice. You might like to pick a relatively small scale business such as a travel agent's or a restaurant.

4. This activity invites you to engage in an (imaginary) social act and consider its relationship with language and discourse. Imagine you are dissatisfied with some expensive product you have purchased (for example, a computer, a refrigerator, or a camera); what means do you have for complaining?

   Consider whom you would contact (participants in the potential exchange), how you would contact them (possible modes and genres), what responses you would expect, what your intended outcome would be, and how you would hope to achieve it. Consider how you feel with respect to your relationship with the company that produced the product in terms of power relationships. Do you feel in a position of power or weakness?

Further study

For background information on general linguistics, a useful reference book is David Crystal's *The Cambridge Encyclopedia of Language* (1987). This book provides an introduction to many aspects of linguistics and its applications and has a good glossary, index, and list of references.

For reference and extra explanation of some areas, you may wish to consult books on discourse analysis, for example, Gee (1999). Older books covering more foundation topics are de Beaugrande and Dressler (1981), and Coulthard (1977), dealing mainly with spoken interaction. These may not be available new but copies can be found in most university libraries. The seven standards of textuality listed in Section 1.3 are edited from de Beaugrande and Dressler, Chapter 1.

For a good introduction to links between applied linguistics and sociology, read Sealey and Carter (2004), which emphasizes the role of discourse as social action and should be of particular interest to readers interested in language education.

If you would like to read examples of articles on discourse studies, there are various good collections: van Dijk (1997a and 1997b) has articles providing an introduction to the subject. Fairclough and Wodak's (1997) article is especially recommended. Another good collection is Jaworski and Coupland (1999). This book includes work on both general discourse analysis and CDA. In the main, it presents a socially relevant approach to discourse studies. To give you a prior taste of CDA in action, try looking at articles on poverty by Meinhof and Richardson (1994), and Caldas-Coulthard and Coulthard (1996), a collection of research reports in CDA, which includes work on a variety of areas, including racist and gender issues.

Journals that publish CDA research and theory include *Discourse Studies* (Sage Publications), *Critical Discourse Studies* (Routledge) and *Text and Talk* (de Gruyter).

2

Discourse and social context

The force and cogency of most language behaviour derives from the firm grip it has on the ever-recurrent typical situations in the life of social groups.

(Firth 1937: 113)

2.1 Sign, context and meaning

This chapter provides an introduction to the analysis of context, an important aspect of CDA. First, we consider the relationship of *context* to meaning, and then we consider ways of specifying context.

Making meaning

Meaning is created when a sign occurs in a specific context. This is as true of visual symbols as it is of language: a red flag on a lifeguard's pole on a beach has different signification from a red flag held by the supporters of a political party marching at a demonstration. A simple cross (X) can be negative or positive, depending on context. When made on a student's exercise book by a teacher, it can indicate an error, but a cross made by the same teacher on a ballot form in an election may indicate the selection of a candidate. The same punctuation mark in different positions can indicate either (1) the end of a constituent in a sentence, or (2) possession, or (3) the conclusion of reported speech. We give them each a different name (comma, apostrophe, and inverted comma) but the shape of the sign is the same in each case. In conversation, gestures, such as pointing, and facial expressions, such as smiles and frowns, carry meaning. The relationship of sign to meaning is known as *semiosis*, and the study of signs as *semiotics*.

In each of these cases, the choice of the sign and of where and when to put the sign are both governed by human intervention. When we consider language as a carrier of meaning, a more complex picture emerges. Language is often thought of as a system of signs but it is not a simple or straightforward system.

An example of its complexity can be seen in what are known as *performatives*. A performative is an utterance which is itself an act of doing something, or, to put it another way, an act is 'performed' simply by the fact that the words have been spoken. For example, at a certain point in a marriage service, a legally appointed official or a spiritual leader tells the couple, 'I now pronounce you husband and wife' – or the equivalent in the appropriate language. The speaker thus performs the act of marrying the couple. However, if the same words are uttered by an actor in a play to a couple of actors pretending to get married, no marriage actually takes place. The context of the utterance has to be the right one because certain conditions have to be met for the words to function fully as a performative.

A less obvious case is where the emotional impact of an expression differs according to the context in which it is spoken. The words 'I love you' spoken by a mother to a small child carry different connotations from the same words spoken by a young couple to each other; yet they both express positive emotions.

Meaning, sense and reference

There is another important relationship between meaning and context. Read the following sentences to see what you understand:

1. Their parents lent them a credit card.

This sentence is written in words that adult English speakers understand. It is grammatical, and the grammar is not complex. The chances are that most readers will say that, of course, they understand it. They know the meaning of 'parents', 'lent' and 'credit card', they know that 'lent' tells us that the event took place in the past.

And yet, as the sentence is printed in this book, we can have only a limited understanding of it. Presented as it is, as a context-free example, there is lot more information that is needed for a complete understanding of the sentence. First of all, the reader can only guess at who constructed the sentence and why it was spoken or written. The reader cannot tell whose parents are referred to. Who are 'they'?

Moreover, in (1), is the information that their parents lent them a credit card the answer to a question? And if so, did the questioner ask, 'Where did they get the money?' Or, 'What did their parents lend them?' Or some other question? That is to say, what is the *information focus* of the sentence? We can appreciate the information focus only if we know more about the context in which this was uttered (who said it to whom, when and why). We need to know the *function of the utterance*.

We can, of course, invent a context for this sentence. We could create a story with characters and a plot in which the nouns and pronouns referred to actual people and events, but, as it stands, the sentence is only an example, presented here to illustrate features of language, and, except as part of the argument of this book, it stands apart from *discourse*.

Now consider example (2):

2. For now, Bridget was being put through her paces on the island of Tenerife.

In (2) we do not know who Bridget is or why she is on Tenerife. We can guess that she is in training, but we do not know what for. Nor can we know when 'now' was. We say that the sentences (1) and (2) lack *reference* because we are not at all sure who or what is *referred* to.

In this book, however, they *do* have a communicative function – that of *illustration* – because they are illustrating a point in an argument. This has little to do with the *content* of the sentences themselves and everything to do with their *context*.

Their original contexts were very different. Sentence (1) is from a newspaper report about a successful business that belonged to a young couple who had borrowed their start-up money from their parents. Sentence (2), perhaps more surprisingly, is from a report about a vehicle robot, designed to travel on the surface of Mars. She (!) was named Bridget by the scientists and engineers who made her.

Language can properly construct meaning only when it is part of a wider social event. It both needs context and helps create context at the same time. Some philosophers distinguish *meaning* from *sense*, keeping the word 'meaning' for the type of meaning that words and sentences hold inherently (as in the meaning of words listed in a dictionary). They use *sense* for the full discoursal meaning of an utterance in context. However, other philosophers and linguists, particularly those calling themselves functional linguists, currently use the word 'meaning' more broadly to incorporate sense and communicative function as well, as in this book.

In systemic functional linguistics, a language, in an abstract sense, has *meaning potential*, which is to say that the words (lexis) and grammar along with the sound systems of the language are available for us to use to make meaning. The meaning evolves (or is 'unfolded' in Halliday's term) in specific instances within contexts of situation. Thompson (2004: 5–6) makes the point that 'communicating meanings in particular contexts' is seen by most people as the primary function of language.[1]

In the case of spoken discourse, phonology (the sound system of the language, made up of vowels and consonants), intonation and stress, is also important. This close link between grammar and meaning is the reason we see some aspects of linguistic studies as useful in discourse analysis.

2.2 Language in use

Socially shared knowledge

Socially shared knowledge – sometimes known as *mutual knowledge* – is knowledge that is used by participants in a communicative act. We need shared knowledge to communicate even in a one-to-one conversation. Sometimes a speaker assumes a shared understanding which does not exist. In such a case, communication could break down. It may be possible to 'repair' the breakdown by questioning, as in the following invented example where the first speaker assumes that the second speaker has some knowledge of Bridget:

1st speaker: They're sending Bridget to Mars next year.

2nd speaker: Who's Bridget?

1st speaker: Oh, Bridget is that robot with a mobile laboratory.

In this example, the lack of shared information was simply the fact that Bridget was a robot. However, not all knowledge involves subject matter of this type. It can be useful to look at some attempts that have been made to categorize knowledge if only because it helps us to understand the many ways in which communication breakdown can occur when interlocutors lack some knowledge or set of values that they are assumed by others to possess. Although such a 'breakdown' can, of course, be the starting point of negotiation or debate, in the worst scenario, it can be the basis of serious misunderstanding or quarrels.

Mutual knowledge can be categorized into the following types:

1. knowledge of certain facts relating to subject matter;
2. wide cultural knowledge, ranging from an understanding of major celebratory festivals, religious and/or ethical customs, to the legal system;
3. knowledge of how people behave with respect to their social roles within social hierarchies;
4. knowledge of the institutional practices of specialist discourse communities, such as workplace groups, schools, government, clubs and societies and their related genres;
5. knowledge of the moral values of the groups to which participants belong;
6. knowledge of the co-text and context in a specific communicative event;
7. knowledge of the individuals involved as discourse participants in the immediate communicative event.

Each of these categories incorporates issues of identity and power. The value systems of a social group, to which all of the above categories contribute, make up its *ideology*.

More importantly for critical discourse analysis, propagandists and advertisers often deliberately assume agreement on a topic in order to take an argument in the direction that they wish. An example concerns attitudes to age, which vary from one society to another. In societies where older people hold – or have traditionally held – relatively more power, age is valued, and the elderly generally receive respect. However, in some places at the present time, including much of Europe and North America, an assumption is made that everyone agrees that it is better to be young than to be middle-aged or old.

The idea that 'looking young is desirable' is exploited by both manufacturers and advertisers. A current advertisement for skin moisturizing cream shows two almost identical photographs of the same middle-aged man with slightly greying hair. Under the first picture are the words:

You think you're aging well?

and under the second are the words:

She thinks you're letting yourself go.

No specific woman is referred to. Presumably this advert is designed to appeal to men who are concerned about their attraction to women. Words in smaller print beneath the pictures read:

Signs of aging, sagging skin and wrinkles? Fight back!

and tell us that use of the advertised product

Reduces the appearance of sagging skin on face and neck.

The suggestion that men who use the advertised skin cream will look younger and hence be more desirable to the opposite sex is based on the widely shared cultural notion that ageing is unattractive. Since advertisements of this type do – in some societies at least – succeed in increasing sales, we must assume that many people share the belief that it is better to look – and possibly to *be* – young. However, this is a socially constructed concept rather than an indisputable fact. There are still societies, for example in some parts of Africa, where to gain certain social privileges and respect, one must be elderly. Even within Europe and America, there are groups that do not accept this position, for example, in certain religious sects where power is enshrined in 'the elders'. However, we rarely see objections raised to the assumption that youth is preferred to age and there is little doubt that advertisements reinforce that view.

Everyone absorbs the established values of their own social groupings and follows the practices they have learnt (more or less unconsciously) in matters such as age, authority, gender, race, and so on, unless they have contact with other cultures or are exposed to social practices or philosophies that lead them to reject or rationally question aspects of their home culture. The set of established values held by social groups makes up their *ideology*.

The critical discourse analyst must work to become aware of assumptions that are made in the name of cultural practice or which reflect the ideological basis of the discourse and be prepared to investigate them with a fresh and open mind.

2.3 Purposeful communication

Certain aspects of language in use are commonly referred to as the *pragmatic features of discourse*. Pragmatics is a branch of study related to, but separate from, linguistics, because it purports to explain aspects of language and communication that have not been – or cannot be – explained by linguistic studies.

Systemic functional linguists, however, seek to account for so-called pragmatics as part of their linguistic theory. Some recent studies support this view, but it is complex and not directly relevant to critical discourse studies. In this book, for convenience, then, we will generally use the term 'pragmatics' when we refer to work published under that name even though we are sympathetic to the SFL position. Discourse features frequently discussed in the literature of pragmatics are *reference, communicative function, presupposition and implicature*, which are all introduced in this chapter.

Purpose and context

When we learn a language, we gradually learn to recognize and name a set of discourse events that are common in the social circles we move in. We not only learn the unspoken rules of conversation, but also those that are handed down from one generation to the next, such as the concern for appropriate behaviour, which may differ from one social group to another. In some societies, for example, it is perfectly acceptable for children to join in conversation with adults uninvited, but in others, it is strictly forbidden, and a child should speak only if spoken to first by an adult.

Part of our socialization is gaining familiarity with a range of discourse types or genres. Some of these we may acquire through exposure and others have to be taught. Thus children might learn an appropriate way to participate in a telephone conversation simply by observation of their parents, but they may need instruction in how to write a laboratory report. Genres are text types that are socially constructed over time to fulfil certain social functions. They tend to follow agreed social rules or customs, and we learn the rules of recognition and production slowly, usually through education or sometimes by contact with the discourse community that uses them.

We learn to recognize genres even when there is a deliberate attempt to disguise them. For example, we may realize that a telephone call is a commercial call, rather than one from a friend, because of certain openings with which we are familiar:

> Hello. My name is Debbie and I'm calling from Travel U.S. to let you know that you have been selected for a free holiday cruise in the Caribbean.

Although, at first, the message may appear to be announcing a piece of good fortune, the purpose of the call is to sell you a product or a service. The speaker refers to herself familiarly, with her first name, as a friend might, in the hope that you will listen further. But she then follows this incongruously with the name of a company and proceeds with the message, more or less directly. Experience leads most listeners to put down the telephone receiver after the first sentence. They have conducted a piece of personal critical discourse analysis and realized that there is likely to be a catch. (In this case, the catch was that the holiday company charged an exorbitant price for airfares to Florida where the cruise began.)

A speaker's intention is part of the interactional nature of an utterance. It is closely related to the notion of *speech act*, which encapsulates the idea that when we are talking to each other we are 'doing things' with our words. We may, for example, be making an offer, selling something, or refusing an invitation. Since speech acts are an integral part of *meaning* (although not the whole of it), critical discourse analysis may need to look carefully at a speaker's or writer's intention, especially when there is some possible ambiguity or disagreement.

2.4 Reference, identity and role

Reference in a grammatical sense is extremely important in the cohesion of texts because of the way in which language allows us to substitute pronouns for nouns (such as *her* for *Bridget* in example 2 or *I* for a speaker) and other pro-forms for other parts of speech, phrases or clauses, such as *here* or *there* for places, *that* for something which has been done or said, as in *She said that*, and so on. This is an important area of study in general discourse analysis which can be relevant to CDA, particularly with relation to how individuals place themselves. In CDA there is a special significance attached to the ways in which identity is realized in discourse because people tend to identify themselves with their own social groupings (Self) and often place themselves in opposition to other social groupings (Other).

As well as playing various roles, we identify with different social groups. To some extent we are able to choose how far we identify with a group. We may each think of ourselves as members of a particular religion and/or a profession. We may choose to identify with our home nation, our favourite football club and our religious group – but we may decide not to.

Analysis: pronouns in the construction of identity

Our knowledge of the world and our experience of social reality influence the way we use and interpret individual words. Evidence for this comes from a growing body of research in CDA that investigates the use of personal pronouns in the construction of identity, where 'identity' refers to the way people see themselves in relation to others and to society at large. Plural pronouns (*we, us, you, they* and *them*) refer, of course, to more than one person. However, each of them can refer to different collections of people.

We can illustrate this by looking at how writers from different backgrounds use the inclusive 'we' to place themselves in relation to different social groups. In each of the texts which follow, the authors have a similar common purpose of fighting inequality and racism. In this sense, they are all 'on the same side' (Self). Racists and oppressors are on the 'other side' (Other).

Example (3a) is from a radio broadcast given early in the Second World War by E.M. Forster, the English novelist and Cambridge academic. Forster's talk was an argument against the notion of racial purity, which was a tenet of the Nazi war machine. He proposes the idea that the British citizens of today all originate from racially and nationally mixed marriages that have taken place through history (a position now supported by DNA evidence). Notice that he uses the word 'we' to refer to himself as part of the social group that he has been discussing: the British anti-Nazis. By placing himself and the listeners as members of the same group, a group consisting of 'mongrels' (which is to say 'mixed race'), he positions Nazis and all racists as the enemy:

> **3a.** We only know that we are all mongrels . . . and that we must learn not
> to bite one another. We can see comparatively clearly into the
> problem of race, if we choose to look, and can do a little to combat
> the pompous and pernicious rubbish that is at present being prescribed
> in the high places of the earth.

We recognize the referent of *we* because of the words in the rest of the talk (the co-text), and because of what we know of the persecution of the Jewish people at that time (mutual knowledge). In another broadcast, he wrote:

> **3b.** Take the evil of racial prejudice. We can easily detect it in the Nazis;
> their conduct has been infamous since they rose to power. But we
> ourselves – are we guiltless? We are far less guilty than they are. Yet is
> there no racial prejudice in the British Empire? *beliefs.*

Thus, he presumes that his listeners hold the same anti-Nazi position as he does, but he is also inviting them to join him in questioning their own attitudes to 'race' in general. *We ourselves* in (3b) allows the author to declare his identity and share the burden of guilt for racist behaviour with his listeners, a characteristic that was to become a significant force later in the century when anti-racist programmes maintained that it was necessary for those holding positions of power to recognize the racist tendencies in themselves before progress towards equality could be made.

Some early black writers of resistance texts in the USA used the inclusive 'we' and 'our' with a different referent, in this case to identify with the specific group of oppressed black peoples of North America, excluding non-black Americans. A poet, Contee Cullen, used 'we' and 'our' in this way:

> **4.** We shall not always plant while others reap . . .
> So in the dark we hide the heart that bleeds
> And wait and tend our agonizing seed.

With a similar use of the pronouns, Marion Morel,[2] a journalist in South Africa, identified herself with the 'coloured' readership of *The Drum* when she wrote:

5. I heard a sad litt' ... r
engagement to b ... in
complexion thar ... :r
wants her future ... y the
same colour as h

What a miserabl ... to
put up with alrea ... ese
petty apartheid d ...

An American writer, Jan ... xamples
taken from Baldwin (197 ... :mpt to
identify with people from ... racism.
In (6) *we* refers to 'the bla ... ericans,
regardless of colour.

6. We know that we, ... :n,
and are, the victim ... y
god is profit ...

7. Some of us, white and black, know how great a price has already been paid to bring into existence a new consciousness, a new people, and an unprecedented nation. If we know, and do nothing, we are worse than the murderers hired in our name.

And in (8) we find further evidence of his commitment to a broader identity than one constrained by the perception of race:

8. In short, *we, the black and the white,* deeply need each other if we are really to become a nation – if we are really, that is, to achieve our identity, our maturity, as men and women. (Our italics)

This is a conscious contribution to the attempt to re-construct group identity in terms other than 'colour', a struggle that is still continuing.

As we shall see later in this book, the critical discourse analyst is often concerned with the perceived identity of the speaker or author. It is important to recognize where a participant in the discourse positions himself/herself as a member of a social group and where others position him or her.

2.5 Assumptions and the co-operative principle

The term *presupposition* has a long and complex history in philosophy and has been used to refer to a number of distinct concepts. As far as CDA is concerned, it is enough for now to explain presupposition as an assumption made by a writer/speaker concerning the knowledge or views of the reader/listener.[3] We all presuppose certain knowledge or understanding when we try to communicate with others.

The interpretation of assumptions is as context dependent as any other aspect of meaning. To say that an assumption is true or false, or right or wrong, depends on the position and beliefs of the interactants and these may depend in turn on such factors as the time in history when the assumption is made or the received culture of the discourse. Some assumptions are so current in society at a particular time that they will automatically be accepted without question. Thus, in some cultures, no one would question the assumption in 'God is good', which is that God exists. People with different belief systems might not accept this assumption.

An assumption may be perfectly valid and lead to conciseness in a verbal exchange, but often assumptions are invalid – sometimes deliberately – and simply reinforce inaccurate or untrue situations. We have already considered the point that there is presupposition that people prefer to look young rather than old. We could call this a cultural assumption. Another cultural assumption in the current moves towards a global economy is that 'big is good' (*the growing economy, increasing our markets, more for your money, world-wide networking*). Resistance groups and individuals can question these assumptions, of course, but it can take a long time to change broad cultural assumptions, and most people go along with received values.

Grice's maxims

In order for communication to work at all, the participants in a discourse must share some common principles of how it does work. For example, if I believe that nothing that you say has any relevance to anything that I say or do, or that anything you say will be a lie, not much communication will take place. If I systematically talk according to the principle of making the message I wish to convey as obscure as possible, or always give masses of unnecessary detail, or say only a little bit of what I mean, and if you assume that that is what I am doing, communication will not be facilitated, to put it mildly.

The philosopher, Paul Grice (1975) argued that meaningful discourse proceeds on the basis of a general understanding between participants, which he calls the Co-operative Principle (CP), and which states:

> Make your conversational contribution such as is required, at the stage at which it occurs, by the accepted purpose of the talk exchange in which you are engaged.

He is particularly concerned to account for *implicatures*, meanings that are evident although they are not explicitly stated. (Grice uses this term because the more usual word *implication* has a distinct meaning in philosophical logic.)

An implicature is the sort of meaning that people refer to informally by such expressions as 'reading between the lines' or 'dropping a heavy hint'. Such indirect meanings are essentially in conformity with the CP and rely on it in order for the implicature to work. Grice specifies four maxims that underpin normal interaction; as shown in Figure 2.1. This is put more briefly in Figure 2.2

Grice gives the following example of how the maxim of Relation (which we will call Relevance) occurs:

A: I am out of petrol.

B: There's a garage around the corner.

If B knew that the garage in question was closed, his statement would not be relevant. Hence, A will assume it to be open, or probably open. We might add that if B knew that it was probably closed, having once made the utterance cited above (admittedly, not a helpful contribution), the Quantity maxim would oblige him to add information to that effect, and so both maxims apply here.

Quantity
1. Make your contribution as informative as is required for the current purposes of the exchange.
2. Do not make your contribution more informative than is required.

Quality
1. Do not say what you believe to be false.
2. Do not say that for which you lack adequate evidence.

Relation
Be relevant.

Manner
1. Avoid obscurity of expression.
2. Avoid ambiguity.
3. Be brief (avoid unnecessary prolixity).
4. Be orderly.

Figure 2.1 Grice's maxims

Quantity – say as much as is needed.
Quality – tell the truth.
Relation – be relevant.
Manner – be clear.

Figure 2.2 Grice's maxims simplified

If you have not heard of Grice's maxims before, you are probably thinking that this is all very nice but people do not actually always observe these guidelines in practice; people lie, waffle, digress, and so on. This is true, but Grice's point is that these are underlying assumptions for the success of communication. The maxims are not really instructions but tell us what we normally do instinctively unless we are deliberately trying to mislead. It is true that they are not always strictly adhered to, but even when they are not, the CP may still be operating because the listener may assume that the speaker is following them.

A participant can opt out altogether by refusing to speak, though it is arguable that even this may often be construed as implicating something; for example, that I do not agree with what you have just said.

Cooperative principle

Occasionally, one or both parties may not wish to be co-operative and may violate the maxim of Quality, by telling a lie or deliberately obscuring the meaning, but the assumption or the pretence that the CP applies is still there if the lie is to succeed. Speakers and writers often intend to mislead and the success of their deception depends on the receiver's (the hearer's or reader's) assumption that the maxims are being observed.

For example, in an interview, a politician may concede that some sector of the school population is under-achieving and that swift action is necessary; this is then followed by a statement that the government intends to reduce the control of local authorities over schools, transferring the power to other groups and individuals. Although there is no obvious reason to suppose that the proposed action will solve the problem, the audience assumes that the maxims are being observed, and that the speaker is saying as much as is needed as clearly as possible so that the two statements must be logically connected, i.e. that the action will somehow improve the lot of deprived children. The speaker thus gives the impression that he or she has offered a solution to the problem without spelling out how this action can improve the situation, which might be more difficult. A speaker can depend on the audience's assumption of relevance to get away with this. Media interviewers are aware of these strategies and occasionally challenge an interviewee with a direct question: 'Yes, but how will this improve the situation?' The interviewee is then obliged to apply some new stratagem for misleading the public while appearing to conform to the CP.

Sometimes there may be what Grice calls a clash of maxims, where two or more maxims are in conflict. So, for example, if someone asks a friend, 'Where exactly is Tallinn?' and he says, 'It's in one of the Baltic States', he is failing to meet the Quantity maxim (sufficient information for the purpose), but he is forced into this by his desire to observe the Quality maxim (tell the truth) since he does not know exactly where Tallinn is.

Most interesting, though, is the way that speakers exploit the maxims in what Grice terms *flouting* a maxim or blatantly failing to fulfil it in order to trigger an implicature.

If someone asks, 'What is his latest book like?' and receives the reply: 'It weighs half a kilo', the Relevance maxim is being flouted. However, there is a probable implicature that the book is boring or that it was so lacking in merit that there is nothing to comment on except its weight.

In the case of the hypothetical exchange about Tallinn, if the friend says 'It's in one of the Baltic States', knowing full well that it is the capital of Latvia, he may be (1) violating the quantity maxim in order to restrict the help he gives to the questioner or (2) flouting the maxim in order to trigger an implicature such as 'This is a bore and I can't be bothered to be more precise.'

Irony or sarcasm, where people say the opposite of what they believe to be true, is one common instance of the flouting of the Quality maxim. Commenting on a report that a young famous football player is to write his autobiography, a journalist stated:

I would equate it with the first folio of Shakespeare.

(Simon Heffer on Saturday, *The Daily Telegraph*, 11 March 2006, p. 25)

As readers, we know that the journalist cannot intend us to believe this. So, assuming that he is being co-operative and wants to tell us something, we think that he is implying that grandiose claims for this publication are ridiculous. The co-text bears this out; he has already mentioned 'evolution in action' and the story is accompanied by a photograph of what is presumably the footballer and two other men in ape-like postures walking out of the sea; the picture bears the caption: 'The Rooney family contemplating the next literary masterpiece'.

Suppose that someone says to a man who has strong feminist sympathies, 'I am surprised that your sister didn't go to university,' and he replies, 'Oh, girls don't need an education, do they?' Someone who does not know him may think that he is stating his opinion directly (that is, there will be a breakdown of communication because of his miscalculation about mutual knowledge). But anyone who does know him will think something like, 'He can't possibly believe this and there is no reason for him to lie, so he must be getting at something else. He is mocking traditional attitudes to education for girls.'[4]

2.6 The analysis of context

Since context plays such an important part in the construction of meaning, many attempts have been made to find a useful way to characterize contextual features. It has long been acknowledged that the analyst needs to be selective in identifying the features of context that are significant for any specific case of interaction. The narrowest case of context is co-text. This can also play a significant part in the meaning of propositions. In the following example, the truth of the first proposition is contradicted in the co-text:

> 'All the guests are French', said Searle, but I didn't believe him. Later he admitted that what he had said was not true.

Most often referred to as the starting point of modern theories of context is the work of Firth (1937) who believed that 'Meaning is best regarded as a complex of relations of various kinds between the component terms of a context of situation.' These 'component terms' included, for Firth, the setting of the event – or at least what was relevant in the setting – the people involved (the participants) and their behaviour, including the speech, or conversation, that is taking place:

> The force and cogency of most language behaviour derives from the firm grip it has on the ever-recurrent typical situations in the life of social groups and in the normal social behaviour of the human animals living together in those groups.

One aspect of this view of context that is sometimes difficult to grasp is the way in which language use itself is seen as part of the context that constrains language. There appears to be something circular in this argument, but in human society so much is governed by language – literally and figuratively – that this approach is unavoidable.

Theorists often add to the confusion by talking about 'establishing clear relations between language and context' as though language was external to its context and could be mapped onto context at discrete points – an impossible task. In this book we have followed Firth in seeing both context and language as inextricably bound together in the production of *meaning*.

The context of a discourse event changes imperceptibly with every contribution. Context is *dynamic*.

Models of context

As we have indicated above, 'context' has often been considered under the two separate headings of *context of culture* and *context of situation*. The context of culture includes the traditions, the institutions, the discourse communities, the historical context and the knowledge base of the participants (which may, of course, be mono-cultural, cross-cultural or multi-cultural). Like situations, culture is under a process of continuous change. Cultural and situational elements are often so closely intertwined that it is extremely difficult to see them in isolation.

Roughly, the context of situation focuses on the various elements involved in the direct production of meanings in a particular instance of communication. Since analysts working within the CDA model generally work with specific texts, or *instances* of discourse, they need to take account of the setting (or social environment), identity of the participants, and so on, for the specific texts in order to be able to make valid generalizations.

Thus, in matters of politeness, for example, the ways in which we show respect (either linguistically or otherwise) and the rules for who should show respect to whom are a part of the context of culture, but in the course of a specific conversational exchange, the power relationships between the participants and whether or not they conform to social expectations are part of the context of situation.

It is useful for the critical discourse analyst to have an acute awareness of contextual influences on the creation of meaning even though in any specific instance it may not be necessary to conduct a full contextual analysis. What the analyst needs to be able to do is to identify those features of the context that govern or reinforce the interactional processes that take place through language, such as the use of language to control other people either by direction or persuasion.

One approach to analysis that is specific to a given text is to pose a series of questions that relate to the production of the text. Many of these a reader or listener would ask intuitively when engaged in a communicative event. One such question, often mentioned in the literature of discourse analysis, is: 'Who is talking to whom about what?' This question addresses important discoursal factors, both the *interpersonal* and the *ideational* functions of language, each of which plays a part in establishing the form of language that is used. And yet the question is deceptively simple. It appears to ask for the names of the participants and the matters they are discussing, but in reality it requires more complex interpretation. An answer might require an assessment of all the people involved in the communicative event (the participants in the discourse, and anyone overhearing). This might include information on such matters as their geographical origins (as revealed in dialect or accent), their social class/es, status, maybe their ages, relative wealth, professions, gender, or membership of discourse communities. Since their social roles directly affect the *tenor* of the discourse, it is important to recognize that each of us plays many social roles (see Chapter 1).

One severe limitation of the above approach (concerning participants and topic) is that it does not necessarily take into account the force of established institutional discourses, which many feel should be the starting point for looking at context. Any speech event, for example, will rely on a *mode* of delivery. It may be simple face to face interaction: two or more persons talking to each other in the same place over the same period of time. It may, however, be a telephone conversation or an internet discussion group or a radio broadcast. It may be business correspondence or a work of literature or a business report, or one of many other modes of communication. Each type of speech event carries its own distinctive features and constrains the participants both in what they may say and how they may say it.

People who work in top-class hotels which are part of a chain are trained to follow a certain 'script' in their dealings with the customers, addressing them in a certain way and using specific forms of politeness as part of the 'house style', a type of institutionalized discourse.

Similarly, the answer to the question 'about what?' can prove problematic since there is usually a wide range of possible answers. For example, a professor may be talking to a seminar group on an engineering course. The seminar might cover a number of different topics, each of which needs to be identified. Even if only one topic is covered, we can approach the analysis in different ways. In broadest terms, we might say that he is talking about the *field* of engineering, but there could be a range of answers – each of which is true. For example, we might get:

> engineering – electrical engineering – electrical supply systems – electrical circuits – contact breakers – danger factors in the use of obsolete contact breakers

A range of this type covers what are called *levels of delicacy*, moving in this example from the most general to the most specific level of delicacy. *Topic*, then, can be seen as a more delicate realization of the field of discourse.

Which of the answers is most appropriate will depend upon why you are considering the question at all. For example, if the analyst is concerned with the issue of safety in the workplace, only the most delicate (concerning danger factors) might be relevant.

Another problem can be that the wording of the question 'about what?' carries the implication that language interaction is primarily concerned with propositions about the world or clearly definable topics, but this does not take into account the matter of communicative function or speech acts discussed above. There is also what is known as *phatic* communion, which consists of greetings or other such expressions that aim to establish contact or solidarity:

Hello!

Cheers!

Love you (at the end of a telephone call)

See you later.

Ups a daisy!

No, thank you.

Additionally, this model of context does not attempt to distinguish fact from opinion and it does not pick up a speaker's or author's attitude. Since these are often the most crucial factors for critical discourse analysis, a model needs to incorporate questions concerning *intention* and *purpose* where these are accessible from the context.

In certain contexts, such as debates, conversation, correspondence, we may also need to consider the reaction and interpretation of the interlocutors in extra-linguistic terms such as gesture or facial expression. This would extend our original question to

> Who is talking to whom about what? Why? What is their purpose? What effect are they having (or trying to have)?

A practical approach to context

Discourse analysts normally work with *texts*. Sometimes they are present in the situation where the original linguistic event took place, but often they are not. In Chapter 1, we explained that the word 'discourse' is sometimes used in contrast to 'text', where 'text' refers to actual instance of written or spoken data. For the purposes of analysing spoken discourse, it is necessary for the text to have been preserved in some way either as an electronically recorded, filmed or written record. The term 'text' can also be used for larger collections of verbal records being used for analysis (also called *corpuses* or *corpora*). Since they may be separated by time and distance from the original discourse event, critical discourse analysts have to be sensitive to the nature of the context in which the act of communication actually took (or regularly takes) place. Usually, this is not too difficult because the language closely reflects its discoursal situation.

To pin down some of the issues we have already mentioned in this chapter, we can say that, at the most practical level, for a given context, the analyst will seek to identify:

- ○ the setting (or place/s) of the event;
- ○ time or times and aspect of the event;
- ○ mode and medium of the event (face to face; one speaker to many listeners; written to be read; television; illustrated text, for example);
- ○ participants and their roles in the event;
- ○ topic/s, themes (including distance of participants from the topics);
- ○ purpose of the discourse event and purposes of the participants;
- ○ attitude of the participants;
- ○ the dynamics of the situation (How do events, participants, topics, attitudes, and so on, change during the course of the discourse event?)   *r/Jack succumbs*
- ○ the genre (where applicable).   *to Gladys suggestion*

There may be cases where not everything in this list is relevant to the critique in hand, and there are certainly times when it is not possible to acquire all this information. Nevertheless, it is useful to approach the analytic task with a check list of this type.

2.7 Institutional constraints

There is one important issue in the study of the nature of context that we have not looked at in any detail so far in this book. This involves the nature of institutions and the constraints that they impose on practices that take place both within and outside the institution. Many companies specify the types of text that the employees will work with, and each text type will have a stated purpose and be preformatted. For example, receptionists in an international hotel chain might work with a discrete set of forms (usually computerized), one for each professional act that the job involves, such as recording reservations, checking in guests, checking out guests, registering complaints, recording and transmitting messages. Receptionists will receive training in the various aspects of the job and this will include instruction on how to process appropriate texts. Thus the management can maintain strong control over the working practices within the company. Of course, each of these texts has itself been created by people who work in the institution and will usually have had experience in the very work they are now involved in controlling. Thus, the context of discourse is created by discourse.

An obvious case is that of legal institutions. In most cultures today, the law has produced a large number of institutional practices which range from the international law of the sea to the way regional courts are organized. Most practices require the use of specialized legal documents, each with its own format, layout and structure. Within the traditional operation of the law, there have developed many formal discourse genres, which professionals need to master and which can cause problems for the lay person. These genres, spoken, written and a mix of spoken and written, become established through custom and general agreement of the communities involved, changing gradually as social needs change or as technologies dictate. These genres include written *court procedures*, which specify the legal participants (for example, judge, jury, defendant, prosecuting council, defending council, court recorder, and so on), the order of events, the formal methods of announcing a verdict, or sentencing. Around the core genres, there also develops a set of fringe genres that draws on the central institutional genres; in the case of the law, we find newspaper court reports and insurance and business contracts, for example.

A similar state of affairs operates in government, education, business, the police service, the army, branches of science, in the arts, religion and even in organized sport. Other formal genres are well established in the news media, entertainment industry, and some games and hobbies. Institutional discourses are important to critical discourse analysts because it is here that the power structure of a nation (or smaller social group) is enshrined.

Activities

1. In section 2.2, we discussed some issues relating to the idea that looking young is preferable to looking old. Is this a valid idea in the social groups to which you belong? Has the situation changed throughout history? Are there any situations in which you feel that the opposite might be the case, that is to say that it may be better to look older or even elderly? Consider this issue in relation to *gender*. (Notice that advertisements for men's skin care products have appeared relatively recently compared to similar ones for products for women. Why do you think this is?)

2. Consider when you would use the pronouns 'we' and 'our'. That is to say, when do you think you would identify with specific social groups? Consider groups such as family, political party, clubs, university, nation, and so on. Do

you have any problems in deciding? Are there any groups with whom you would not identify yourself, whatever the circumstances?

3. Read these words from a popular singer, Ronan Keating, recalling his time with the band Boyzone in 1995 and consider what assumptions are carried by the final sentence:

> We were making a fortune and I started spending my money on clothes. … was mad for labels – I had to have the Gucci hat, the sweater with the big D & G on the front. At that age, it's all that matters.
>
> (Reported by Naomi West, *Flashback*, in *Telegraph Magazine*, 20 May 2006)

4. In Section 2.5 we quoted a journalist's report about a young footballer's auto-biography. Another journalist asked the question: 'How will it be possible to pack such an enormous life into just five volumes?' What is the implicature here? Account for this in terms of Gricean maxims.

Further study

This section directs the reader to books where ideas are explained in more detail and also to research relating to ideas in the chapter.

The nature of context of situation was considered by Firth (1937), referred to in Section 2.6, who gave early recognition to the importance of social roles and social identity in the development of distinctive styles in speech events.

For more about context, see Halliday (1978: Chapters 1–3) and Hasan's work on social systems and social roles (1996: 191–243). Van Dijk is currently working on the further development of a theory of context. An alternative, but related, model of situation is that of Mediated Discourse. See Scollon (2001, in Wodak and Meyer, Chapter 7).

The classic early works on speech act theory and communicative functions were written by the philosophers Austin (1962) and Searle (1971). Their ideas are sum-marized in most introductory texts on discourse analysis and pragmatics, for example Mey (1993), but beware of Mey's use of the term 'discourse' which he appears to limit to spoken conversation. A more difficult and sometimes controversial work is Levinson (1983). Students who have an interest in philosophy might like to try some of the chapters in Grice (1975).

See Jäger (in Wodak and Meyer 2001), for a discussion of the work of Foucault. The main work on ideology in relation to CDA is van Dijk (1998a).

Interesting accounts of the use of pronouns and identity are those of Ward (2004), who analyses the use of what he calls 'pronouns of power' in a trades union context, and Faiz Sathi Abdullah (2004) writing about the use of pronouns as markers of identity in Malaysia, where people originating in three distinct ethnic groups work towards one *national* identity. A classic article on the grammar of pro-nouns in relation to gender issues was written by Bodine (1975), who describes their use as 'one of the most socially significant aspects of language'.

Other examples of critical discourse research based on the principles introduced in the chapter can be found in Coulthard (1992a), Caldas-Coulthard and Coulthard (1996), Jaworski and Coupland (1999), and Young and Harrison (2004).

3

Positioning and point of view

3.1 Position and attitude

In Chapter 1, we said that as discourse analysts, we need to be aware of our own position in relation to the object of our analysis since our beliefs and attitudes are likely to colour the way we interpret what we hear or read.

Just as we, as analysts, observe the discourse from our own ideological positions, we need to realize that all speakers and writers take up some position in relation to the propositions they make. We can call it *speaker stance* or *authorial stance*. Readers and listeners, as well, take up positions in relation to the discourse.

We need to consider this from different perspectives, however. Let us take the case of a prepared text such as a speech or a radio programme, a newspaper report or a business report. First of all, the text may be prepared by one or more individuals. The messages in the text may be those of an individual writer or the writer may be representing the views and the attitudes of an institution or group. To complicate matters even further, the stance taken may be *explicit* (also known as *overt*) or *hidden* (*covert*), and may be either *conscious* (also known as *inscribed*) or *unconscious*.

As analysts, one of our main jobs is to try to recognize the *stance* that is taken. In the case of many well-established genres, our knowledge of their social purpose gives us certain expectations of what the stance taken will be, but these expectations may not be realized on further examination.

In the next section, we will look at four distinct types of discourse practice, using written texts, from the point of view of the stance taken by the authors and the methods by which we detect it.

1. Reviews of books and films [conscious stance: explicit].
2. Promotional business letters [conscious stance: hidden].
3. Potted biography [unconscious stance: explicit].
4. History texts [conscious or unconscious stance: explicit or hidden].

A specific area of research that relates to this chapter is *appraisal analysis*. When, in written or spoken discourse, writers comment on something, such as a film, an event, someone's behaviour, they may comment positively, negatively or neutrally. Some of the work of appraisal analysis involves the recognition and classification of stance. Analysts have worked on a semantic system that provides a taxonomy for different types of appraisal, such as the expression of emotion (*I felt overjoyed*) as opposed to making a moral assessment of an event or person (*His behaviour was unforgivable*). Here, the first type is known as 'affect' and the second type as 'judgement'. The system overall has complex sub-systems which we do not have room to describe in detail in this book. However, it is likely that the framework will play an increasing part in CDA.

3.2 Stance in film and book reviews

We have said that all speakers and writers come to the action of speaking and writing with a point of view regarding their position towards the topic, but there is considerable variation in how far a person gives overt and explicit expression to their point of view.

The analysis of stance in reviews is not something that CDA is usually concerned with since reviews are not primarily involved directly with power or control, although on occasion the review or the object of the review may address a certain social problem or reveal significant social attitudes. The reason we are discussing reviews here is simply to illustrate techniques for the analysis of stance.

A serious film or book reviewer discusses the pros and cons of a film with the purpose of recommending or not recommending a book or a film to the readers of the review. Reviewers also sometimes see themselves as also having the more complex task of influencing writers or film makers for the better.

Interestingly, reviewers tend to avoid personal evaluations of the type:

> The film made me feel depressed. [Affect and negative appraisal.]

> In my opinion, the acting was excellent. [Judgement and positive appraisal.]

When a reviewer is writing about a film, the use of 'I' and other pronouns referring directly to the writer is rare. The first element of each clause, which indicates what is being written about, is more often the film itself or some component of the film, such as the acting, the plot or the camera work.[1]

Readers *expect* a reviewer to hold some opinion of the film since a reviewer's primary *role* is to evaluate or give value to something. The public reads the review, at least in part, to discover the stance the writer has taken. Thus, the reviewer takes on the identity of an 'expert' on film and offers that view with confidence and without attribution, even though it is recognized that some people would disagree.

A reviewer's stance may be entirely negative. Text 3.1 is the first sentence of a film review. It is not necessary to read further in order to understand that the author has an unfavourable opinion of the film. The remainder of the short review (not given here) summarizes the main points of the plot.

Text 3.1 From a film review

> This tatty exploitation piece is simultaneously manic and repressed, silly and cynical.
>
> (Review of *La Mome Pigalle*, from *Time Out Film Guide*, 2000, p. 691)

In this straightforward example of *explicit evaluation*, the film is referred to as an *exploitation piece*, suggesting that it is a work of art that 'exploits' the viewers' emotions for no genuine purpose. The term 'exploitation piece' is well known as a critical term; it is explained in *Brewer's Cinema* (Law 1995: 188) as 'a low budget film of little or no artistic merit that is crudely targeted at a particular section of the movie-going public'. The adjectives *tatty* and *silly* directly indicate the author's disapproval, and *cynical*, which, in some contexts, might conceivably be used as praise, in this case clearly carries unfavourable connotations, especially as it is linked with the dismissive 'silly'. It is difficult to precisely interpret *manic and repressed*. However, we can only read the expression as one of disapproval, implying, as it does, some ambivalence or contradiction in the film.

In the book review, printed here as Text 3.2, the author again uses adjectives but this time as a part of longer nominal groups to express her approval of the crime thriller: *superb action sequences, constant surprises, an ultimately satisfying and haunting book*. She also employs positive adverbs in *beautifully handled, well rendered*. However, although the reviewer's stance is generally positive, she expresses some reservations about the unreliable narration in the book and the unlikely manner of the final revelations.

Text 3.2 A book review

Ben Truman, a police chief in Versailles, Maine, a one-horse town where a drunk taking potshots at street lights is the limits of criminal activity, becomes caught up in a series of gang-related murders in Boston before realizing, too late, that the heart of the mystery lies in his own back-yard. Full of suspense, with *superb action sequences* and *constant surprises*, Mission Flats also contains the humor and pathos that are essential to a fully-fledged crime story. While not original, Truman's impromptu partnership with retired cop John Kelly is beautifully handled, as is his tentative relationship with Kelly's daughter, a spiky Boston DA. On the whole, the moral ambiguity of Truman and his fellow law-enforcers is well-rendered; the unreliable narration does begin to grate towards the end, and the necessary withholding of vital information from the reader leads to some of the final revelations being made in an unlikely manner, but these are only minor detractions from an *ultimately satisfying and haunting book* (our italics).

(Laura Wilson: Review of Mission Flats by William Landay, Corgi. The Guardian,
24 October 2005, p.19. Copyright Guardian Newspapers Limited 2006.)

An interesting linguistic point concerns the implied transitivity in the expressions *constant surprises* and *satisfying and haunting book*. Although the reviewer does not mention herself, the verbs *surprise*, *satisfy* and *haunt* each imply a human participant. Here the reader understands that it is the reviewer who experienced these feelings even though she does not say so explicitly.

When these feelings (mental processes) are expressed as verbs, we normally refer to a human Senser or Sensers, as we can see from the underlined words in *I was surprised* and *We were satisfied* or *The film surprised me* and *The meal satisfied us*.

Because the verbs in these clauses are transitive, the human referent can potentially appear in different positions in the clause depending on whether the clause is active or passive. The grammatical analysis is explained further in Tables 3.1 and 3.2. In the active clauses (Table 3.1), the persons who are surprised, haunted and satisfied are realized as Sensers in object position. In the passive clauses (Table 3.2), they are referred to as Sensers in subject positions. 'Senser' is a technical term for the person or animal that suffers the mental process being expressed. 'Phenomenon' is another technical term that refers to the event, thing or person that is the source of the mental process, as you can see in the tables:

	ACTIVE	
Phenomenon/Subject	**Mental process/Verb group**	**Senser/Object**
The incident	surprised	*me*
The book	haunted	*him*
The ending	satisfied	*everyone*

Table 3.1 Phenomenon as Subject

	PASSIVE	
Senser/Subject	**Mental process/Verb group**	**Phenomenon/Adjunct**
I	was surprised	by the incident
He	was haunted	by the book
Everyone	was satisfied	by the ending

Table 3.2 Senser as Subject

In the review, it is the reviewer who is *satisfied, haunted* and *surprised*, but, by suppressing references to herself, she suggests that any readers would experience the same feelings.

As we have said, the expressions *beautifully handled* and *well-rendered* are also evaluative. This is the result of the adverbs 'beautifully' and 'well' that reflect the reviewer's judgement of the work. No-one is actually named and the social actors of the processes are *suppressed*. The reviewer relies on the readers' knowledge of the world, which allows us to appreciate who did the handling and rendering and who made the judgement. In order to express the participants, the reviewer would have had to produce something like this paraphrase of the third sentence: 'I thought the Landay handled Truman's impromptu partnership with the retired cop beautifully even though it was not original.' This degree of detail would be clumsy and unnecessary.

By choosing to read a review in a newspaper or magazine, the reader willingly enters into a specific type of discourse – a discourse of debate. Reviews are about attitude and opinion and as readers we approach reviews knowing that we can agree or disagree with the author or, if we prefer, reserve judgement. We do not expect an impersonal or detached author even though writers of reviews sometimes avoid the use of direct reference to themselves.

We now turn to a very different type of text, an unsolicited letter, which has a different purpose altogether and a different way of transmitting its message.

3.3 Stance in a promotional letter

Unsolicited letters are a part of the constant barrage of promotional literature that we are all subjected to. Unlike direct advertising, however, the message in such a letter is often disguised and may mislead an unsophisticated reader.

One morning, a few years ago, one of the authors of this book opened the mail to find such a letter. It had been sent, by the normal postal service, in a plain white envelope. This letter is reproduced, with minor changes, as Text 3.3. The name and address of the company have been changed.

Text 3.3 A circular letter

Finezal House

Finezal House Investment Services (Midlands) Limited
Pensions and Investment Brokers
14 Lowland Road, Harborne Road, Birmingham B17 8LN

12 September 199-

Ref: DCR/PM

Professor Bloor
[address]

Dear Professor Bloor

Many people are not aware of some of the legal ways by which tax can be reduced or, in certain cases, avoided altogether.

We have found that this applies to a surprisingly large number of people in the academic professions – probably due to their dedication to their chosen field.

No doubt you are worried about the effects of inflation. Also you will be aware of the taxation penalties levied on the results of your diligence and prudence. Perhaps you are thinking that it is time you did something about it and would welcome some unbiased advice.

We see it as our responsibility to ensure that our clients are well – and regularly – informed of the opportunities and alternative lines of action open to them, so that they can act both wisely and profitably. We are not unmindful that individual objectives will vary according to intentions and personal circumstances but generally we can provide a worthwhile solution to meet most requirements.

Being cautious, I make no promises that we can reduce your tax liability until your financial position can be examined. I would welcome the opportunity to meet you to discuss these matters on some future occasion and confirm that this would be <u>without cost or obligation</u>.

I hope you will receive this letter favourably and not deem it an intrusion when I telephone you shortly, with a view to arranging a mutually convenient appointment. If, in the meantime, you wish for some other information to be sent to you, please get in touch with me at once.

Yours sincerely

[Signature]

Brian J. Sharman

As we read it, we realized that this was an unsolicited commercial letter, a copy of which had certainly been sent to many more university academics, each of whom would have had their own name and address printed on the note paper. The letter was what is known as a 'circular' letter, in this case one designed to advertise a service. We often think of advertisements as being concerned with *goods* rather than *services* and as having established verbal and visual formats in magazines, newspapers or on television or billboards, but this letter is a variation of a more traditional advertisement. The main intention of the writer of the letter was to *persuade* the reader to use the services of the company for financial advice. This letter has a deliberate, conscious but covert message. The writers set out to *sell a service* as though they were *offering advice*.

Analysis of messages in a promotional letter

Although it quickly becomes clear that the underlying intent of the letter is to sell a service, at various points in the letter, the writer, on behalf of the company, adopts different positions *vis-à-vis* the reader. The letter carries a series of messages, which together make up the *rhetorical structure* of the discourse.

The writer begins the letter by suggesting to the readers that they have a real need for help. In the first paragraph, after the statement about most academics' 'ignorance of tax matters', the writer directly excuses them for their ignorance by saying that this is 'probably due to their dedication to their chosen field'. With this phrase, he turns a possible insult into a flattering compliment: academics are ignorant about tax matters but only because of their love of their subject and their hard work.

Paragraph 3 begins by suggesting that the reader is worried about the effects of inflation, something they may never have been concerned about. This implicitly carries the message that the reader *should be* worried. Then we find words that almost directly contradict the earlier suggestion that the reader is ignorant of tax matters: '*you will be aware of the taxation penalties* on the results of your diligence and prudence'. The last four words here are nothing but extreme flattery. The writer, of course, knows nothing of the characters of the persons to whom he has addressed the letters and yet he marks each potential reader out as *dedicated, diligent* and *prudent*. The writer, on behalf of the company, positions himself as an admirer of a reader who is wise and busy and yet unconcerned about material matters like money and taxation.

The rest of the letter subtly turns the argument away from the prospective client to present what Finezal House can do for its customers:

- provide unbiased advice;
- inform clients of opportunities (i.e. to avoid tax);
- inform clients of alternative lines of action;
- act to suit intentions and personal circumstances;
- provide a worthwhile solution to meet most requirements;
- send further information as required.

Having made the claim that the company can be of service to its clients, the letter then adds the clear hedge:

> Being cautious, I make no promises that we can reduce your tax liability …

The words 'being cautious' suggest that the company is not reckless but reliable and so carry a further promotional message, but the main point here is that the company literally makes 'no promises'. This is an attempt to cover itself legally from any threat of misrepresentation of a product, which could be illegal.

Significantly, there is another key characteristic of the messages in this letter. This is an underlying indirect appeal to the readers' greed. This is introduced subtly while at the same time proposing that the academic is not interested in money at all. At no time does the letter state that the reader is worried about tax or wishes to avoid tax, only that the reader is 'no doubt worried about inflation', indirectly suggesting that the reader *is* concerned about financial matters. In the fourth paragraph, the word *profitably* is slipped in:

> We see it as our responsibility to ensure that our clients … can act both wisely and profitably.

And in the fifth paragraph, we are assured that our first meeting with the firm would be 'without cost or obligation' (underlined), once more suggesting that the potential client is not a person to waste money unnecessarily. There is, of course, no promise that subsequent advice would be without charge. Nevertheless, since the company makes its money from providing financial advice, there will be a price to the customer either directly or indirectly.[2] The company leaves out any information about fees or indirect charges. This is an example of *exclusion*, the intentional *suppression* of relevant material.

We have looked at the messages carried in this letter in some detail to set out how a careful and critical reader might see through the persuasive techniques used in it even though they may not analyse it consciously. We see that the rhetorical structure incorporates various moves, including seven that are set within a general framework of persuasion (see Chapter 9 for further discussion):

- naming the product or service and provider;
- informing the reader;

- ○ flattering the reader;
- ○ implying a need;
- ○ making a positive evaluation of the product or service;
- ○ giving instructions (on how to access the product or service);
- ○ making an offer.

Visual and aural presentation may also play an important part in a persuasive text, as we can see from the use of pictures, music and script style in TV advertisements. While appearance may not seem so significant in a written text such as a letter, companies often employ designers to consider the visual impact of a text. We now examine the visual presentation of the letter as well as the style of language used to express the moves outlined above.

Analysis: style and format

Each person who receives a letter such as the one in Text 3.3 interprets it in their own way. Different readers may take different messages from the text, and even the same reader may interpret the meaning differently on a second or third reading. Thus some readers might respond favourably to the interpersonal nature of the above letter, but others would feel it an imposition on their privacy.

The writer has a choice of informal and formal formatting, depending on the type of letter. In English, notes to close friends are texted, sent by e-mail or hand-written. The receiver is addressed by nickname or first name and the note often ends with 'yours' or 'love from' and the writer's name. A formal letter follows strict rules but there is still a wide choice of formats ranging from a traditional business layout to a modern more relaxed layout. A variety of formats can be found in any standard word-processing computer program.

With a circular letter, the company wants to project a professional air so we should expect some degree of formality, such as the use of a printed letter heading, addressing an unknown reader as Sir or Madam, including full addresses of the sender and receiver, the full date, and closing the letter with 'yours faithfully' (for first contact) and 'yours sincerely' (for second and subsequent contacts). There would be a professional designation after the signature. The font selected is frequently traditional. However, a company may wish to give the impression of friendliness and easy accessibility but without too much intimacy. This is clearly the case with the writers of Text 3.3. To this end, they chose a less traditional typeface and addressed the intended reader by name. This less formal opening was matched with the complimentary close, 'Yours sincerely'.

In Text 3.3, we can see the visual and linguistic signs merging to give an overall impression of business correspondence but with an individualized touch. With respect to the presentation of the page, we find a mixture of fonts, including a modern font for the company's name, possibly to give the impression that it is an up-to-date business that is familiar with present-day problems, and we have a relatively informal form of address and closure. What is perhaps more significant is that the body of the letter is written in a style that merges formal and informal language.

Analysis: linguistic characteristics

With respect to variation in styles, there are certain techniques that have been used to measure characteristics of texts. While this is not, as yet, a precise science, statistically there are certain tendencies that occur across varieties, disciplines and genres. For example, research has demonstrated measurable differences between spoken and written discourse concerning factors such as sentence length and lexical density (see Chapter 10 for a measure of lexical density). In written texts, longer sentences are more likely in formal genres (legal contracts, for example) than in popular news reports, longer paragraphs are more frequently found in history books than in detective novels, personal pronouns (for example *you, we, I*) are more frequent in speech than in scientific reports. Not all measures confirm the obvious: for example, UK football reports, even in popular newspapers, tend to have longer sentence length than the rest of the newspaper.

Word length and sentence complexity can also be indicators of difficulty. Of course, what one reader finds difficult, another may find simple, depending on background knowledge, but a vast body of research in the USA has matched schoolchildren's reading ability in each school grade against a set of textual characteristics to arrive at what are known as readability scores. Such measures are becoming much easier to apply with the development of computer programs to assist in the process.

A straightforward computer measure (using the tools in Microsoft Word) of some characteristics of the unsolicited letter discussed above gives:

Number of words	265
Number of words of 3 or more syllables	42
Number of paragraphs	6
Sentence length	23.2 (words per sentence)
Passives	36% (of verbs in text)
Readability level	Grade 12.4

The sentence length is as long as that in many serious textbooks and the vocabulary is relatively adult. In addition, the readability level indicates that it is appropriate for university level students (slightly above Grade 12, the highest class in US high schools). These figures alone would be indicative of a reasonably formal register.

However, there is a high number of personal pronouns (for example *you, we*) in the letter. This number of personal pronouns is usually associated with spoken English or very informal texts, such as friendly letters. Surprisingly, for a business letter to a stranger, there is only one sentence in the whole letter – the first – which lacks a personal pronoun as subject of the main clause.

There are twenty-four personal pronouns in the text as a whole which averages more than two per sentence, a relatively high frequency. Fifteen of these are in subject position and are either Theme or part of a complex Theme, and five are in object position. The remaining seven are part of nominal groups, in either object or subject position. (For further explanations of the grammatical terms used here, see the Glossary and the Appendix.)

Personal pronouns as subject

e.g. *You* will be aware of the taxation penalties levied …

I make no promises that we can reduce your tax liability …

'you' as subject	5
'we' as subject	5
'I' as subject	4
'they' as subject	1

Personal pronouns as object

e.g. … when I telephone *you* shortly ……

… please get in touch with *me* at once

'you' as object	4
'me' as object	1

Personal pronouns as possessives in nominal groups

e.g. … we can reduce *your* tax liability

… due to *their* dedication to *their* chosen field …

'their'	2
'your'	3
'our'	2

What are the implications of this high frequency of personal pronouns in this text in comparison, say, with the number in the other texts we have examined in this chapter? First, we can see that the writer is attempting to establish some kind of personal relationship with the client, by mimicking aspects of a conversational style or personal friendly letter. The frequent use of second person singular pronoun (*you*) is an attempt to indicate a personal interest in the reader even though they have never met or spoken before. While in the first part of the letter the writer uses 'we' to refer to the company, in the two final paragraphs he switches to 'I', moving away from identifying himself as part of an impersonal company and increasing the effect of intimacy between writer and reader. This is particularly appropriate because he is moving here into an increasingly interactional message:

1. He suggests a meeting.
2. He asks the reader to 'welcome the letter favourably'.
3. He warns the reader of an impending telephone call.
4. He invites the reader to get in touch with him personally.

This is the equivalent of 'Let's meet', 'I hope you want to be friends', 'I'll call you', 'But feel free to call me first' in a colloquial conversational style.

Thus, we have a letter that maintains a degree of formality in its layout, sentence length, and vocabulary and yet moves towards establishing a business–client relationship that more closely resembles a relationship between friends. This is likely to be company policy rather than the individual decision of the man who signed the letter. A person's financial affairs, income, wealth, and taxation are generally considered to be personal matters in the UK, where this letter was received. Many people would find it difficult to discuss such matters with a stranger without embarrassment. Maybe this letter is an attempt to break down such barriers at an early stage?

Ron Scollon, discourse analyst in the USA, wrote as part of a study involving the social action of having a cup of coffee in a café:

> In the past two decades or so, in North America at least, there has been an increasing erosion of the distinction between institutional and non-institutional actions. That is, waiters have come to be expected to treat their customers as if they were not only customers but friends and family.
>
> (Scollon 2001)

This seems so close to the merging of similar distinctions in the circular letter that the critical discourse analyst might be tempted to look further for the same phenomenon in other instances of social practices involving contact between business companies and their clients or customers. We return to marketing and related issues in Chapter 9.

3.4 Unconscious stance in racist and sexist discourse

In our discussion of a review and the unsolicited letter, the genre and purpose of the texts were relevant to the identification of stance. In the example which follows, neither the genre nor the topic of the text is our particular concern. What is important is that the author's attitude to the topic he is writing about is coloured by his own prejudices. Considering the time when this text was written (1930), it is possible that the opinions revealed are totally unconscious. However, similar positions can, of course, be taken consciously. Prejudice can pervade discourse and it can often go unnoticed except by those who are its target. Perhaps the most important function of CDA is to shed light on this kind of disguised attitude.

The extract (Text 3.4) is from an anthology of French poetry for British schools originally written in 1930 and reproduced here from a 1945 edition.

Text 3.4 Baudelaire's life

> Baudelaire's life was extremely unhappy. Ever since his mother's remarriage he never knew what it was to have a home. He lived in lodgings until his death, and though he had many acquaintances he made few friends. He had expensive tastes and a lofty contempt for money; while, with scanty means and a very limited earning power, he was constantly in debt. These difficulties were increased by a quixotic conception of his moral duty to an unworthy woman, Jeanne Duval, who had come into his life when he was only twenty-one, whom by a curious aberration (she was a half-caste from San Domingo) he idealized, and for whose needs he thought himself in honour bound to provide, even when he had not enough for his own, until alcoholism drove him to a miserable death in hospital.
>
> (H.E. Berthon, 1945, Introduction, in *Nine French Poets*, London: Macmillan)

Our concern here is with the constructed identity of Baudelaire's lover, Jeanne Duval. Let us first deal with the single ethnic label in the text: the word *half-caste*, which is used to describe her. Denotationally, this indicates someone whose parents are of different race. While many racist terms have been consigned to history, *half-caste* is a term that still occasionally surfaces. It is widely perceived as an offensive term, but the term *half-caste* cannot of itself be taken to indicate racial bigotry. It is not inconceivable that someone writing in 1930 or even 1945 might use the term with no sense of its pejorative associations. As we have said, it is necessary to examine the co-text to see to what ends the term is used.

The unhedged use of the adjective *unworthy* to describe the same woman suggests a confident moral standpoint on the part of the author. It is not clear whether the term is intended to suggest that she was unworthy of the devotion of Baudelaire (a poetic genius and a drug addict and alcoholic, suffering from syphilis) or whether she was just generally lacking in worth. It may in fact be not merely an epithet – a description grammatically akin to *tall*, *kind*, *stupid* – but rather a classifier, assigning her to an identifiable sub-class of women – comparable to *married*, *professional*, *French*. If the latter, it may be that the expression *unworthy woman* is a paraphrase for *fallen woman*, *woman of ill-repute* or *prostitute*. Whatever our reading of this, we cannot fail to perceive it as reflecting a sweeping and simplistic approach to the categorization of individuals, or perhaps more particularly of women.

What is even more significant for the critical reader are the words that come immediately after *a curious aberration*, the parenthetical statement:

> *(she was a half-caste from San Domingo)*

The most important point here is the precise location of the clause. The crucial fact is that this clause is presented not merely as additional information about Jeanne Duval, but rather as an explanation for the author's observation that Baudelaire's idealization of her was *a curious aberration*. There is no other explanation of the placement of these words in this parenthetical position.

It is evident that to 'idealize' such a person is considered curious and aberrant – not because of the unworthiness mentioned previously, but because she was *a half-caste from San Domingo*. The reader will almost certainly assume that there is a connection here, but even so it is not signalled with total explicitness. This is the reason we call the stance of the author *covert* (or hidden). An explicit statement of stance would be *since she was a half-caste from San Domingo*. Or to be even more explicit, he might have written *I call his idealization of her 'a curious aberration' because she was a half-caste from San Domingo*. However, although the lack of such an explicit signal might leave a loophole for the author to wriggle out of, his decision to place the words in the middle of another clause leaves the reader in little doubt as to the intended slur.

Given the date of publication of this text, it is unlikely that the author would have had any conscious perception of possible negative responses or that any accusation would have been forthcoming. Present-day writers might be less flagrant in exposing this aspect of ideological positioning. Thus a single offensive word in this text turns out to be a significant element in identifying a marked racist stance, which, at the same time, indicates the author's stereotypical moral position concerning expectations of how women should behave. What is more, the implied criticism of

Baudelaire for behaving in a responsible way toward this woman (which was, in fact, honourable behaviour by the poet) reveals a less sympathetic stance by the author. Readers might like to consider whether such a passage could be published in a school book at the present time.

3.5 Stance in history textbooks

History textbooks, written by 'experts' to be read by children in an educational context, are not generally thought of as likely sites of authorial attitude or opinion. A common expectation of child and student readers is that the textbook will present certain factual events from history (the 'truth', as it were) in a relatively unbiased and objective way, without much comment on the part of the author. However, it is not unusual to find clear indications of an author's stance, presented either overtly or covertly.

Analysis: true makers of history

In the following text (Text 3.5) where the author deliberately presents his position about history we find both conscious overt opinion and unconscious covert stance.

Text 3.5 The true makers of history

> In order to know and understand how political history came about, we have to look beyond the big events, beyond the high traditions and the rulers of magnificence and power. We have to listen behind the din of armies on the march and the bitter crash of battles. We have to observe, if we can, how ordinary people lived and worked and organized their lives.
>
> Those who want to grasp the fuller meaning of the history of Africa must manage to catch the click of the farmer's hoe, the thump of the housewife's pounding stick, the hiss of the iron-smelter's bellows. They must somehow watch the trailing caravans on their toiling march across the hills and plains . . . . . .
>
> And behind these sights and sounds of everyday life, they must imagine the farmers and their wives, the miners and the traders and the seamen, who were the true makers of history and the real creators of wealth.
>
> (B. Davidson. and J. Mhina, 1968, *East and Central Africa to the Late Nineteenth Century*, Harlow: Longman)

The text encourages the child reader to engage imaginatively with history but also sets out the author's position with respect to the relative importance of the powerful (rulers and armies) and the powerless, pointing out that without the work of the ordinary people there would have been no wealth and no history. Yet, in spite of this progressive and original approach, the text reveals an unreconstructed view of the role of women in history. Men are presented as taking the productive roles and women are reduced to 'the housewife's pounding stick', a reference to women's role in preparing food or being the wives of farmers. This is particularly surprising since in much of Africa the women have traditionally been farmers and everywhere have undertaken many jobs (basket making, pottery, spinning, leather work, jewellery making, hairdressing, cosmetic preparation, to name just a few).

Analysis: Sayyid Said

When an event is *presented as fact*, there is a tendency for readers to accept it as fact if it is written or spoken by an authoritative person. When we read Text 3.6, about a ruler of Oman and Zanzibar, we may well accept it as a series of objectively presented facts and, moreover, facts that are indisputable. Any fact is potentially verifiable, but, unless we are specialists, we are not likely to go off and check the dates of Sultan Bin Ahmad's reign or argue that Said was only 12 when his father died. Most readers accept the text without question. Such an assumption is the inevitable consequence of the Co-operative Principle that we discussed in Chapter 2. Unless we have some reason to behave otherwise, we follow Grice's maxims, in this case, the maxim of Quality.

Nevertheless, when we look at a text critically, we can see that it is sometimes difficult to sort out fact from the author's interpretation – or more accurately *construction* – of historical events. The account of Sayyid Said's reign is extremely brief – even for a school textbook – and it may well be the maxim of Quantity that makes readers question the contents of the account. We feel that more explanations and details are required, and a close examination of the text can reveal more about the author's position.

Text 3.6 Sayyid Said

Sayyid Said was a boy of thirteen when his father, Sultan bin Ahmad, died in 1804, and his cousin Badr seized the throne. But Badr was assassinated in 1806, and Said became ruler. Though still only fifteen, he at once showed skill in government. He ruled for fifty years, dying in 1856.

(B. Davidson and J. Mhina, 1968, *East and Central Africa to the Late Nineteenth Century*, Harlow: Longman)

The writer is more sympathetic to Sayyid Said than he is to Badr. We are told that Sayyid showed *skill in government* (positive appraisal). The use of the word *seized* suggests that Badr was in the wrong to take the throne since the word is associated with force and violence; 'to take hold of, suddenly, with force' is one dictionary definition. We are not told precisely why or how this took place. Did Badr have any legal claim to be Sultan? Did he perhaps doubt the ability of a 13-year-old to rule wisely? Clearly he did not *kill* Sayyid Said when he took over the country, an act one might have expected if his motives were entirely selfish. Then, there is the question

of Badr's death. We are not told who assassinated him or why, but from the information we are given, it suggests that the most likely assassin was Sayyid Said or his
supporters. And, on the basis of the text alone, we cannot accept the validity of the
claim that 'he at once showed skill in government'. Since no evidence is given, we
may well assume that this is just the authors' opinion.

We are not accusing the authors here of deliberate bias (but see Activity 4). It is
possible that they recorded the only facts available to them at the time of writing.
But we can see from this illustration how authors construct historical stories from a
certain point of view even when that point of view is not explicitly stated.

3.6 Some conclusions

Stance may reflect an individual writer's opinion or may represent the attitude or
purpose of a commercial organization, as in the letter from the financial advisers.
The way in which opinion or attitude is realized in text may be *conceptual* or
linguistic, and different linguistic and discoursal techniques are used by writers
depending on the genres and social practices within which they are working.

Similarly, expectations of the reader are based on socially agreed conventions with
respect to issues of fact, opinion, objectivity and bias. In most contexts, writers take
advantage of these expectations and present their ideas according to the conventions
of the particular discourse. This is most clearly evident in advertising and other persuasive texts, but can also be seen in textbooks and other genres. Myers (1998)
considers the ways in which different genres follow different conventions in the
expression of opinion.

Part of the job of the discourse analyst is to identify the linguistic and discoursal
features of language varieties and hence to show how stance is represented in specific contexts of situation.

In this chapter, we have used both conceptual and linguistic modes of analysis,
some of them overlapping; we have applied these techniques to samples from
different genres in an attempt to identify the writers' positions with respect to the
message.

Activities

1. Choose a book or film that you have read or seen recently. Write a short, gen-
    erally favourable, review of your choice. Then, by adapting the first review,
    write a generally unfavourable review of the same work. Give your reviews to
    a friend and ask which they find most convincing. Discuss why this is. Then list
    which words and clauses indicate that your stance is positive or negative.
    Discuss any problems you may have.

2. Text 3.6 comes from one of the first books written in English for African
    schoolchildren about African (rather than colonial) history. If you have access
    to the internet or a good library of African or Middle Eastern history, find out
    what you can about Sayyid Said and his reign. Can you suggest any reasons
    why the authors may have written such a brief account? Can you suggest any

educational or political motivations for these omissions? (Hint: if you are searching the internet, use dates as well as names since there have been a number of rulers in the Middle East and Africa with similar names.)

3. Identify the positive appraisal features in the following advertisement for a holiday. Are there appraisal features that you – or anyone – might find negative or neutral?

Distinctively alluring, decidedly intriguing Vietnam beckons with lush jungles, turquoise lagoons and limestone cliffs that shape this ever changing landscape. Imagine setting sail from Bangkok for the tropical paradise island resort of Ko Chang in Thailand. From here we venture to the 'Pearl of the Orient', Ho Chi Minh City with its elegant neo-classical architecture and beautiful pagodas. .

4. Read the following accounts of Edward Ganolese and identify the stance of the author in each case. The first account was taken from an American detective novel. The second two were constructed. Which do you think could have been written by Ed's own defence lawyer? Why? What features of the language help you to decide on the stance?

(a) I thought about Ed Ganolese. I would call Ed the man with the finger in the pie. Any pie. Show me a pie and I'll show you Ed's finger.

You may never have heard of Ed Ganolese, but he is a very important guy in your life. At one time or another he has probably bought a politician for you to vote for. If you ever came to New York for a convention and did things the little woman shouldn't know about, Ed probably wound up with some of your cash. If you ever guessed three numbers for money, Ed got part of your dime. Likewise, if you have ever given money to horses or other sports stars, or drunk much beer, or ever heated a spoonful of white powder over a candle, you have helped make Ed Ganolese the wealthy and happy man he is today.

A man with so many varied interests obviously can't watch all of them at once. So Ed has people working for him, people whose job it is to stand on the edge of the pie plate and make sure that nobody runs off with the filling.

(Donald E. Westlake, 1988, *The Mercenaries*, New York: Carrol and Graf Publishing)

(b) Mr Edward Ganolese has numerous business interests. He invests widely in the entertainment industry and has assets in casinos and clubs. Much of his income comes from the promotion of sporting events, the alcohol industry and the pharmaceutical industry. These wide ranging investments have given Mr Ganolese a strong financial standing and enabled him to offer support to political parties.

Owing to the variety of his business concerns, it has been necessary for him to delegate responsibility to subordinates, who protect his financial interests.

(c) Edward Ganolese has a controlling interest in many illegal activities in New York and has frequently been involved in political corruption. He has strong financial interests in nightclubs, gambling and prostitution. Much of his high income comes from the illicit drug trade and the sale of alcohol without a licence.

Because of the dubious nature of his business concerns, he has found it essential to place his own men in key jobs in the city.

Further study

Hunston and Thompson (eds), *Evaluation in Text: Authorial Stance and the Construction of Discourse* (2000) is a collection of articles reporting research relating to the topic of this chapter. In the first chapter, the editors give three reasons for the importance of studying 'evaluation', as they call it. The first of the functions of evaluation given by the authors (p. 6) is 'to express the speaker's or writer's opinion, and in so doing to reflect the *value system of that person and their community'* (our italics). In Chapter 1, they provide clear examples of three types of analysis: *lexical*, *grammatical*, and *textual*. Their textual analysis section incorporates what we have referred to as *rhetorical analysis* in this chapter. Their lexical analysis section incorporates *corpus analysis*. For an example of a corpus analysis of stance, see the article by Biber and Conrad (2004: 40–56), and for a range of work on corpus analysis see Stubbs (1996) and Coffin *et al.* (2004).

From time to time in this chapter we have used *appraisal analysis*. However, it is likely that the framework will play an increasing role in CDA and readers may find it a useful area to pursue. An introduction to appraisal analysis can be found on the Appraisal website (current address www.grammatics.com/appraisal). The work of Martin and White (2005) is a much fuller description of the framework with example analyses.

Those readers who are interested in literary criticism might like to read Toolan (1991), which has a chapter on 'narrative as political action' and contains a summary of Labov's (1972) study of stories told by American boys, showing how the expression of the story-teller's opinions is a significant part of successful oral narrative.

Crystal (1987: 379) lists the American Plain English Society's recommendations on 'readability and design', with some reference to business letters. These are not accurate representations of how genres are actually written but are interesting because of the influence they may have had on the way people write – especially in the USA. A brief introduction to the measurement of readability (Grade levels, etc.) can be found in Crystal (1987: 252) and a more detailed explanation is in Stauffer *et al.* (1978: 151–8).

4 Intertextual analysis

No text is ever the text of a single speaker or writer. All texts show traces of differing discourses, contending and struggling for dominance. Texts are therefore the sites of struggle, and in being the sites of struggle, texts are the sites of linguistic and cultural change. Individuals … are the bearers and agents of that struggle.

(Kress, 1989: 32)

4.1 Chains and networks of text

Discourse analysts writing about media reporting have argued against the idea that there is really such a thing as 'hard news' that can be reported impartially.[1] When journalists record or describe events, they are usually reporting on other texts, citing speeches, attributing ideas, and where they are reporting acts that have occurred, they inevitably interpret reality on the basis of the way they viewed the event or the way they heard about it. Often, newspaper texts do not report what has already happened at all but report what 'is to' happen (hypothesized by drawing on such things as press releases from film distributors, research bodies or government press conferences).

All facts are open to a process of creation or re-creation in text in the light of the changing cultural or historical contexts. A further example of this process can be seen in business discourse. The social practice of committee meetings may include short reports from members of the committee on matters in hand. These may then be discussed. The discussion, in turn, may then be summarized by the minutes secretary and later presented to the members in written form and discussed again. Thus is created a succession of related spoken and written texts.

Fairclough (2003) has called this reiteration and re-creation of texts *chains* of texts. Where such chains move and re-link across different media and contexts, *networks* of texts develop. For example, if a business committee makes a decision to make employees redundant, further texts will be created including instructions to managers, letters of dismissal, and so on. If it is a large company, the decision to lay off staff is likely to be reported in the press or on television.

Closely related to text chains is the notion of *intertextuality* (from Bakhtin 1981; 1986), which is the main topic of this chapter. Bakhtin was much concerned with context, even historical context, and how specific utterances were produced and understood 'against the background of other concrete utterances on the same theme'. Intertextuality involves both the intrusion (or adoption by the speaker/author) of aspects of previous texts into a new text either through citation, attribution or reference, and also the hybridization of one genre or text type with another. The rest of this chapter illustrates the analysis of intertextuality within a context of culture.

That is to say, where possible, we consider how the cultural settings (in terms of historical time, domain and social practice) interrelate with text in the creation of meaning.

4.2 Prediction and fact in the media: an example

Newspapers often present future events as though they were facts even though the outcome may be in doubt. Here are some examples from newspaper headlines:

Dutch told to return land they took from the sea

Sinking islanders are facing mass evacuation

Web-sites may be hit by curb on junk food adverts

Walkout warning by Euro-MPs

Cash-hit hospital to lay off 1,000 workers

Church wedding rules may be eased

In headlines such as these, writers can exploit the grammatical potential of language to condense propositions by joining together two or more processes, each reflecting a different present, past or future state or event. In the first example, *told* (present or past verbal process) is joined *to return* (future material process) and *took* (past material process). In the second example, present processes (*sinking, are facing*) are linked to a possible future event, where the process is expressed as a noun (*evacuation*). These somewhat complex examples incorporate grammatical metaphors, to which we return in the next chapter.

Often a prediction is fulfilled and sometime later the newspaper reports the same event again, this time as an actual occurrence. However, inevitably, at times, such headlines predict events which do not actually occur. This may be because the prediction is a hypothesis, dependent on some condition which is mentioned or implied in the main text. At other times, headlines predict events which could not *possibly* occur.

We now look in more detail at a news item that is unlikely to be fulfilled, in part because it becomes clear from the article that the writers do not precisely state what they are predicting:

> EU plan set to put up inheritance tax.

This headline (from *Daily Express*, Monday, 6 March 2006) suggests that in future the European Union (EU) will increase inheritance tax in Britain. This appears to be a strong prediction which, if not a fact in itself, is based on factual evidence. However, a closer reading of the article shows that it begins with a modified proposition, making clear that the article is only a prediction of what might happen:

> Families affected by inheritance tax *could be* exposed to a new threat.
> (our italics)

Could be exposed is a lot weaker as a prediction than the headline suggests. The second sentence reads:

> Moves to harmonize death duties around the EU *could see* people stung for charges on property *passed on during their lifetime.*

Here again we have the modal verb of possibility and the more substantial point that the European Commission is considering tax on gifts given when people are still alive, a very different idea from the one stated in the headline since 'inheritance tax' in Britain is a tax on wealth left by someone on death to their heirs. Thus the tax is on *inherited* wealth: hence its name. We might imagine that this is just an error resulting from the journalist's ignorance of tax matters, but, in fact, this point is made clear in the article itself, in effect, contradicting the headline:

> Here [that is 'in the UK'], a person's estate for the purposes of bequests is deemed to be what he or she owned at death.

The rest of the article reveals that these are only proposals which are being debated and that there is considerable opposition to them in Scotland and England from both government and lawyers.

What is going on here? First, we need to ask *why* the editorial staff chose a headline which apparently states as fact an idea which has only been put forward as a possibility and, what is arguably worse, even misrepresents the idea. To find the answer we have to consider the wider discourse context in terms of the ongoing ideology of the paper. In our view the article seeks to promote two of its favourite issues: (1) its opposition to the present amount of an individual's estate taken in inheritance tax, and (2) its opposition to Britain's membership of the European Union.

The *Daily Express* has been running a long-term campaign of protest against the government about British inheritance tax. This is called, by the *Express* itself, 'The Daily Express Inheritance Crusade', and, in the centre of the layout of the article, there is a copy of a form which readers are invited to sign and submit to the paper.

To Gordon Brown, the Chancellor of the Exchequer, I believe that there is no justification for the unfair inheritance tax and demand it should be abolished immediately. Signed ....

We will pass your voucher to Downing Street.

Those readers who are familiar with this action will understand that the phrase 'unfair inheritance tax' relates to the *Express*'s view of British inheritance tax and has little to do with the European plan mentioned in the article's headline. However, new readers might well think that they are signing a protest against some threatening 'new' law rather than the non-event reported in the article.

On the second issue, the *Daily Express* is known to its regular readers as an extremely nationalistic paper that has consistently opposed Britain's membership of the European Union and has taken every opportunity to report news which may be read as evidence for Europe's flaws. To this end, it has presented the British (and sometimes the English) in the role of Self (that with which the paper and its readers identify) and the European Union ('Europe') as Other, regardless of the facts that Britain is part of the geographical continent of Europe, is actually a member of the European Union, sends representatives to the European Parliament and recognizes the European Court. This is supported in the article by the use of 'here' to refer to Britain.

4.3 The uses of intertextuality

In our analysis of the 'inheritance' text in the previous section, we relied on our knowledge of the newspaper and its political concerns in order to offer explanations for the way it reported the news story. The petition 'to Gordon Brown' provided a link to other anti-tax stories with the words 'the proposal comes as tens of thousands of Daily Express readers continue to send in coupons backing our crusade to end the iniquity of inheritance tax'. Our understanding of its consistent opposition to this tax and to the policy of European union was dependent on *intertextuality*.

Intertextuality is a discourse process which is closely linked to the notions discussed above of re-creation, reiteration and interpretation. Within CDA, *intertextual analysis* has two main functions: (1) it plays an important role in revealing speakers' and writers' strategies in reinforcing or re-formulating ideas and beliefs; and (2) it can reveal traces of the dominant ideology or evidence of ideological struggle and cultural change.

Sources, referencing and plagiarism

We have referred above to *sources* of an author's material. The use of the word *source* reminds us of another use of the word: the geographical point at which a spring or river begins. Metaphorically, the word is used in discourse studies – and generally in the academic world – to refer to the place or places in which a certain idea or set of ideas originate. Scientists, for example, commonly talk or write about sources in terms of quotations or citations that allow readers to find where related ideas came from. This is seen partly as a conventional form of respect for other members of the discourse community and partly as a means of making a 'short cut' by allowing writers to leave out at least some of the background details of the work in hand. This subscribes to the traditional idea that all new ideas are based on what has gone before and that we rely on our forebears for any scientific or artistic achievement.

This is commonly referred to as 'standing on the shoulders of giants', an expression often attributed to Sir Isaac Newton, the British scientist. In 1676, he wrote to a friend, 'If I have seen further, it is by standing on the shoulders of giants', the idea being that we can see further and hence achieve greater success if we build on previous work. It is not known for certain, but it seems likely, however, that Newton was familiar with the work of John of Salisbury, who wrote in the year 1159:

> Bernard of Chartres used to say that we are like dwarfs on the shoulders of giants, so that we can see more than they, and things at a greater distance, not by virtue of any sharpness of sight on our part, or any physical distinction, but because we are carried high and raised up by their giant size.

Whether Newton knowingly adapted the words of Salisbury or whether the idea had by that time become part of a popular heritage, we shall never know, but it is a clear example of the movement of voices through time and the resources that the language makes available to its users. Incidentally, the poet and critic Samuel Taylor Coleridge wrote (1818), 'The dwarf sees further than the giant, when he has the giant's shoulders to mount on' (*The Friend*, vol. 2, 'On the Principles of Political Knowledge') and even more recently, the expression 'Stand on the shoulders of giants' has been used as the slogan of the Google internet research site 'Google Scholar'.

The effect of referring to the work of others is a clear and obvious way of introducing 'other voices' into a text. These voices may simply contribute additional information or opinions or they may support or refute the meanings that are created by the main author. The use of other voices can help a writer or speaker to bring extra richness to a text by incorporating different levels of meaning and by evoking, for example, other places and other times.

A current issue in intertextuality studies is that of *plagiarism* (or 'copying') in students' work. While students are always encouraged to read widely and to draw on the work of 'giants' in their field, there are written conventions that need to be learned about how the ideas that they glean can be incorporated into their own writing. A basic principle is that, where the exact wording of a previous written text or even spoken text (such as a lecture or broadcast) is used, the exact source should be given. If the accepted conventions of academic genres are not followed, a student may be accused of plagiarism, a 'crime' that is punished with disgrace and even dismissal when it appears to be a deliberate act of deception.

Students in higher education occasionally fall into the trap of unintentional plagiarism. In secondary and high schools, children are often encouraged to find information for their essays and projects on the internet. They may be encouraged to 'cut and paste' what they find into their own work as a stage in the process of learning how to cope with discourse in different registers. In some cultures, undergraduate students are expected to reproduce in examinations exactly what they have learned from lectures or course books. However, the time comes when they need to be able to control the conventions of intertextuality appropriately in writing their own work.

Although there is no copyright on ideas, students are credited for knowing the sources of their ideas and it is normal for academic writers to give credit to others where possible.

The ways in which authors legitimately refer to previous publications vary across genre and discipline. For example, in (1), taken from a book on child development, the author makes certain points about infants' cries and then refers to research reports where the reader can find the evidence for the information that has been given.[2]

1.   The baby's cry is a complex auditory stimulus that varies in intensity, from a whimper to a message of all out distress (Gustafson and Harris, 1990). As early as the first few weeks of life, individual infants can be identified by the unique vocal 'signature' of their cries. Recognition of their own baby's cry helps parents locate their infant from a distance and is especially advantageous once their babies move on their own (Gustafson, Green and Cleland, 1994).

(L. Berk, 2000, *Child Development*, fifth edn. Boston and London:

Allyn and Bacon, p. 134)

However, not all authors summarize or comment on their references when referring to a source. They simply assume that the reader will already be familiar with the work referred to or will be prepared to follow up the references and read the work elsewhere. This is usual in the hard sciences, especially in journal articles. When writing for an expert readership, writers can simultaneously 'advertise' their own scholarship, show respect to fellow academics, and provide a resource for the reader.

Other voices

In another form of reference, a direct quotation may be made from a source text, as in example (2). Where the quotation is self-explanatory, neither a summary nor prior knowledge is required. In (2), somewhat surprisingly written by a professor-consultant of obstetrics and gynaecology, the author, discussing the role of patient–doctor discourse in surgical cases, writes:

2.   In theatre, the surgeon has to be able to ignore everything expect for the job in hand. Before and after the operation he cannot afford too much empathy. AJ Cronin in 'Dr Finlay's Case Book' had his hero, immediately after finals, apply for a post as assistant to a great surgeon. When asked why, Dr Finlay said, 'You saved that poor woman's life. I want to do that'. The great surgeon turned him down, telling him that with so much sympathy he was better suited to general practice.

(J.O. Drife, 1998, 'Narrative in Surgery', in T. Greenhalgh and B. Hurwitz,

Narrative Based Medicine, London: BMJ Books, p. 113)

Here, Professor Drife is not addressing fellow experts in obstetrics and gynaecology (expert-to-expert discourse); instead he is writing an article for inclusion in a book on the humanistic dimensions of medicine in which doctor–patient interaction is seen as an important factor in health care. The first two sentences make a generalization about the role of surgeons. Drife then provides a short narrative to support his point that empathy is not generally seen as a quality that surgeons need. This is not written for the expert reader. Readers will be medical personnel from different branches of medicine – but may also include a general readership or academics interested in communication.

In example (2) he cites the words of a character in a fictional text (a novel by A.J. Cronin). There is probably an assumption that the reader will be familiar with the novel from which the quotation is taken since it is a successful work that has been adapted for both film and television. There are then a number of linked texts incorporated into the example. At the most embedded level we have the conversation between Dr Finlay and the great surgeon, consisting of the words attributed to Dr Finlay himself, given in direct speech, and the response from the surgeon given in indirect speech. We then have the voice of Cronin, presented as 'writer' of the fictional text. These texts are incorporated *within* the main text – the words (and argument) – of Professor Drife's. To complicate matters, it is quite possible that Cronin, who was himself a qualified doctor who had been a general practitioner, was drawing on a real-life experience in constructing the story about Dr Finlay's interview. In this way, actual spoken discourse can pervade written discourse and then be reproduced in later texts. In using the quotation from Cronin, Drife re-positions it. In the novel, it is seen as a moment of revelation for the doctor, who, as a result of the conversation, becomes a successful general practitioner and a social innovator. It is a turning point in the narrative structure of the book. In Drife's article, however, it has a different function altogether. It is presented as supporting Drife's argument that 'surgery is a technical business' and doctor–patient interaction, while important in diagnosis, could prove a hindrance to good surgery if the surgeon becomes too sensitive to the patient's feelings. He writes: 'Narrative requires honesty about emotions, but the fact that operating involves inflicting mutilating and potentially painful wounds militates against the operator showing sensitivity.'

As we have shown, one contrasting element in examples (1) and (2) above is the nature of the texts drawn on by the authors. In Berk's text, all the citations are to other academic works and there is no mixing of genres. Drife's text, in contrast, draws on a number of different genres and styles in the textual mix, including everyday conversation and fiction (the novel). This type of mixing of genres is sometimes known as *interdiscursivity*, but the term overlaps with *intertextuality* and it can be difficult to distinguish between them in specific instances.

In media discourse, journalists use intertextuality to introduce other voices into their articles or reports. This may be simply a matter of attributing some idea or opinion to another, but in some places it is a way of bringing the people who are the topic of discussion directly into the text. This can perform the function of revealing the personality and position of a person in a way that the journalist might hesitate to do more directly. For example, in the obituary of the Southern Baptist leader Adrian Rogers (*Daily Telegraph*, 19 November 2005), the writer does *not* accuse Rogers of promoting homophobia, religious hatred, gender inequality or racial discrimination. Instead, he writes of him:

3a. As well as opposing homosexuality and female ordination, he promoted the evangelization of the Jews, and ordered a boycott of the Disney Corporation because of its liberal employment policies towards homosexuals. He described capital punishment as 'spiritually ordained' and emphasized the primary role of fathers: 'We have dads today that are only interested in sports, business and sex,' he observed. 'They've forgotten their God-given assignment to teach the Ten Commandments'.

20 / POST WW1, prohibition. ←70's Vietnam corruption
40 WW2. Contrast packs, period War.
so toriety / drunkness
mob.

58 | The Practice of Critical Discourse Analysis

'Women', he pointed out, were instructed by the Bible to 'submit' to their husbands.

3b. Rogers' belief in the literal truth of the Bible sometimes proved awkward: when asked on one occasion about Biblical justifications for slavery, he observed that slavery was 'a much maligned institution', and added that if it had not been abolished 'we would not have such a welfare problem', though he later signed up to a revised *Baptist Faith and Message* to the effect that all races were equal before the Lord.

Thus, the journalist establishes Rogers' attitudes, which he clearly sees as open to criticism, and, at least in the case of the slavery issue, contradictory and unacceptable, but he reveals them in the preacher's own words, letting him condemn himself. In this way a new level of meaning is added to Rogers' own presentation of his views of the world by the way in which the new author summarizes and juxtaposes major points of Rogers' doctrine so that this religious leader appears to be intolerant, illiberal, discriminatory, and reactionary. (More of this obituary can be seen in the Activities section at the end of this chapter.)

4.4 Intertextuality in literature

It has been suggested that every text carries resonances of all the texts that have preceded it, and that all discourse is the sum of past discourse. A text is also said to stand in contrast to all other texts since it reflects the specific context of its creation. This sounds somewhat mystical and unlikely at first, but it is not so strange if one thinks of how both ideas and the form of language and human interaction change and develop over the centuries. We may not always recognize the influences on the way we speak or write and, even when we do, we can only pick up on the more obvious examples. As with a family tree, the more generations one goes back from the present, the more difficult it is to identify the details. Here we will look at one literary example in some detail.

A well-known example of intertextuality from literature can be seen in Eliot's poem *The Waste Land* (1922). Not only does he lift from texts of different historical periods but also from different languages: German, French, Latin and Sanskrit among others. Intertextuality is exploited by Eliot in all his poetry, but in *The Waste Land*, it is so intensive that Eliot was obliged to provide six pages of notes at the end of the poem to elucidate it for the readers. The notes, however, in the main give only brief references, often to obscure texts, and yet there can be little doubt that a knowledge of the primary texts adds meaning to the poem.

For readers who are not familiar with Eliot's work, one section of this complex poem tells the story of a typist returning home to a simple London home, preparing tea for a boyfriend, a house agent's clerk. She is described as 'bored and tired'. The following eight lines immediately follow the account of the young woman's seduction by the boyfriend, in whom she shows little interest:

She turns and looks a moment in the glass,
Hardly aware of her departed lover;

Her brain allows one half-formed thought to pass:
'Well now that's done: and I'm glad it's over.'
When lovely woman stoops to folly and
Paces about her room again, alone,
She smoothes her hair with automatic hand,
And puts a record on the gramophone.

The reader is presented with a picture of woman unconcerned and unexcited by a casual sexual act. She is presented as having little emotional reaction to what has happened. A note to the fifth line of the above selection refers the reader to 'the song' in Goldsmith's *The Vicar of Wakefield:*

When lovely woman stoops to folly
And finds too late that men betray.
What charm can smooth her melancholy?
What art can wash her guilt away?

The reader of *The Waste Land*, who, on reading the poem, is aware of the origin of the line 'when lovely woman stoops to folly' has an added dimension to their understanding. The two texts, Eliot's and Goldsmith's, are brought together for a purpose. The contrast between them is striking. Where Eliot presents a picture of a woman's casual indifference to an intimate sexual act, Goldsmith stresses the significance of what has happened and the social shame and distress that a woman in that situation is expected to feel.

Elsewhere in the poem, Eliot seems to stress the splendour of the past with scraps of text from earlier poets, religious books, Shakespeare. This has been interpreted by critics as a way in which Eliot points to the squalor and desolation of present-day society ('the waste land') in contrast to the glory of the past, but this is not the only possible interpretation. Not all past references are to splendour; some, from the Bible and Webster, for example, are to horror and death, and there is an end-note to the effect that the same people appear in different guises at different points in the poem. He writes: 'so all the women are one woman and the two sexes meet in Tiresias', referring to the Tiresias of ancient Greek stories, who changed his persona and even his/her gender from time to time. He is described by Eliot as 'the most important person in the poem, uniting all the rest', which suggests that he is not only concerned with change, but also with what remains the same. The poem is a series of contrasts, pointed by the instances of intertextuality, in which *here* and *there*, *then* and *now*, *life* and *death*, are inextricably brought together.

We have seen in this section that texts are frequently dependent on previous texts in terms of meanings, wordings. We have also seen how these can be mixed and restructured in new texts to create new meanings. However, from the discourses of the near and distant past, we inherit not only meanings and wordings but also generic conventions, orders of discourse, and aspects of culture. Perhaps the strongest pervading inheritance is from a society's religious and ceremonial texts, both written and spoken, and from highly valued works of literature or science.

What we might call intertextuality has a similar social force in the visual arts, architecture and music. Jazz 'quotes' from other pieces of popular and classical music. Orchestral music has been based on folk songs. Films contain references to other films, sometimes with parodies of scenes, sometimes quotations from a script, sometimes visual stylistic references. Clips from older films often appear on a television screen that a character is watching. Frequently, an author or speaker might refer to another person's work and include not only citations of language, or summaries of ideas, but also diagrams or pictures.

4.5 Intertextuality in scientific discourse

We have already mentioned the way in which sciences build on previous research (and therefore on previous texts) to push knowledge forward. This is a classic case of intertextuality that we do not have room to consider in any depth here. However, we give some space to scientific discourse for additional reasons: first, because it is an example of how language use changes through social pressures, and, second, because it serves as an example of how specialist meaning is constructed. Both these issues are important in CDA since expert discourse is often seen as socially divisive because the language used by specialists (scientists, lawyers, for example) is often inaccessible to the non-expert.

We use the word 'scientific' here in a broad sense to include the hard sciences and also other disciplines that have formally established knowledge bases, theories and research methods.

What is generally known as the 'scientific register' of English usually refers to expert-to-expert discourse in the written mode rather than the popular versions of science that we find in the media or informal discussions of scientific issues. We tend to think of 'science' as a set of truths about the nature of the world, but, in fact, science might be better described as a set of models constructed by people who have carefully observed and studied the world. It is interesting to see how the discourse of science has changed over the centuries and how this is revealed in the structure of the English language. This change can be seen as largely cultural since it is tied to the development of international scientific communities, within which members share idealized cognitive models (frames) and a common language. Much of the arcane nature of scientific discourse is the result of expert-to-expert communication taking place in a context where there is already a large body of shared knowledge. To the lay person, this becomes inaccessible and to the novice scientist it is part of the subject of study.

In the title of an article on the language of science, Halliday (1993) uses the words 'the construction of knowledge and value in the grammar of scientific discourse'. Some readers find this strange because, popularly, scientific language is characterized by its vocabulary rather than its grammar. It is true that one of the main features of scientific discourse is specialist lexis, but this itself is often dependent on grammar for its formulation and its use.

Words are often incorporated in long nominal groups (*a commercially available immunoassay kit; effects of radical resection on liver metastasis*). Scientific written language tends to use more *grammatical metaphor* (see Appendix) than the language of many other domains. This has not always been so and there are exceptions even today, but it has been a general trend in many branches of science as well as in what might be termed 'fringe' sciences, such as economics. A simple example, taken from cancer research data, is in the nominal group:

the evaluation of the effects of radical resection on liver metastasis

Here four processes often expressed as verbs are construed as nouns (Table 4.1). The nominal construction allows the writer to leave out any references to the participants of these processes (the scientists, the surgeons, the resection and the tumour). Such omissions can make texts opaque to uninitiated readers, but they give a higher lexical density (see Chapter 10) and make the nouns available for modification, as in *radical* resection or the constructed example:

The recent evaluation of the long-term effects of radical resection ...

Verbs	Nouns
evaluate (the scientists evaluated the effects)	evaluation
resection (the surgeons resected the liver)	resection
affect (the resection affected the metastasis)	effect
metastasize (the tumour metastasized to the liver)	metastasis

Table 4.1 Nominal construction

Gledhill (2000) demonstrated how long nominal groups are gradually built up in scientific texts by re-contextualizing words that had been previously referred to in the same text, a type of grammatical intertextuality. (We demonstrate grammatical metaphor in political discourse in Chapter 5.)

Scientists' findings are often presented as *claims* rather than facts because researchers recognize that their observations or experimental research are only small steps towards our better understanding of the natural world. Moreover, they know that they themselves have played a part in the construction of their contribution to scientific knowledge. This is easy to understand in the case of theoretical science, where the scientists involved have arrived at theories on the basis of their investigation of previous work, but it may be less clear in the case of more empirical science. However, the minds and consciousness of the scientists are always involved in the production of scientific meaning. In the case of descriptive or analytical work, they may have devised hierarchical classification systems which can draw out the different characteristics of natural structures. In the case of experimental work, they may have not only devised the methods of research and put them into practice, but also collected the results and reported on them. In either case, the scientist acknowledges that what is discovered today may be refuted or superseded tomorrow.

The way in which lay people 'see' the natural world is reflected in their use of language. Discoursally, a contrast has been made (Myers 1990) between a narrative of science and a narrative of nature. The narrative of science refers to what experts address to experts about their work. The narrative of nature refers to the way lay people speak or write about the world.

Clear examples are the ways in which medical specialists discuss illnesses, the ways in which non-specialists discuss illnesses, and the ways in which specialists communicate with non-specialists on the same topic. We may consider the specialist discourse to be more precise, more rational, more 'evidence based', but there is still a social need for a less explicit, more personal, more experiential discourse which must be used by both doctor and patient in the consulting room, for example. The process of diagnosis requires an understanding of the patient's experience of symptoms: pain, discomfort or progress.

4.6 Expert discourse and issues of power

An important social consideration in the issue of 'expert' discourse is that in most institutional situations the specialist is the holder of power. The experts hold the key both to the expert discourse and to the non-expert discourse as well, while the non-experts and novices are privy only to the non-expert discourse. Analysis of the doctor–patient interaction almost always shows the doctor in the position of *controller*. The doctor asks the questions, the patient answers; the doctor interrupts, the patient remains silent; the doctor prescribes treatment, the patient accepts it, and so on. This extends to institutions in general. The law is a parallel case, where the lay person has to rely on the expertise of the solicitor, the barrister or the court, and almost always feels at a disadvantage, in part because of the overpowering force of the conventional structures which he or she does not fully understand.

Another issue is the way in which 'expert' discourse is in constant change. New laws are made, new medicines are discovered, new technology is developed, new research provides further evidence of environmental damage, and all the innovation that is reported involves new terminology and new structures of discourse. Yet the non-expert or the novice is unable to keep up with the changes, either conceptually or linguistically.

Expert discourse (legal, medical, educational, administrative, scientific, technical, political, economic, and so on) is, on the whole, valued and respected in social life. Of course, we complain when we are excluded from exchanges that affect us, such as not understanding a contract or how to apply for a mortgage, but the command of expert discourses is understood as evidence of education and as part of 'knowing' a subject and having specialized skills, and we have to pay good money to those who hold the skills to operate within specialist discourse.

The French social theorist Pierre Bourdieu (1991) proposed the notion of *cultural capital* to account for what is symbolically 'valued' in society. While we agree that the distinction between expert and non-expert discourse is crucial in respect of power in contemporary society, we cannot accept what our reading of Bourdieu seems to indicate: that the dominant classes have control of all 'expert' discourse. To us, linguistic expertise is not directly related to class as a stratified economic structure (although we do not deny the importance of social classes), but to a complexity of structures within which each *discourse community* has its own experts, who control the linguistic capital of that community, and also has its own novices – who are preparing to become experts – and its interested lay people. These discourse communities may operate within one social class or cut across them. Social clubs and hobby groups also form discourse communities that are not always class based. Swales (1990) gives the example of an international stamp collecting society, which had evolved its own specialist genres, terminology, and modes of communication and has no basis in class.

Of course, some areas of expertise are more closely positioned in social classes and this is often a product of the length or type of training required. It is the case, in Europe at least, that a consultant surgeon is classified as middle class while a car mechanic is a member of the working class, but each has their own areas of dominance and power and each employs highly specialized discourse in specific contexts. Moreover, each of them is equally likely or unlikely to use relaxed articulation, slang and coarse language from time to time in certain contexts, something which Bourdieu appears to deny.

Everyday language and scientific concepts

Even if we are experts in a particular field, our everyday language will not necessarily reflect our expertise. Even when we understand a scientific concept, our everyday language may not show it. To take a simple example: Is it a fact that the sun rises in the east and sets in the west? Most people would unthinkingly agree that the sun rises in the east and sets in the west with some deviation towards the north and south according to the time of the year. However, a little consideration of the issue will remind those of us who have studied elementary science that, according to the scientific account, the sun does not *rise* at all. In that account, which is generally believed, the earth turns on its axis towards the east, the sun comes into view and *appears* to rise. We know what we mean when we say 'the sun rises' and yet most of us do not *perceive* the reality of the situation. Of course, if we stop to think about it and know enough science, we are at liberty to express the idea in a different way, but this would seem inappropriate in situations other than educational or academic ones because, on the whole, we accept the conventional modes of speaking even when they are factually misleading.

What seems to be happening here is that either (1) the naïve way we perceive the world (our 'commonsense' interpretation) is more powerful than our education when it comes to everyday discourse or (2) we have inherited an ancient (pre-Galileo) discourse of the state of the universe that pervades our sense of reality.

Although explanation (2) seems unlikely, there are many similar cases in language use as, for example, in the case of North American 'Indians', who are now known as Native Americans. They were given the name 'Indian' by European explorers in the sixteenth century because of the sailors' mistaken impression that they had reached India. Nevertheless, long after it was well known that this was a mistake, indeed right into the final quarter of the twentieth century, English speakers referred to them by that name and some still do.

Activities

1. Read the following two texts. Text A is an historian's account of attempts to restrict child labour by law, written recently. Text B is a section from Lord Ashley's actual speech in the House of Commons over 170 years ago. Comment on the linguistic and rhetorical differences between the two texts. Do you think that the writer of Text A was familiar with Text B? Identify any examples of intertextuality here.

A. Child labour in the nineteenth century

On 16th March 1832 Michael Sadler introduced a Bill in Parliament that proposed limiting the hours of all persons under the age of 18 to ten hours a day. After much debate it was clear that Parliament was unwilling to pass Sadler's bill. However, in April 1832 it was agreed that there should be another parliamentary enquiry into child labour. Sadler was made chairman and for the next three months the parliamentary committee interviewed 48 people who had worked in textile factories as children. Sadler discovered that it was common for young children to be working for over twelve hours a day. Lord Ashley carried out a survey of doctors in 1836. In a speech he made in the House of Commons he argued that over half of the doctors interviewed believed that 'ten hours is the utmost quantity of labour which can be endured by the children' without damaging their health. However, Lord Ashley admitted that some doctors that came before his committee did not believe that long hours caused health problems. Children who were late for work were severely punished. If children arrived late for work they would also have money deducted from their wages. Time-keeping was a problem for those families who could not afford to buy a clock. In some factories workers were not allowed to carry a watch. The children suspected that this rule was an attempt to trick them out of some of their wages.

B. Lord Ashley, speech in the House of Commons, 9 May 1836

Of the thirty-one medical men who were examined, sixteen gave it as their most decided opinion that ten hours is the utmost quantity of labour which can be endured by the children, with the slightest chance of preserving their health. Dr. Loudon reports, 'I am of the opinion no child under fourteen years of age should work in a factory of any description more than eight hours a day.' Dr. Hawkins reports, 'I am compelled to declare my deliberate opinion, that no child should be employed in factory labour below the age of ten; that no individual, under the age of eighteen, should be engaged in it longer than ten hours daily.'

2. In Section 4.4, we discussed the added dimension that was brought to *The Waste Land* by the reference to Goldsmith's poem 'When lovely woman stoops to folly' and we cited four lines from the poem. The full poem has eight lines; the rest of it is given here:

The only art her guilt to cover,
To hide her shame from every eye,
To give repentance to her lover,
And wring his bosom, is – to die.

Does reading this make you question our analysis of the effect of this instance of intertextuality? What extra force does it give the eight lines from the Eliot poem? If you know that the Goldsmith poem is presented as a song in a light-hearted novel (*The Vicar of Wakefield*), does it affect the way you read Eliot's version?

3. Here are two more short passages from the obituary of Adrian Rogers, discussed in Section 4.3. Re-read the selections in that section and then read Text A below. What do you think the writer means by 'formidable force for conservatism in American politics' and 'an uncompromising agenda in domestic and foreign affairs' (which we have underlined). Do you think the author is sympathetic to Rogers' political position? Give your reasons.

A. Adrian Rogers, who died on Tuesday aged 74, served three terms as president of the American Southern Baptist Convention and was instrumental in turning it into a formidable force for conservatism in American Politics.

Rogers was elected in 1979 on a platform of 'biblical inerrancy' (the literal truth of the Bible) and stamped his authority on the subject, securing the dismissal of more liberal minded seminary professors and requiring all employees of the denomination to swear loyalty to a statement of faith set out in a document entitled *Baptist Faith and Message*. He taught that Christians have a duty to be involved in government and promoted an uncompromising agenda in domestic and foreign affairs. (*our underlining*)

Comment on the use of language in Text B below, particularly on the use of the epithets *courageous, even-handed, democratic* and *terrorist-infested* in terms of positive and negative evaluation. Why, do you think, has the writer chosen to quote some of Roger's exact words rather than summarizing his ideas?

B. In May 2003 Rogers was one of a number of religious leaders who signed an open letter on foreign policy to President George W. Bush, commending his 'courageous decision to go to war in Iraq', but warning him that he would be 'morally wrong' to be 'even-handed' as between 'democratic Israel … and the terrorist-infested Palestinian infrastructure.'

4. Read and discuss the following quotation in the light of the work in this chapter:

The more one studies narrative, the more one realizes how complex the bridge between teller and listener actually is. For instance, the act of telling a story changes the story … The narrator cannot ever tell exactly the same narrative again. On the listener's side, none of us ever truly 'hears' a story exactly as it is told by the narrator. Each story inevitably has gaps of meaning and significance, and we fill in these gaps as we imagine the world to be and as we imagine the teller intended. Thus, rather than hear a story, it is rather more accurate to say that we construct for ourselves a story about what we think we are hearing.

(H. Brody, Introduction, in Greenhalgh and Hurwitz, 1998, *Narrative Based Medicine*)

Further study

Related to our discussion of predictive newspaper headlines, Fairclough identified three types of statement: *statements of fact, predictions*, and *evaluations*. He includes hypothetical statements in the 'prediction' category (see Fairclough 2003: 109).

Bakhtin (1981; 1986) is usually credited with the original work on intertextuality. Most books on CDA contain some discussion of the process, particularly Fairclough (1999 and 2003: Chapter 3). Fairclough is particularly interested in the influx of media and promotional discourse into educational and local authority genres.

Roudiez (1981) attributed the word *intertextuality* to Kristeva, who used the concept in the analysis of literary texts in a rather more abstract way than we have introduced it here. On plagiarism and cross-cultural issues in academic writing, see Bloor and Bloor and other articles in Adams *et al.* (1991), Angelil-Carter (2002) and Coulthard (2006a). See also Ivanič (1998).

For work on scientific language and discourse, see Halliday and Martin (1993), which includes accounts of both expert-to-expert discourse and the teaching of scientific discourse in schools; M. Bloor, T. Bloor and other articles in Sanchez-Macarro and Carter (1998: 155–73). The data on grammatical metaphor in scientific discourse comes from Gledhill's (2000) study of collocation in scientific text. Brennan (1994) studied the problem of expert-to-lay-person discourse in relation to cross-examination in court, particularly of children. Greenhalgh and Hurwitz (1998) has a number of articles on doctor–patient discourse.

An interesting contributor to work on discourse and culture – and particularly work relating to facts in the media – is Stuart Allan (1998), who wrote: 'I argue that televisual news accounts encourage us to accept as *natural, obvious* or *commonsensical* certain preferred definitions of reality, and that these definitions have profound implications for the cultural reproduction of power relations across society.' See also Fowler (1991) for a critical approach to the news media.

5

Figurative language, metaphor and message

Rhetoric … is essentially geared towards the persuasive communication of preferred models of social events, and thus manages how recipients will understand and especially how they will evaluate such events, for instance as a function of the interests of the participants. It is therefore not surprising that rhetorical structures play such an important role in ideological manipulation.

(van Dijk, 1998a: 208)

5.1 Rhetorical devices in discourse

This chapter is about the rhetorical devices that speakers and writers use to construct their messages. Public speakers, advertisers, politicians, journalists and others deliberately use this resource knowingly to enhance the way they use language. However, we all – even small children – use some rhetorical devices unconsciously in everyday communication.

No doubt most cultures – not only literate ones – have some type of rhetorical tradition and many have a tradition of commentary and critique as well. Certainly, in the Arab world and in India and South-East Asia as well as China and Japan, traditional approaches to rhetoric are valued and new ones develop. In Ethiopia, there are regions where oratory competitions are traditionally held and judges discuss the various merits of the speakers' techniques, even referring to the characteristics of highly valued speakers from the past. Similarly in Shona discourse, oratory and oral story telling have a long tradition, and the use of figures of speech and in particular the ideophone (onomatopoeia used to represent sounds, such as 'bang!' or the sound of hooves) is incorporated, often with gesture, into the narrative.

5.2 Aristotle's *Rhetoric*

The study of rhetoric dates back though history. In Europe, we attribute the first description of rhetorical devices to classical Greece, where there were schools of rhetoric in which students were taught the art of persuasion and argument, particularly with respect to public speaking. There was a demand for such training because of the power wielded by effective speakers in the assembly, where the enfranchised men of Athens (about 25 per cent of the total population) were free to debate issues of city government and had the scope to create and revise laws as well as to operate them. Isocrates, for example, who first made his living writing speeches for politicians, opened schools of rhetoric in Athens and Chios (by 387 BC), training orators in the techniques of persuasion, and became a rich man as a result. However, for our purposes in CDA, the most important of the Greek rhetoricians was Aristotle, who opened his own school, the Lyceum, in Athens in the year of Isocrates' death (338 BC). We say 'for our purposes' because there is a lot in the work of Aristotle that reminds us of the objectives and practices of critical discourse analysis.

The importance of Aristotle was that, although he was also interested in teaching public speaking, he had two other concerns. The first was to consider rhetoric as an intellectual field worthy of study in its own right, not just as part of a general skill of oratory. He saw it as a branch of philosophy ('Thus the study of rhetoric, instead of being a philosophical outcast, transcends its humble and practical origins to become an important component in the general study of man'[1]). The second was to see rhetoric as a component of communication. This meant that he was not only concerned with the productive aspect of rhetoric but also the receptive, which is to say the way audiences interpret discourse and the extent to which they are persuaded by stylistic devices.[2] Hence, part of the academic study of rhetoric involves training in the ability to recognize and analyse such devices, and, as a result, not only to be able to use them but also to be able to see through them.

Aristotle's vision of 'ethics' as being related to the 'political' may seem somewhat incongruous in the cynical twenty-first century, and it is likely that it appeared equally idealistic during his lifetime. Aristotle required the rhetorician to *make a moral case* for his position. As a means to this end, he said that the politician needed to understand character, virtue and happiness, social value, justice and criminality, war and peace, nobility, revenue and many other aspects of the human social condition. He believed that part of the role of the orator was to praise ('the noble is that which is praiseworthy') and to argue for what is good for the realm on the basis of 'proofs' (what today we would probably call *evidence*). Another role was to censure the criminal and the unjust.

Having established his argument, the orator must then consider the style and arrangement of his speech and to this end Aristotle provided a taxonomy of skills 'to render the facts persuasive'. 'It is not sufficient to have a grasp of what one should say, but one must also say those things in the way that one should, and this makes a great contribution to the character that the speech projects.'[3] The most accessible of these are listed in Figure 5.1 in a summary form.

These devices are all in current use in the twenty-first century, as most key speeches of leading politicians around the world testify.

In addition to concern about the substance of the speech, Aristotle attended to matters of style as revealed in the use of figurative language. Many of the techniques that Aristotle discussed have been incorporated into the study of literature. The nineteenth century was perhaps the major period when literary criticism incorporated a study of such devices, and, in English, it provided students with lists similar to Aristotle's.

In the next section, we look at some types of figurative language and other rhetorical devices and consider how people use them in discourse.

Shruch

70

Argue NCR

1. **The use of the voice:** to express emotion: Particularly in terms variation of speed, volume, accent and rhythm.
2. **Use of example:** (a) mention of facts supporting/refuting th
                        (b) comparison.
                        (c) use of analogy. Here one may use fables or invent stories which mirror the present case. *fable knows best*
3. **Use of repetition:** To emphasize the main points of the speech.
4. **Use of maxims:** A general assertion. Listeners are delighted when a point is generalized which they happen to presuppose in the particular case. Use general truths to support or refute arguments. 'One should guess at the sort of opinions that the audience happen already to have pre-supposed, and then speak in general about them.'

Figure 5.1 Aristotle's forms of rhetorical presentation

5.3 Metaphor

Where one entity is said to be like another, we say that a *simile* has been used. Daniel, a 3-year-old, enjoying eating runny custard for the first time, said, 'Custard is like a drink', creating a *simile* that he had almost certainly never heard before to express a concept which was new to him. The same child, observing the letter 'J' on a keyboard, said, 'That's like grandma's walking stick'.

A *metaphor* is not very different from a simile. It has been described in the literary context as making a comparison by transferring a name from one thing to another, 'a shift, a carrying over of a word from its normal use to a new one'. The use of simple metaphors of this kind is normal in all human communication. Aristotle gave the examples 'Achilles like a lion leapt' (simile) and 'the lion leapt' (metaphor), the latter example referring to Achilles as the lion, since 'they are both bold'. Many of Aristotle's examples are difficult to interpret nowadays without a close knowledge of the Greek politics and history of the period, but he also gave some striking complex examples of metaphor from contemporary speeches and comedians. One that is particularly applicable today, on women delaying the age of marriage, was *My daughters are late for their own wedding.*

At its simplest, metaphor has been seen as a tool for representing one entity or event in the terms of some other related entity without explicitly stating a likeness, and has sometimes been presented as a poetic device which can add interest, wit or complexity to a text. Although metaphor can be used in this way, it is, more importantly, an extra resource that language offers to construct meanings. The child who compared custard to a drink was commenting on the food's consistency and, no doubt at the age of just three years, was unfamiliar with the words *liquid* or *viscous*, but found a way to make his meaning clear.

Handwritten annotations at top: up/down, metonymies — referential, al, orient ch.al, ontological. Lakoff / Johnson.

Students have sometimes been advised by teachers to write clearly and avoid metaphor. This is an impossible task since all language is imbued with metaphor and almost all new meanings involve metaphor. We use metaphor unselfconsciously because it is integral to the language: we *hide* our talents; we *find our way through a maze* of arguments; we *see the point* when we understand something; we *fill our children's minds with rubbish*, and we *clear our heads* with a *breath of fresh air*.

Lakoff and Johnson (1980) in their influential book on metaphor show how 'argument' and 'love' are both often represented metaphorically as *war: take up a position, fight it out, go into the attack, conflict of opinions; win her love, conquer her heart*, and when we look at much of the media today, we find a vast range of concepts represented as war or as some related act of aggression.

A problem is a war

In the following example, *constantly bombarded* is an example of a metaphor where a verb describing a type of military action is used to represent the idea that we are often warned about possible ill health:

> We are *constantly bombarded with warnings* about cancer, terrorism, bird flu, obesity. But what's the real risk?' (See page 32)
>
> (*The Guardian*, Review Section, 1 April 2006, p. 2)

The *Oxford Dictionary* definition of *bombard* is 'to batter with shot and shell'. The newspaper's use of metaphor is an example of hyperbole (exaggeration). It uses a war metaphor to suggest that somehow these warnings are threats and that they are not for our benefit. In spite of the fact that 'bombarded' with this meaning has become a cliché through overuse, it is still more striking than 'We are often warned about cancer, … etc.' The words which follow (*cancer, terrorism, bird flu, obesity*) are also likely to worry the average reader, – perhaps to exploit the readers' fear of disease.

Why would a journalist use such a metaphor in this context? We have to consider the writer's intention here, which is to attract the readers' attention to other parts of the paper. The two sentences appear in a separate section of the paper from the article they refer to, in a small block of their own (5.5 cms × 3.5 cms) in relatively large print.

The use of metaphor can sometimes entail complex grammatical reorganization of the structure of a sentence, often to fit in with a preferred information structure. In the example above, the verb *warn* has been nominalized (changed into the noun *warning*) which is an example of what has been called a *grammatical metaphor* (see Grammar appendix). It realizes a *verbal process* (the act of warning) as a noun instead of a verb and makes it available for use as the object of the preposition 'with'. This suggests that the warnings themselves are like shells that have been sent to injure us, *we are bombarded with warnings*.

Other military metaphors appear regularly in headlines (our italics):

> *Invasion* of the company *snatchers*
> [Overseas companies are buying British companies]
>
> (Business News, *Daily Telegraph*, 11 February 2006)

US *wages* indiscriminate visa *war*.

(Article by Vicki Woods, *Daily Telegraph*, 1 April 2006, p. 26)

The first headline here not only exploits the military metaphor, it is also an interesting example of intertextuality since most readers will pick up the reference to the horror film *Invasion of the Body Snatchers*, thus introducing humour and also displaying the newspaper's negative stance towards the events reported.

This second headline introduced an article about the problems British people have had in getting visas for the USA. The main story was about the news that a famous British orchestra had to cancel a planned tour in America because of the difficulties and expense they faced in getting visas. The journalist writing the article went on to recount problems she and other journalists had in gaining entry to the USA. She cited a US consul general as commenting, 'We are all paying a cost because of terrorism'. The 'war' of the headline then is related to what the American government terms (again metaphorically) *the war against terrorism*. But the headline does not refer to a real war – only to an *indiscriminate visa war*. The stories that are told in the article point to the ineffectual quality of the war since the wrong people are being targeted by the US immigration authority – not terrorists but musicians and journalists.

Critical discourse analysts have considered in some detail how the realities of war and aggression are frequently presented euphemistically by making the horrors of war appear less serious than they really are.[4] Metaphorically, we can say that the examples above are the other side of the same coin. While an actual battle becomes a *conflict* or an *engagement*, a disagreement with a banker becomes a *battle*:

Stressful *battle to beat* the banks
[A complaint about the difficulties the writer had in claiming back unjust charges from two banks]

(*Daily Telegraph*, 1 April 2006, Money section)

In both cases, war appears to be trivialized. In our examples above, relatively minor issues are represented as war or attributes of war. Yet when governments promote real wars, they tend to choose less aggressive imagery. Well-known examples include the following:

war	*armed conflict; hostilities; action; liberation*
civilian casualties	*collateral damage*
torture	*interrogation*

Of course, hyperbolic metaphor draws not only on military matters, but on other types of aggression as well (from *The Guardian*, 1 April 2006):

Supermarkets *turn on* Tesco.

[about supermarkets' disagreements]

Last *big* Tory *beast stalks Cameron*.

[about two conflicting views of the same political party's agenda]

Personific~~ation~~

Another he~~ading~~

> Slaves t~~...~~ k.
> [about l~~...~~ ours]
>
> ~~(The...~~ 06. Work section, p. 1)

This conta~~...~~ be of metaphor where
something ~~...~~ being. In the first sentence, the ~~...~~ ve owner; in the second
sentence p~~...~~ again that it is the inan-
imate obj~~...~~ nine as a person is a traditional m~~...~~ century and certainly
common j~~...~~ ters and computer programs are ~~...~~ ter specialists who consciously e~~...~~ e processors (*intelligent,
sensitive*) ~~...~~ y require a human agent:
select, beh~~...~~

Metonymy ← *The t(oke) / organisation* *personified/entity*

In *metonymy*, a word is used as a way of referring to something which is normally associated with the entity that it denotes. For example, political commentators often use
the expression *Washington* for the US government or *the White House* to refer to the
US President or to the President and his team; *the Pentagon* can, on occasion, mean not
the building itself but the US Department of Defense, which is housed there, e.g.:
Kremlin

> Hawkish noises have been emanating from the Pentagon.

Similar examples are *the Kremlin* and *Downing Street* for the governments of Russia
and Britain respectively, and the *Quai d'Orsay* for the French Ministry of Foreign
Affairs.

Business executives are colloquially and disparagingly referred to as *suits*, especially in the context of the entertainment industry. UN troops may be referred to as
blue berets or *blue helmets*, e.g.:

> Several blue berets witnessed the event.

5.4 Soundbites, slogans and stock phrases

Aristotle discussed the use of stock phrases (termed 'frigidity' in some translations) as
important in oratory. These are short fixed expressions that become well known to an
audience and evoke certain reactions of emotions usually as a result of association.

Politicians, advertisers, journalists and comedians all exploit short fixed expressions that carry 'received' messages. This practice is so well established that, as with
genres, there are socially accepted names for them, names such as *catch phrases*
(used almost exclusively by comedians for humorous effect), *slogans*, and *sound-
bites*, each of which has its own currency.

Slogans are fixed expressions, usually chosen carefully by organizers and activists, which are often chanted by political groups (*liberté, égalité, fraternité*) and protestors at demonstrations (such as *no paseran, stop the war, troops out, feed the world*). Slogans are also widely used by advertisers (*your very own Ireland*) and encouraged by football teams.

A *soundbite* is a quotable short piece of text, a snappy answer to a question or merely an extract from a recorded interview or speech that pungently characterizes the essence of a message.

Because of the way they have been used in the media and by politicians, stock expressions carry positive or negative connotations. Some appear to be thrown into current politicians' speeches and interviews simply for their connotations so that an utterance can be given a positive or negative slant (Table 5.1).

Individual speakers tend to favour certain metaphors and the phrases associated with them. Nautical metaphors are long established and popular in English: *steering a straight course, keeping the boat steady, launching new policies, rocking the boat,* and so on.

Stock phrases of this kind reflect and maintain ideologies. Thus, politicians will select and sometimes create phrases that will project their own beliefs while triggering ideological support. They are often *euphemisms*, substituting a less distasteful word or phrase for something unpleasant. To avoid describing a company as sacking or dismissing employees, we find expressions like *downsizing, rationalization, staff economies, increasing efficiency.* In examining stock phrases, we are engaging in an embryonic type of ideological analysis. The use of such expressions often reflects the ideological position of the speaker or writer, sometimes without the conscious expression of opinion, but, in the case of politicians, there is always the possibility that they use them cynically, simply to evoke a particular response, and, perhaps because our parties are so similar to each other in ideology, they borrow them from each other.

An expression that was much discussed during the 1980s when Margaret Thatcher was Prime Minister of the UK, was *Victorian values.* The expression was introduced to the politics of the day in 1983 by a BBC television interviewer, Brian Walden, when he was questioning her after she had been condemning people for

Positive	Negative
family values	nanny state
launching (a new policy)	rocking the boat
reform agenda	change for change's sake
leafy suburbs/stockbroker belt	sink estates/no-go areas
responsible citizens	anti-social youths
hard-working families	problem families
	nuisance neighbours
	neighbours from hell

Table 5.1 Stock expressions

taking part in demonstrations and strikes in order to 'get a bigger share' for themselves. She was claiming that they expected 'their standard of living to be guaranteed by the State' while others 'really strived to do better'.

Brian Walden: You've really outlined an approval of what I would call Victorian values. The sort of values, if you like, that helped to build the country throughout the nineteenth century. Now, is that right?

Thatcher: Oh, exactly, very much so. Those were the values when our country became great, but not only did our country become great internationally, also so much advance was made in this country.

Thatcher hereby associated herself with the moral imperatives of establishment Victorian England, which included the admiration of imperialism, the economic exploitation of the colonies, a generally aggressive foreign policy, reliance on charity to manage social problems, and discrimination against women in the workplace and in education. By-products of Victorian ideologies were extremes of wealth and poverty in Britain, the use of children as cheap labour in industry, and considerable moral hypocrisy. Nevertheless, the expression found favour with those in Britain who felt disaffected by aspects of modern society and imagined that such 'values' could solve crime and increase Britain's international standing.

Later in the same interview, she praised 'freedom and democracy' but specifically rejected 'equality' as a political goal, saying:

Nations that have gone for equality, like Communism (*sic*), have neither freedom, nor justice, nor equality.

Victorian values, as a catch phrase, did not go unnoticed by other political parties or by comedians, who made much of the phrase, and there was much debate between those who liked the idea of Victorian values and those who were horrified by it. Its appearance in speeches was often used as a soundbite to attract media attention.

Not surprisingly, politicians since then have not been so taken with the Victorians as Mrs Thatcher, but they have not forgotten 'values'. The phrase was quickly adapted to *family values*, much loved by all British political parties. Tony Blair specifically rejected Victorian values, which he contrasts with libertarianism, which was also out of favour with Blair. He was searching for something in between the two, catch phrases that sounded positive to all his listeners across the political spectrum. In his speech to the general meeting of the Women's Institute in June 2000, he said:

We have moved beyond debates about Victorian values and the libertarianism of the sixties.

(Prime Minister Blair's speech to the Women's Institutes' General Meeting, 7 June 2000)

Instead, at various points in the same speech, he refers approvingly to *traditional British values; good old British values; our values, our traditions and our history*.

Interestingly, this respect for traditional values is peppered throughout this speech, a speech which seeks to justify possibly unpopular social change that included limiting any rise in old age pensions (Basic State Retirement Pension) in favour of means-tested benefits ('help for the poorest') and changes in postal services ('revolutionised by new technology'). At that time many local post offices were being closed; he acknowledges this but only in these words:

> So we can give rural post offices a future but I would fail in my duty to you if I don't also say that it has to be a future allied to future reality.

In spite of his efforts, the audience, according to the press, booed the Prime Minister at this point.

In the final stages of the speech, he returns to chauvinistic praise of Britain and its future, and to praising the Women's Institute and the women who make up his audience, using the type of flattery that is so typical of persuasive discourse. Finally, he once more evokes 'values':

> So, I say today: respect for the old, for what it still has to teach: respect for others, honour, self-discipline, obligation, the essential decency of the British character. Let us take these old values and blend them with the challenge of the new world to fashion a Britain able to take on the world, strong in new daring and old wisdom, looking to the future while guarding what is best of the past. That is what we seek and all of you can help us to find it.

His speech is a typical example of oratory that draws on rhetorical devices that date back to Aristotle.

Another phrase much favoured by British politicians of all parties is *hard-working families*. Tony Blair used the phrase in countless speeches in 2000 and has been using it ever since:

> 3 February 2000
> Our goal is … supporting *hard-working families* up and down the country.
>
> (Speech to farmers in the West Country, challenging 'yob culture')

> 18 February 2000
> Not just as a Prime Minister, but as a parent too, we (*sic*) want to support *hard-working families* and make sure we engage in a real battle to combat a surge of drugs.
>
> (Broadcast on illegal drugs)

> 3 November 2000
> *Hard-working families* had been hurt by high interest rates, unemployment and house recessions.
>
> (Speech to University of Northumberland)

The juxtaposition of 'hard-working' and 'unemployment' in the last example is of particular interest.

5.5 Metaphorical framing

The *family* has a long history as a solidarity metaphor to bring together people who have a common set of beliefs or a mutual political interest.

Religious groups have used the family metaphor for centuries. Some Christians, for example, refer to *God the Father* (an appellation that some religions consider blasphemous) and Christ as his *son*, while fellow believers call themselves *brothers* and *sisters*. In the New Testament, Paul addresses his correspondents as *brethren* and, throughout history, the Church has used family names to address religious professionals (the Pope – father; priests – father; monks – brother; nuns – sister).

American slaves traditionally addressed each other as brother and sister, which may have had origins in religion but certainly became widespread as a demonstration of political solidarity. Interestingly, though, by the time of the major anti-discrimination struggles of the 1950s and 1960s in the USA, some black activists were prepared to use family terms to non-blacks who supported their struggle, and in one notable case to other non-blacks as well. James Baldwin, the American author of the great resistance text *The Fire Next Time* (1963), wrote a letter to his 15-year-old nephew in which he discussed the complexity of the relationship of blacks to whites at that time. In the middle of the letter, he wrote:

> Please try to be clear, dear James, through the storm which rages about your youthful head today, about the reality which lies behind the words *acceptance* and *integration*. There is no reason for you to become like white people and there is no reason at all for their impertinent assumption that *they* must accept you. The really terrible thing is that you must accept them. I mean that very seriously. You must accept them and accept them with hope. For these innocent people have no other hope. They are, in effect, still trapped in a history which they do not understand; and until they understand it, they cannot be released from it. They have had to believe for many years and for innumerable reasons, that black men are inferior to white men. Many of them, indeed, know better, but, as you will discover, people find it very difficult to act on what they know. To act is to be committed, and to be committed is to be in danger. In this case, the danger, in the minds of most white Americans, in the loss of their identity. …
>
> But these men are your brothers – your lost younger brothers. And if the word *integration* means anything, this is what it means: that we, with love, shall force our brothers to see themselves as they are, to cease fleeing from reality and to begin to change it. For this is your home, my friend, do not be driven from it.[5]

But just as the family metaphor has been used to express solidarity and inspire unity, it has also been widely applied, sometimes explicitly, to reject other groups. When Rhodesian white conservatives unilaterally declared independence from Britain to pre-empt independence and inevitable majority rule, their supporters in Britain repeatedly exploited the lexical unit *kith and kin*, meaning that 'we' (white British and white Rhodesians) are of one family (Self), a corollary of which is that black Rhodesians are outsiders (Other). Similarly, British Neo-Nazis and Nazi sympathizers have argued that Britain should not have fought Germany in the Second World War because the Germans and the British are *brothers*. These two examples are specifically racist because they suppose a genetic racial link between groups of people that they imagine have the same ancestry.

Lexical items are important here because their use triggers the desired conceptual image: the family as a self-contained group of loving and mutually supportive members united against the outside world.

Another example of metaphorical framing, one which is less reliant on lexical items, was identified by Lakoff (2004). He called this the 'Nation as Person' metaphor. He discussed how the US government persuaded the American people to support the first Gulf War by using a frame based on *traditional stories*, the 'Self-Defense' story and the 'Rescue' story. In stories of this type, there are three main characters: an innocent hero, a villain, and a victim. There is a crime committed by a villain who is so evil and irrational that it is impossible to negotiate with him; the hero has no choice but to kill him. According to Lakoff, when President George Bush (Sr) made his first case for Gulf War 1, he used the self-defence story. Iraq was presented as the villain who was threatening the free world by making weapons of mass destruction (at that time, specifically a very large gun!). America would, therefore, have been acting in self-defence in invading Iraq. When this argument did not convince the American people, he tried the rescue story by presenting the case for 'rescuing' Kuwait from Iraq. Thus, the hero (America) was seen as rescuing a poor, defenceless, 'friendly' Kuwait from the clutches of the villain, Iraq. Oil did not play any major part in Bush's story of the liberation of Kuwait even though much of the world believed that it was the motivating factor.

When preparing for Gulf War II, Bush (Jr) had two stories, both of which were used. Saddam Hussein was now accused of making nuclear and chemical weapons. The phrase 'weapons of mass destruction' became such common currency that it was referred to as WMD in some reports. Additionally, it was suggested that Saddam Hussein was somehow responsible for the Al-Qaeda attack on New York. Hence the US itself was threatened, and Bush could use the self-defence story. However, this was a difficult thing to argue since there was no evidence of any connection between Saddam Hussein and Bin Laden. In fact, since Bin Laden is apparently an Islamic Fundamentalist and Saddam led a secular state, it is highly unlikely that any links existed. If this story failed though, Bush could still try the rescue story – as long as the Iraqi people could be presented as the victims of Saddam's terror. In this case the USA and her allies (including Britain) could be seen as the rescuers, in spite of the indiscriminate bombing by the Americans. It is this second story which still leads in the media in the USA and Britain at the time of writing. In the lack of evidence of Saddam ever having had 'weapons of mass destruction', the favourite stock phrase now is his 'crimes against the Iraqi people'. Only time will tell how the history of this war will be framed.

5.6 Analysis: a political article

Towards the end of 2003, David Blunkett, the British Home Secretary, introduced a bill to change laws on immigration and asylum, making life more difficult for many asylum seekers and unapproved immigrants. Among other things, this would deny asylum seekers the opportunity to work or claim benefits while waiting for legal approval. This would mean that they might not be able to support their families, and their children would have be 'taken into care' by the state or by charities.

These elements of the bill attracted strong criticism from left and liberal factions, including supporters of Blunkett's own party, Labour, and the government was accused of reactionary policy-making. The *Guardian* newspaper was one source of criticism, describing the new policies as 'beyond belief'. In response, Blunkett published in the same newspaper a fairly lengthy article defending his position (*The Guardian*, 27 November 2003). Here we shall examine only a tiny proportion of the text.

The article was printed under the headline 'I am not King Herod', a semi-quotation from his statement in the body of the article: 'I did not come into politics to be King Herod,' an intertextual reference to the king in the Bible who notoriously slaughtered the innocent children shortly after the birth of Jesus.

Blunkett takes two lines of defence, or, to use another metaphor, two approaches to selling his bill to a predominantly Labour-voting, liberal left readership:

1.   If I don't do this, the far right will come to power and do worse.
2.   These steps are in the interests of 'genuine' asylum seekers and legal immigrants.
     (Our interpretation and wording)

The first of these is a common device for excusing policies that meet serious resistance. There are expediency arguments in both lines of defence, but they are presented as being in the interests of the very people who will suffer as a result of the bill should it become law.

Exploiting both grammatical and traditional metaphors, he presents his personal predicament as a general truth and diffusely reframes his 'Herod' image as that of a champion of decency and moderation against forces of extremism and impracticality. In the process, without actually making the point explicitly, he tries to identify opposition to his policies with political extremists rather than with the traditional supporters of his party that he is primarily addressing, but he also separately suggests that irresponsible and impractical left-liberals are defective in that they fail to see that he is doing what must be done.

Since it is virtually impossible to communicate linguistically in a normal way without using metaphor, we are not suggesting that Blunkett is always aware of his exploitation of this resource any more than that he is always aware of his use of grammatical structures, but the investigation of these aspects of the text sheds some light on how it creates its meanings. In fact, Blunkett's use of metaphor does not display any marked attempts at rhetorical manipulation. Exploitation of metaphor is typified by his conventional use of:

> Sticking one's head in the sand is not an option …
> We need to have the same story to tell …
> … the less ammunition there is for the extreme right to fire

Near the beginning of the article, Blunkett uses a grammatical metaphor:

> Being a Labour Home Secretary in the 21st century means fighting a
> constant battle against both extreme right and extreme left.

He is clearly talking about his own position (as it were: I am a Labour Home Secretary and so I must …), but the generalization plays down the personal aspect; he is implying that his actions go with the job. The embedding of the proposition [*x be a Labour Home Secretary*], (that is to say: somebody – unspecified – is a Labour Home Secretary) as a non-finite clause:

being a Labour Home Secretary

and the similar treatment of [*x fight a constant battle*] (somebody unspecified fights a constant battle) as:

fighting a constant battle

enables him to link the two propositions in an intensive clause, a relational process where one clause functions as Subject and the other as Complement:

[clause 1]   *means*   [clause 2]
Subject   Complement

The message is that it is not merely the case that the Labour Home Secretary *happens to behave* in this way; it is rather that behaving in this way is *a crucial attribute* of being the Labour Home Secretary.

Exploiting the conventional 'politics is war' metaphor, Blunkett positions himself as a warrior *fighting a constant battle* against extremists. (Yet, at another point, he says that his plans are *necessary medicine*. This time we get Blunkett as doctor, saving people's lives with nasty but necessary treatments.)

He uses a tactic much favoured by mainstream politicians when he links right and left together, condemning both simultaneously and on the same grounds. He does this several times, another example being the following metaphorically complicated sentence.

What both sides share is a dogmatic belief that there is no middle ground to be occupied.

The linguistic structure *A dogmatic belief that [proposition]* is another grammatical metaphor. It is the nominalization of

someone believes [something]

or, slightly more formally:

x believes *p* (where *p* is a proposition).

Believing is a mental process, but here it is reified, that is represented as a 'thing' (*belief*). This makes it grammatically possible to modify with the disparaging adjective *dogmatic* and to render it semantically as something that can be shared.

Non-metaphorically, *sharing* is a material process. When Actors share a material object, say, a cake, each ends up with only a portion of the whole. In metaphorical sharing like this, each may have the whole thing, in this instance, a belief. The persons who believe (*Sensers*, in SFL terms) are not specified here though they can be understood from the co-text as *both sides*.

The expression *Both sides* encapsulates extreme left and extreme right in a single nominal group, blurring their distinct identities as bitter antagonists with opposing ideologies. Incidentally, it carries on the war metaphor (*sides* as contending forces in battle).

No middle ground to be occupied is another war metaphor. Armies occupy enemy territory or, as in this case, the ground between the two sides – no-man's land. The use of the passive voice means that the writer can omit the agent, the actor who occupies the ground.

The use of the *what*-structure (technically known in some grammars as pseudo-clefting) enables Blunkett to set up the structure he used to resemble an intensive clause, e.g.

Napoleon	was	a Corsican
What both sides share	is	a dogmatic belief that there is no middle ground

Except for a degree of emphasis, this option adds little that would not have been achieved by the non-clefted equivalent: *Both sides share a dogmatic belief that there is … no middle ground to be occupied.*

Blunkett likes the clefted structure, though, and follows with two more examples in the same paragraph:

> What few in the Westminster village and the chattering classes seem prepared to acknowledge – but what the public instinctively understands – is that there is no contradiction between enthusiastically welcoming legal migrant labour to strengthen our economy, while ensuring we have a robust, functioning asylum system at the same time, protecting those fleeing persecution.

In this case, the use of this structure sets up the possibility of two contrasting grammatical subjects as Given, with the long clause-complex (*that .... persecution*) as New. This is grammatically complex and, in fact, the writer loses control of the syntax, writing *while* instead of *and* to introduce the embedded nonfinite clause beginning *ensuring we have* .....

Contrasting pairs figure from time to time in the full text: *right and left; difficult but sensible; too soft or too tough; not <u>draconian</u> but reasonable; the more x the less y; my plans are not beyond belief [....] they are necessary medicine [....].* In the last two examples, we have two contrasting clauses, and the same is true of the longer structure from the paragraph quoted, which we now analyse:

A.1. what few in the Westminster village and the chattering classes seem prepared to acknowledge

contrasts with

A.2. what the public instinctively understands

And further

B.1. enthusiastically welcoming legal migrant labour

contrasts with

B.2. ensuring we have a robust, functioning asylum system at the same time, protecting those fleeing persecution.

The writer is making the point that the second two are compatible, but the rhetorical pattern of contrast is still present, although any contradiction is denied.

The nominal group complex *the Westminster Village and the chattering classes* combines two distinct metaphors. *The Westminster village* is a slightly pejorative standard metaphor for the occupants of the Houses of Parliament, potentially including Members of Parliament, staff, reporters, lobbyists, and so on; it carries connotations of pettiness, rumour and a lack of wide perspective. It may seem an odd term for an elected minister of government to choose, but ironically the government (the Prime Minister and the Cabinet) is often in conflict with the rest of Parliament or large sectors of it, including members of the governing party, and tends to regard Parliament (and its own party members) as a brake on serious governing. This was very publicly evident at the time of this article.

The chattering classes is an even more pejorative stock expression, which is applied to what in other countries might be called the intelligentsia. It is a way of referring to people who publicly express views with which the speaker does not agree, and it is most often applied to liberal or left-wing intellectuals by politicians who resent criticism or even disagreement. It carries connotations of ineffectuality as well as loquacity.

The implied distinction between *the Westminster Village* and *the chattering classes* on the one hand and *the public* on the other is very striking. Of course, the 'chattering classes' must be a sub-set of the public, but the discourse here implies that they are not. In fact, Blunkett is implicitly attributing to the mass of the population agreement with his decisions. The concept of the sensible ordinary citizen – or the collective body of such citizens *(the people, the public)* – is frequently appealed to by politicians, especially when opposition comes from informed sources with whom the more acquiescent public can be favourably contrasted. These same politicians often bemoan public apathy, but clearly it is preferred to opposition. Blunkett's hope here is that the reader will wish to identify with the understanding public and not with the chattering classes. Note that he attributes the public's understanding to instinct ('what the public *instinctively* understands') rather than to intellect. Reasoned thought is not encouraged.

The verb *acknowledge* presupposes the truth of the propositions expressed in everything following the word *that*, namely:

> [they] acknowledge that ... there is no contradiction between enthusiastically welcoming legal migrant labour to strengthen our economy, while ensuring we have a robust, functioning asylum system at the same time, protecting those fleeing persecution.

If the lexical item *believe* were used instead of *acknowledge* (i.e. if these groups were said not to be *prepared to believe that p*), no such assumption would be present. The verb *understands* has a similar presuppositional force to that of *acknowledge*. When we say *the public understands p*, we presuppose that *p* is true.

He opts for the impersonal economic abstraction *migrant labour* rather than the emotionally charged *immigrants* and limits its scope with the modifier *legal*. *Robust* is a currently fashionable word, denoting strength and substance, and is useful as a euphemism for *stringent, harsh, unyielding* or *ruthless*. Arguments that there may be contradictions inherent in the policy are nowhere considered, of course.

Let us now return to the headline:

I am not King Herod

and the statement in the text from which it is taken:

I did not go into politics to be the King Herod of the Labour Party.

Although a negation, this is a traditional metaphor and hence an obvious choice of metaphor for a mass child-murderer. Although his critics are not suggesting he is considering murder (although they are suggesting that his policies might cause children to suffer), Blunkett takes a risk in denying the aptness of the metaphor because the proposition 'I am not King Herod' presupposes the possibility of the proposition 'I am King Herod'. As Lakoff observes of the former US President, Richard Nixon:

He stood before the nation and said, 'I am not a crook.' And everybody thought about him as a crook.

(Lakoff 2004)

And indeed just over a month later, also in *The Guardian*, the journalist Nick Cater selected 'Bully-boy Blunkett' as 'villain of the year', writing of him as:

David 'Herod' Blunkett … starving asylum seekers out by refusing them benefits while stealing their children into care.

(Nick Cater, *The Guardian,* 23 December 2003)

The dating of Cater's observations, just before Christmas, gave them an added bite.

Activities

1. 'The nanny state' is a popular critical term used to refer to governments which impose and enforce petty bureaucratic laws which unreasonably interfere with our individual freedom. Yet these laws are often established in the people's interests to improve the environment, protect children from injury, improve health and safety in industry, for example.

   'Soft on crime' is a popular term used to criticize governments who do *not* enforce all laws strictly. Read the following section from newspaper reports and decide whether they follow a 'nanny state frame' or a 'soft on crime' frame. Is there any difference between the stance of the government and that of the newspaper editor? On what basis did you reach your conclusion?

   FINED £80 IF YOU DROP YOUR LITTER
   (or if you put bins out on the wrong day)
   By James Slack, Home Affairs Editor

   Armies of wardens have been ordered to hand out £80 fines to anyone dropping even tiny amounts of litter.

   In a call to arms, Environmental Secretary Margaret Beckett said they had 'no excuse' not to punish offenders. She also raised the fine from the current £50 amid suggestions that councils have so far been reluctant to take action.

The crackdown covers all open spaces, including rivers, ponds and private property. Householders could even be fined for putting out their rubbish on the wrong day.

(Daily Mail, 31 March 2006)

2. In the light of Thatcher's dismissal of 'equality' as a political aim (Section 5.4), comment on the following sections from a speech by the Right Honourable Gordon Brown, Chancellor of the Exchequer, in May 2000, 13 years later (Brown was in a different political party):

And we must never forget that poverty – above all the poverty of children – disfigures not only the lives of the poor but all our society. Exactly one hundred years ago in 1900 the consequences of gross inequalities in child health were revealed by the mass recruitment to the army for the Boer War.

Today, as we tackle global competition in the new economy, the glaring inequalities in educational opportunity and skills make it once again central to our national interest to tackle child poverty.

Our five year olds who will finish school after 2010 and graduate from university and college after 2015 will be our teachers, our doctors and our scientists, our employers and our workforces. The future of our country lies with the hopes and dreams of these children.

Indeed in the new century, economies that work only for the privileged few and not for everyone will ossify and their societies will become ever more divided and poor.

3. Read the quotation below from the end of the same speech by the Chancellor of the Exchequer. Analyse it in terms of its message – and hidden messages, if you see any – and its use of rhetorical devices and figures of speech:

This is the thinking behind the new children's fund.

It will encourage local initiatives and community action in a war against child poverty.

It will offer government money to back non-government initiatives to tackle child poverty.

It will involve the biggest voluntary and community organisations and the smallest.

It will support anti-poverty projects for children of all ages.

Its emphasis will be on prevention and not just on coping with failure.

It will operate not just at national level but also at local level.

The network of local children's funds – perhaps up to fifty – that we plan to establish are designed to mobilise the forces of compassion and care in every community …

And at the national level, we will seek to build a new alliance for children.

An alliance of government, community organizations, voluntary and charitable sectors, and all those who share the ambition, your ambition, of ending child poverty in our country.

Further study

Though pre-dating CDA as we know it, an early work that provides a clear introduction to language in use is Bolinger and Sears (1981), which includes sections on functions (such as *suasion*) and language variation, as well as the rhetorical use of English, including collocation, connotation, idiomatic usage and figures of speech. Chapters 6 and 7 are particularly relevant to CDA.

Lakoff and Johnson (1980) made a revolutionary contribution to thinking about metaphor and to cognitive studies in general with their analysis of the way that metaphor permeates human language and thought. These ideas are developed further in Lakoff (1987); see also Lakoff (posted 18 March, 2003 on www. alternet.org) for the short, practical political application referred to in Section 5.4.

The term 'grammatical metaphor' comes from Halliday. You will find introductions to grammatical metaphor in Bloor and Bloor (2004: Chapter 6) and Thompson (2004: Chapter 9), and a full, but more difficult account in Halliday and Matthiessen (2004: Chapter 10).

6

6.1 Power

In Chapter 1, ~~...~~ _... tunction of CDA_ was to investigate how discourse helped to maintain power structures and support discrimination. In this chapter, we focus on the significance of language in classifying people with respect to their place in power structures and on how powerful groups, sometimes with the tacit 'co-operation' of the less powerful, can use language to maintain inequality.

It is always in the interests of the dominant elite group if the subjected group can accept their position as an ideological imperative – that is to say, if they believe that this is the way things should be or the best that things can be, if they 'accept their lot in life' as the old expression put it. Towards this end, power structures tend to be institutionalized and fixed by both customs and laws, which encourage people to behave in certain ways and identify with certain groups. In complex modern societies – and to some extent perhaps in all societies – they vary across domains, and are constantly in a state of change.

We do not claim here that discourse is the only factor – or even the main factor – in the establishment or maintenance of dominant groups. For that we might look to wealth, class, political control, military strength, and so on, but there is no doubt that dominance is practised and reproduced through language. _Dominance_ has been defined as 'the exercise of social power by elites, institutions or groups that results in social inequality, including political, cultural, class, ethnic, racial and gender inequality' (van Dijk 1993a).

In Chapter 5 we saw two views of 'equality' as a political project. Although Thatcher's view was very different from Brown's view, they both accepted that inequality exists. There was a _presupposition_ of its existence. However, whereas Brown addressed the issue of childhood inequality, Thatcher considered it not to be the direct business of government. From the discourse point of view, issues of social power and identity are closely related to issues of equality.

6.2 Identity and social roles

We now turn to the question of how individuals come to be defined as members of a group or other social category. There is no easy answer to this question. We have already said that each person will be involved over their lifetime with different social domains and within these domains they will play different roles.

Some of these roles we are born to. They involve the type of family unit we are a part of and our position in that unit (e.g. second child of three boys). Others we might choose, such as our jobs (e.g. doctor) or our leisure activities (e.g. tennis player). Others are thrust upon us by parents (e.g. boarding school student) or other people in control over us (e.g. prisoner). Many of these roles change through life and the power and status associated with those roles obviously change as well. We identify ourselves and others, at least in part, through our roles and the way we perform them.

However, there are certain social classification systems that transcend 'roles' of this type because they impose an identity on individuals that they may find unwelcome. The categories in which people are placed are embedded in official discourses and become institutionalized.

Major systems of institutionalized identity are *national identity*, *racial identity*, *gender identity*, and *class identity*. In this chapter we look at the first three of these categories and consider how they are constructed.

6.3 National identity

We are all familiar with prejudice against people from other nations. This often reveals itself in the stereotyping of people from a particular country or culture and is seen regularly in the popular press, in anti-immigrant discourse (see an example in Chapter 8) and jokes that play on perceived national characteristics. Thus, the Italians might be presented as noisy, the French as sexy, the Germans as humourless, or whatever happens to be the popular stereotype of the time.

National boundaries are often established as a result of conflict, and their institutions, legal practices and other discourses of social control are constructed over time by those holding the power. Historically, stories, myths and other cultural manifestations, such as music and the visual arts, technologies, cuisine and costumes, are built up into what is sometimes called a national culture. Boundaries of any kind keep some people 'in' and others 'out' and support the view of Self and Other that we have met elsewhere in this book.

Many people – but not all – are happy to position themselves as members of specific nations. A nation is identifiable by its government, its laws and its boundaries, but none of these is fixed or stable. Governments encourage those born in a country to participate in nationhood by means of well-established texts and practices, such as registration of births, birth certificates, identity cards, and passports. With the help of social events and celebrations such as national anniversaries like Thanksgiving in the USA, Guy Fawkes Day in the UK, Bastille Day in France, an emotional attachment to the nation is encouraged. Within a nation, people may be pressured to take on typical behaviour patterns, either through upbringing or training in school.

Individuals who go to live in a country not of their birth may be eligible for *naturalization*, another bureaucratic practice that may be more or less complex. The rules and procedures for becoming a UK citizen, for example, have recently become more difficult than they used to be. Since November 2005, a person, even if married to a UK citizen, must live in the country for at least three years (sometimes longer), follow certain 'rules' during that time, and pass a test on 'Life in the UK', before being permitted even to apply for naturalization. Various commercial enterprises have sprung up around this procedure, which, for a fee, will advise on the process and assist with the necessary form filling. Other companies will train an applicant to take the – extremely difficult – test. A ceremony is then held to confer British citizenship.

These new procedures are an attempt to erase the newcomer's former identity. The new citizen is under pressure to adopt the social practices of the host country, which are projected as 'normal' or 'natural' for British citizens. (Hence, perhaps, the term *naturalization*, which dates back to the seventeenth century.)

For some individuals, nationhood raises complex problems, as, for example, with people who are legally entitled to more than one nationality or those who have strong loyalties outside their place of birth or their registered habitat. One loyalty that may clash with national identity is religious affiliation. Many faith groups cross national boundaries and although in most places nowadays there is freedom to practise any religion, there have been cases where religious intolerance has made it impossible for certain faiths or sects to exist within a state, and those persisting have been forced to flee to other places. Individuals – of whatever origin – may experience alienation from the cultural or ideological norms of the nation and prefer not to participate in certain 'normal' practices.

Another problem arises with colonized peoples where conflict arises over identity with the colonized or the colonizer. In the French colonies, indigenous people were entitled to French citizenship. This attempt at egalitarian government did not always work as it was intended. The system conferred certain privileges on people who, in the main, could not take advantage of them. Those who identified with French culture and visited France to study or work, often found themselves up against such racial prejudice and discrimination that they could no longer feel themselves to be French citizens. Yet, when they returned to their home countries these same people found themselves alienated from their own local culture and were laughed at because they had taken on characteristics of the European in terms of style, dress, accent, and so on (see, for example, Fanon, 1970: Chapter 1 and elsewhere).

Furthermore, in some countries, such as those in Africa where state boundaries were drawn by colonial powers in the nineteenth century, national boundaries do not coincide with traditional identity groups; this still leads to political conflict and personal persecution and distress in incidents where cultural groups span national boundaries and refugees from one nation state cross into another to seek help.

6.4 Racial and ethnic identity

Whereas a person's nationality is usually specified by geographic boundaries such as place of birth or parents' birth or by naturalization, racial identity is popularly imagined to be inherent in bodily structure and recognizable from the colour of the skin, shape of the body or facial features. However, race is not physical but discoursal, and the merging of race and ethnicity with nationality in the classification of human beings leads to considerable confusion and unacceptable stereotyping. Thus we find that people perceived as having certain physical characteristics can be associated with specific cultural practices, styles of behaviour, sexual prowess, financial acuity, or even criminality or low intelligence. At its worst, such stereotyping has resulted in inequality, slavery, concentration camps and genocide.

'Ethnicity' is a word with slightly more favourable connotations than 'race'. It has been used to describe cultural characteristics of national groups, but is used differently in official documents in Britain and in the USA. In origin, however, it has the same meaning as race, originating in the Greek word for Gentiles (those other than Jews, or more broadly, those from other racial groups). In the UK, it has fewer negative associations and is used neutrally in expressions relating to cultural artefacts like *ethnic music*, *ethnic food*, *ethnic dress*, although it can also be used discriminatorily in terms like *ethnic minority* and is used by extreme right-wing groups as a derogatory term.

Categories of race are deeply ingrained and are constantly being re-contextualized in new discourses. The aspect of racial identity that we concentrate on in this section is the way in which it is constantly reinforced as a viable concept by official documents and directives. The more a concept is reinforced, the more real it seems and the more difficult it is to challenge. To this end, we look at the ways in which census questionnaires and related papers give racial categorization a respectability that it does not warrant and which we see as potentially dangerous.

Ethnic identity in the British census

Censuses are generally viewed as a matter of bureaucratic routine – a kind of natural accounting. Yet it is our argument that the census does much more than reflect social reality; rather it plays a key role in the construction of that reality. In no way is this more importantly the case than in the ways in which the census is used to divide national populations into separate identity categories: racial, ethnic, linguistic or religious.

(Kertzer and Arel 2001)

National censuses have a long history. In Britain, they date back to 1801 when they simply sought to discover the number of people living in each area of the country. Conducted every ten years, the information gathered increased regularly, and, in 1831, occupations and trades were included for the first time. By 1901, the census recorded name, age, marital status, relationship to head of the household, occupation and location on census night. The population was not required to give any information concerning ethnic or national origins until nearly 200 years after the first census, and this in spite of large numbers of people entering the country in the late 1940s from Europe, in the 1950s from the Caribbean and in the 1960s from Africa (the so-called Kenyan Asians). It was not until the 1991 census, under the Thatcher government, that a question was asked that related to ethnicity. The term 'race' was not used.

The justification for such questions appears to relate to two factors. The only valid one might be as a means of preventing discrimination by enabling a statistical means of verifying whether or not certain groups are not achieving in such matters as educational level, access to work and income. Another is to provide 'commensurate comparability' with other countries, enabling governments, researchers and others to make comparisons. An official paper on the classification of ethnic groups states, 'This is designed to meet a range of user needs' and mentions 'policy needs on health and housing'. Why this should require ethnic data is not elaborated.

The writers of the census came up with an elaborate choice of categories, but still, from the respondents' position, it was difficult to respond to, even for those who accepted that such a classification system was valid. For example, the use of the word 'British' was arbitrary. From the wide choice of boxes to complete, it was possible to identify oneself as *White British* (under the 'white' category), *Asian British* (within an Asian category), or *Black British* (within a 'black' category), but it was not possible to identify oneself as *Mixed Race British* or *Chinese British* since the 'mixed race' and 'Chinese' categories did not include the word *British*. Other obvious problems are that 'black' and 'white' are clearly racial categories whereas 'Asian' and 'Chinese' are (overlapping) regional categories. Needless to say, some people of Chinese origin, especially perhaps those families that have been resident in Malaysia or Singapore for many years, think of themselves as 'Asian', and some people of Asian origin may think of themselves as 'white'.

We have gone into this matter in some detail to illustrate the complexity of applying socially constructed classification systems to human beings. We wish to emphasize that institutional discourse of this type enters into a dialogue with every one of us about how we perceive ourselves. We might reject the racial classification, as many have done in past racial conflicts, but can do so only if we are prepared to break the law since, in Britain, and we believe in most countries, it is a legal requirement to answer this question on the census. There is an uninvited compulsion imposed by the census for each of us to think of ourselves as belonging to a specific ethnic or racial category. This automatically places anyone who is not so designated as Other, which can raise problems, particularly in families and close communities where individual members fall into different categories.

Ethnic identity in other censuses

During the nineteenth century, there were questions on racial origin in censuses in at least some of the British – and other European – colonies. It seems likely that, since race was not considered an issue in Britain at that time, the preoccupation with race in the colonies was, at least in part, concerned with the management of the indigenous people and racist considerations that sought to prevent – or at least control – what was considered to be miscegenation. In some Spanish colonies in Latin America, elaborate classification systems (*castas*) were set up, and civil rights and responsibilities were based closely on what was supposed to be the proportion of European blood that a person had. No less than 47 categories were listed in Spanish although not all were in use in every country.

In other cultures too, some censuses required people to indicate precisely what proportion of their genetic inheritance came from non-white groups. Thus, the slave-owning societies of USA and the West Indies in the nineteenth century developed labels to designate 'deviations' from pure white to those who were considered 'one-eighth non-white', that is to say having one great-grandparent of African descent. The 1890 US census specified the following criteria: Black ¾ or more African; Mulatto ⅜–⅝ black; Quadroon ¼ black. These distinctions had considerable significance in terms of social status and power which lasted for a long time and which affect racial relations even today. As late as 1970, the Louisiana 'blood law' required persons with ¹⁄₃₂ or more of 'negro blood' (ancestry) to be designated as 'coloured' on birth records, and this was upheld in court when a woman who identified herself as white sought to be 're-classified'. However, by the 1970s, there was a strong core of anti-racist protest and a general consciousness of inequality issues.

In 1977, under a directive of the federal government, the US Office of Management and Budget issued a policy directive, *Race and ethnic standards for federal statistics and administrative reporting*. This greatly simplified the construction of race but still recognized racial classification as valid. It also separated the questions on race (choice of one from four categories) and ethnicity:

Categories of race:	American Indian or Alaskan Native
	Asian or Pacific Islander
	Black
	White
Plus	Some other race
Ethnic categories:	Hispanic origin
	Non-Hispanic origin

From this, we might imagine that at least the end was near for the complexities of discrimination that were current in Louisiana, but in spite of this work, the 10-year census in 1990 had 16 checkbox categories and two write-in areas concerning ethnicity.

One of the major objections to this 1991 census question was that it did not allow people to identify themselves as mixed race (or as the US Census Bureau terms it 'multiracial').[1] It was not until 1997 that an official committee reviewed the categories to construct the 2000 census. This still did not offer a 'mixed race' category but it did allow respondents to check more than one category if they wished.

The following text is taken from the US Census Bureau's *Statement on Racial and Ethnic Classification Used in Census 2000 and Beyond*, dated 12 April 2000 (the omissions refer only to information about earlier censuses):

> The most profound change to the question on race for census 2000 is that respondents are allowed to identify one or more races to indicate their racial identity. There are 15 check box categories and 3 write-in areas ... The three separate identifiers for the American Indian and Alaskan Native populations ... have been combined into one category – American Indian or Alaskan native – with instructions for respondents who check the box to print the name of their enrolled or principal tribe. The Asian and Pacific Islander category has been split into two categories: Asian, and Native Hawaiian and Other Pacific Islander. There are six specified Asian and three detailed Pacific Islander categories shown on the 2000 census questionnaires, as well as Other Asian and Other Pacific Islander which have write-in areas for respondents to provide other race responses. Finally, the category Some Other Race, which is intended to capture responses such as Mulatto, Creole, and Mestizo, also has a write-in area. All the responses collected in Census 2000 can be collapsed into the minimum race categories identified in the 1997 revisions to the standards on race and ethnicity issued by the Office of Management and Budget, plus the category Some Other Race.

After a description of changes to formatting and terminology, the document continues by discussing how the data will be tabulated according to preliminary guidelines:

> Data producers should provide the number of respondents who marked (or selected) only one category, separately for each of the five categories, as well as the detailed distribution of respondents who reported two or more races ... For Census 2000, 63 possible combinations of the six basic racial categories exist, including six categories for those who report only one race, and 57 categories for those who report two or more races.

Later we find:

> People of Hispanic origin may be of any race and should answer the question on race by marking one or more race categories shown on the questionnaire, including White, Black (... etc.) Hispanics are asked to indicate their origin in the question on Hispanic origin, not in the question on race, because in the federal statistical system ethnic origin is considered to be a separate concept from race.

In this context it is important to remember that the racial classifications are purely arbitrary and constructed *as text*. The variety and number of the classification systems alone testify to the fact that the categories do not reflect any natural reality. It is difficult to imagine any rational or practical need for census questions of this kind when there is no external justification for such classifications. The detail and complexity almost suggest parody.

The instability of self-identification

As a further indicator of the arbitrariness of the categories, there is evidence that some people do not see their so-called ethnic or racial origins as stable. A research paper on the statistics comparing the 1991 and 2001 statistics (Bosveld *et al.* 2006) reports that people can identify themselves differently at different stages of their lives – even on census forms. On the 1991 census, 'the introduction of additional response categories in 2001 resulted in many people who had been classified as Other Black in 1991 subsequently changing their ethnic category. Only 8 per cent of people classified as Other Black in 1991 retained the Other Black classification in 2001.'

Details are given of many changes of identification between different non-white categories and it is reported that as many as 15 per cent of those checking Other Black and 2 per cent of those checking Chinese in 1991 subsequently re-classified themselves to a White group. All groups showed some shift. Various explanations are offered, including respondent error, but the report admits that 'some will reflect a genuine change of ethnic identification, ethnicity being subjective and liable to change over a person's lifetime'.

Some readers may be asking why the institutionalized social construction of racist categories could be a problem. We see it as a problem because of the systematic discrimination that has been practised over the centuries by one category against another and because the documentation of such categories by legal and official means makes exploitation and discrimination easier. To give just three examples of many, we can point to the slave trade, to the Nazis' persecution of the Jews, and to Apartheid in South Africa.

Institutionally enforced identity

An example of institutional racism on a large scale can be seen in the republic of South Africa under the system known as *apartheid*, where racial identity was forced upon members of the population.

South African colonization was begun by the Dutch East India company in 1652. The white settlers, later known as Boers (Dutch for *farmers*) or Afrikaners, took over large tracts of the country by force of arms. In the nineteenth century, Britain gained control of much of the territory, eventually defeating the Afrikaners in 1902. When the Union of South Africa was formed in 1910 as part of the British Empire, it was largely under Afrikaner leadership and it eventually gained independence within the Commonwealth in 1931.

In 1914, the Nationalist Party (Afrikaner) instituted the policy of *apartheid*, or separateness, which intensified and systematized the long-standing racist organization of the country, excluding 'non-white' people from power and as far as possible introducing segregation of peoples from different racial categories.

With increasing resistance from the African National Congress (ANC) and other revolutionary organizations such as the Pan-African Congress and the Communist Party (all illegal), and, less effectively, by minority constitutional parties, this system continued until the 1990s. In 1984, limited suffrage was granted to 'Asians' and 'Coloured' but not to 'Blacks'. The real end of apartheid began in 1989 under the presidency of a Nationalist leader, de Klerk. The ANC leader, Nelson Mandela, was released from prison in 1990, and was elected president in 1994.

Apartheid South Africa provides striking evidence of the injustice and irrationality of institutional racism. People were categorized as White, Bantu, Coloured, and Asian. Somewhat approximately, these meant respectively people of European ancestry, black Africans, people of mixed race, and people of Asian, mainly Indian, ancestry. Marriage and sexual relations with members of other groups were forbidden by law. Education, taxation, health services, social services were different for different groups. Hotels, bars, restaurants, parks, public benches, and even beaches were segregated; so were sports activities, places of entertainment and other meeting places. In the international flights section of Jan Smuts Airport, Johannesburg, restrictions were slightly more relaxed, but in passing from one non-segregated area to another, passengers were obliged to go through separate doors marked 'Whites only' and 'Nonwhites only'. Not surprisingly, in spite of the elaborate gradations of race, this simple binary division was the most important. Some districts were designated as 'Whites only' areas and members of other categories who worked there – such as labourers and servants – were obliged to travel long distances daily. Territories were set aside as 'Homelands' for Africans, similar to the reservations assigned to Native Americans, on fairly uninviting land. At a personal level, there was considerable hardship and suffering, with parents forcibly separated from their children and marriages broken. This system effectively marked any non-white as economically deprived and lacking opportunity for advancement. Thus apartheid provided cheap labour for the mines, factories and farms and provided a servant class. Whites generally had a high standard of living, good housing and safe areas.

People who thought their neighbours had been wrongly classified could report them to the authorities. People who felt that they had been wrongly designated could apply for reclassification. Sometimes, a person designated White, for example, would ask to be reclassified as 'Coloured' in order to continue living with a spouse. It was more difficult to be reclassified from Coloured to White or from Black to Coloured, thus reinforcing a hierarchy of colour categories with those with the lightest skin given privileges over the darker.

It is worth noting that many Afrikaners, particularly members of the Dutch Reformed Church, consider themselves to be the 'chosen people', selected by God to rule, and the more extremist elements argue that only white people are true human beings. The Reformed Church supported these beliefs. Here, racial identity was seen to be conferred not only by the state but also by God.

Non-Afrikaner white South Africans also profited from apartheid and many supported it, but it is also important to remember that whites, including Afrikaners, were represented among the anti-apartheid activists, demonstrating that not everyone accepted state-inflicted identity – even when it conferred considerable privilege.

6.5 An example: a racial identity issue

In 2006, the ultra right-wing, anti-immigration British National Party tried a tactic that is familiar in accounts of racism and other types of discrimination. It is well known that people accused of racism or sexism may recruit 'token' members to deflect criticism. Given the rationale of the BNP, such an action would be anomalous, to say the least, but it may have happened, in a way.

The BNP chose as a candidate in a local election Sharif Abdel Gawad, causing protests in the ranks of the party 'even when it was explained that he was not a Pakistani Muslim' (BNP spokesman, quoted in *The Guardian*, 8 April 2006, p. 1). Protesters were told that he was, in fact, 'a totally assimilated Greek Armenian' with a Christian grandfather. Irate members did not seem to accept this distinction and classified him as 'ethnic'. An email posting on the BNP's Stormfront bulletin board said:

> The BNP is the last bastion of hope for our people, they too have been let down if just anyone is allowed to join. Ethnics have every single opportunity afforded them, and now they even get to join the BNP. Just like immigration into this country, we were not consulted. When an ethnic wants to join, it should go to a membership vote. We're the ones who do all the work, we should have the say.

(BNP member's posting, quoted in *The Guardian*, 8 April 2006, p. 1)

This is a dispute not just about membership of a party but also about identity with a racial category. On the one side are *our people* and on the other side *ethnics*. Note that the word *ethnic* has now become a noun. Like the *white/nonwhite* dichotomy, it is a simple binary choice. The pronoun *we* in this text refers to members of the BNP, and the nominal group *our people* and the first occurrence of *they* refer to the 'non-ethnic' racial majority that the BNP claims to represent, which, according to the BNP, is 'British Caucasian'.

The third-generation British citizen at the centre of the dispute presumably identifies himself as a member of the racial majority, but some members refuse to accept him as such. They see him not as *one of us* but as *one of them*. Here we have more evidence, if any is needed, that race is a social construct.

6.6 Gender identity

There is a large amount of research in CDA relating to gender issues. Most of it seeks to identify in some way how discourse supports or creates gender discrimination. It falls roughly into four types:

○ the way language itself is gendered – or has become gendered – and looking at the reasons for this as, for example, the way in which a male pronoun such as 'he' can be used to refer to either *males* or *males and females* (but not *females* alone);

○ the way women and men, boys and girls are stereotypically represented in discourse;

○ the way men and women interact in discourse and whether or not there are differences in their styles of talk;

○ the way language is used by males and females in specific discourse events, such as seminars or 'doctor–patient' interviews.

In this chapter, however, since we are focusing on the construction of identity, we shall consider aspects of this work only insofar as they are relevant to the identity issue, but, in the Further Study section, we refer you to a representative range of work on gender.

Gender inequality

Consideration of gender identity is important because in most – if not all – places in the world, there is still considerable gender discrimination in terms of educational opportunity, job equality, income, home ownership, work distribution, and child care provision. There is a concerted struggle going on to rectify the situation. In most cases, it is the men who benefit from the status quo, but not in every case. For example, in Britain, girls have recently reached equivalent levels of educational attainment to those of boys, and to say that the men generally benefit from gender discrimination is not to say that they all endorse it.

Nowhere is this more clearly illustrated than in the percentage of women in governments and other ruling bodies internationally. According to the UN official statistics for 2005, in the UK, women made up less than one in five Members of Parliament (18 per cent) and in the USA, only 14 per cent of the Congress were women. Surprisingly, the number of women with political power is higher in some of the less privileged countries than it is in Britain or the USA: Costa Rica (35 per cent), Namibia (26 per cent) and Mozambique (30 per cent), and approximately 50 other countries all have a higher proportion of women in power.[2]

Gender as a social construct

We claimed earlier in this chapter that both national identity and racial identity are socially and discoursally constructed within an institutional framework. Is this true of gender? If we think of gender in terms of sexual differentiation – as most people do – gender is not a social construct but a biological one. Looked at from this point of view, we could say that whereas we have our national and racial identities thrust upon us, we are born with our sexuality. The argument would go that, for some, it may be possible to resist, refuse, reject national or racial identities, but not our masculine or feminine status. This is registered at birth and legally remains with one for life. Those who are unfortunate enough to have their sex wrongly identified or wrongly registered have a lifetime of problems in most nations of the world.

Although gender may be with us from birth, institutions still play a part establishing *the nature of the gendered identity* even if they do not establish the identity itself. It is not so much biology that leads to gender stereotyping as the differential behaviour and personality traits that are associated with each gender by cultural history.

6.7 Gendered discourse

The social expectations of the relative roles of women and men, carried intertextually, hamper progress towards more egalitarian structures. Discourses of gender are significant in visual as well as verbal media. At the time of writing, for example, children's clothes in British chain stores are strictly gendered: the boys' clothes are blue, black or grey or white or combinations of these colours, often decorated with the colourful symbols of football teams. The girls' clothes are all pink and purple, but some have a concession to national unity in a World Cup year with the word 'England' – often in silver – or a small flag. Boys' and girls' toys are marked strictly for gender as are many television programmes, advertisements, computer games and books. A number of studies of gendered discourse have demonstrated the social pressures on children to conform to masculine or feminine traditional roles. There has been some debate about how far authors of school books should seek to present a more symmetrical view of male and female roles, and it has been argued that many books display more asymmetry than is actually present in society.

This is a long-standing site of struggle for feminists and one that is becoming more significant for males. In 1978, one of the authors of this book co-authored a book for African secondary schools. She objected to the proposed book cover, which was a collage of working people, on the grounds that it represented men and women in traditionally gendered roles (doctor-male, nurse-female, businessperson-male, secretary-female). The publishers agreed to change the cover to present women in professional roles. The result was a cover with pictures of six men (three factory workers, two African representatives at the UN and one library customer), and two women (a librarian and a nurse operating high-tech equipment). As equality grew, visibility decreased.

Reading schemes which had been criticized for sexism in their representation of males and females were replaced in many schools by *The Oxford Reading Tree* in the 1990s. A close analysis (Wharton 2005) of Stage 3 of this series (18 books) showed that although the more obvious stereotyping of masculinity and femininity in traditional roles is avoided, alternative gender differences are constructed that are not advantageous to either boys or girls as models. There are an equal number of male and female characters in the stories but the males are dominant in terms of overall numerical appearances as well as playing a significantly large number of agent roles, as in this sample of the analysis (Table 6.1). The males (boys and fathers) here not only play more active roles in material processes, they also say more and are described more often by the narrative voice.

Process	Participant role	Male	Female	Mixed M/F
Material	Actor	79	44	30
Verbal	Sayer	35	10	9
Relational	Carrier	32	9	6

Table 6.1 Comparison of male and female roles in *The Oxford Reading Tree*
Source: Wharton (2005).

Eleven of the stories have a problem–solution structure. In only one case does a female character have a problem. Seven male characters have problems; the remaining three affect a mixed group. In addition, the majority of problems are solved by female characters. Then there are thirteen cases of what the analyst calls the 'buffoon scenario' where a character is presented as behaving foolishly and humorously. Twelve of these characters are male, either a boy or a father being the buffoon.

The analyst comments:

> Males are dominant in terms of overall numerical representation … yet an analysis of the interaction between gender and narrative suggests that this representation is not entirely advantageous: males are portrayed as incompetent, dependent, and as butts of jokes. One may wonder which gender of readers is more frustrated here: females because of their invisibility or males because of their unattractiveness.

An example: reporting war deaths

It is not always the case that females receive less attention in discourse than males. We illustrate this with a case where a female was singled out for considerable media attention. She was one of five service personnel who were killed in May 2006 when their helicopter was shot down. Over a hundred British servicemen had been killed before that incident as well as thousands of Iraqis and a large number of American servicemen yet the woman's death received massive coverage on radio, television and in newspapers, where front page stories with photographs were supplemented in many papers with articles and editorial comment.

While there is no doubt that this young woman was exceptionally talented and brave, we may wonder why she was honoured and applauded so much more than her male colleagues. The *Daily Mail* Comment section (1) gave a typical response. (we have italicized the sentences that indicate gender differentiation):

1. The loss of any member of our armed forces is painful. *The death of Flight Lieutenant Sarah-Jayne Mulvihill in Iraq is even more so.*

    Killed with four male colleagues when their helicopter came down over Basra, she is the first service woman to fall victim to enemy action abroad since World War II.

    In these days of sexual equality that is not supposed to matter – but it does.

    (*Daily Mail*, 8 May 2006, p. 14; our italics)

The British Army is an example of an institution that has seriously made an effort to treat women with at least some degree of equality, and, as such, it might be expected that the general consensus in the country would be to accept and perhaps support this position even among people who oppose the war in general. However, the subsequent debate revealed considerable disagreement on this point, with some writers revealing that sexism is still alive and well. A male journalist wrote:

2. Even in this age of equality, there are some tasks which our society should continue to hold back from. Among them is surely that of (a woman) emptying a rifle into a man.

    Sarah-Jane Mulvihill's death drives home the message that service in war is brutally different from the civilian world in which women have justly gained equality. Many of us cherish the notion that women should be preserved from the ugliest manifestations of military life.

    (Max Hastings, *Daily Mail*, 9 May 2006)

From a different perspective, a female journalist wrote:

3. They (women) knowingly sign up and know what their responsibilities are, especially to their colleagues in uniform. They also know that this provokes ancient concerns about the role of women and that many of those who object are uncomfortable about dealing with the fact that it is a woman who is being paid to protect and defend, and arguments about their safety shade easily into disapproval of what they are doing, but these days, it is not going to stop them doing the job.

    (Kate Adie, *Daily Telegraph*, 9 May 2006)

The Activities section of this chapter contains an exercise based on extracts from these articles.

Activities

1. In 1967, a committee of 18 experts made up of professors and judges, including biologists, anthropologists and social scientists, produced the UNESCO Statement on Race and Racial Prejudice. This should be read in its entirety

although space does not allow us to reproduce it here. We give here a few of the key points:

○ The conference of experts meeting in Paris in September 1967 agreed that racist doctrines lack any scientific basis whatsoever.

○ All men (*sic*) living today belong to the same species and descend from the same stock.

○ The division of the human species into 'races' is partly conventional and partly arbitrary.

○ The human problems arising from so-called 'race' relations are social in origin rather than biological.

○ In order to undermine racism it is not sufficient that biologists should expose its fallacies. It is also necessary that psychologists and sociologists should demonstrate its causes.

Discuss what contributions CDA might make to undermining racism.

2. **a.** If you are working or studying in a university or other educational institution, try an analysis of the gender distribution among the staff at all levels.

    b. If your institution produces an in-house magazine for staff or alumni, take a recent edition (or more) and analyse the amount of space given to the relative achievements of men and women. Count the numbers of photographs of men and women.

    c. Draw conclusions about the relative positions of women and men in your institution. Can you find reasons to account for this?

3. Compare the extracts below from articles on the death of a young woman soldier in a helicopter crash in Iraq. The first was written by a male journalist, a former war correspondent and newspaper editor. The second is from an article by a woman journalist, a former BBC war correspondent. Consider the following issues:

    ○ What differences can you see in their overall attitude towards women military personnel?

    ○ How do the writers differ in their interpretation of the attitudes of older people?

    ○ Does either writer make dangerous generalizations about other people's attitudes? If so, how?

    ○ What evaluative language is used in these extracts? What is evaluated?

    ○ Can you see any words or phrases that you would call sexist? How are they used?

4.   To people over 40, even in this enlightened age, the notion of a woman losing her life in this way after being put in harm's way remains instinctively repugnant.
        However hard we try to move with the times, most of us still think of war and its inescapable bloodshed as the business of the stronger sex. Yet to younger people, such a death is no more remarkable than a man's sacrifice.

(Max Hastings, *Daily Mail*, 9 May 2006)

5. When Hitler menaced our shores in the second world war, many of
    my mother's generation were willing to stand – literally – on the
    beaches and fight for their country. They thought they would be
    fighting for survival. This feeling outweighed all others. Arguments
    about femininity, 'a woman's place', women as life-givers, not life-
    takers – all these lost out to the gut instinct for survival.

(Kate Adie, Daily Telegraph, 9 May 2006)

Further study

Wodak *et al.* (1999) provide a thorough exploration of national identity in Austria, including its historical construction, and the linguistic means identifiable in the discourse of national identity. Translated from German, it also considers the development of a perceived 'national character'. For discussion of statehood and nationality in relation to identity, see Blommaert (2005: 217–21) , who takes the view that we should distinguish the meanings of 'state' and 'nation state' and their position in an era of globalization.

Identity and alienation of migrant peoples in a host country and issues of citizenship have become subject to some debate in discourse studies. Parekh (2000: 55) makes the crucial point that no-one benefits where migrants are required to reject much of their former identity to pay 'a heavy cultural fee' to become a member of the new society. 'Full acceptance' would allow the host country to be prepared to change or 're-negotiate its norms' to allow for the social practices that the newcomers bring with them. Blackledge (2006) argues that this approach is required in Britain to allow space for the rich resource of languages that are brought into the country by immigrants and refugees. The pressure on immigrants to suppress their original languages is of no benefit to the nation.

On racism in a colonial context, see Fanon ([1952] 1970). On discrimination in the USA and an interesting discussion of stereotypical and racist images of Native Americans in the USA, see Feagin and Feagin (1993: 183–5). For a wide ranging collection of work on language and ethnicity, see Harris and Rampton (2003).

Readers interested in further reading on ethnicity in censuses can find relevant papers on the web-sites www.statistics.gov.uk and www.census.gov. Kertzer and Arel (ed.) (2001) includes a collection of articles relating to census issues.

Background reading on gender in language and discourse can be found in Cameron (1990), especially the section introductions by Cameron herself and the article by Bodine on pronouns. Of direct relevance to this chapter are the articles by Sunderland, Caldas-Coulthard, Coates, and Cameron, in Mills (1995). Sunderland (1994) has articles on the textual analysis of gender in school textbooks and other relevant issues.

Lemke (1995) provides a fascinating discussion (Chapter 5) of how discursive practices work together to construct social types. It includes an account of how the traditionally constructed cultural model of 'two sexes, two genders' is inadequate to account for biology or human behaviour.

7

Politeness, power and solidarity

7.1 Non-verbal communication

Face-to-face interaction requires participants to engage with issues that do not arise in most forms of written discourse or in some kinds of monologue. A significant contribution is made by such phenomena as voice pitch and volume as well as gesture, posture and the physical distance of one speaker from another (known as *paralinguistics*, *kinesics* and *proxemics*). Deference or contempt can be signalled by these means; there is a recognized offence called 'dumb insolence'. Eye-contact or *gaze* is also an issue here.

We recently observed an event in a school playground where various groups and individual children were playing or standing around. A 9-year-old boy playing an impromptu football game made a powerful shot at goal and missed, so that the ball struck on the side of the head an older boy, who was not part of the football group and was standing alone at some distance. The victim immediately picked up a stone and threw it, but it fell short. The boy who had kicked the ball raised both hands, palm outwards and tilted his head to one side with a rueful expression and a slight shrug of the shoulders. The victim half-nodded and walked away rubbing his ear.

Although no words were exchanged, this was clearly a social interaction, involving unintentional encroachment and offence, hostile reaction, apology and acceptance. Such behaviour plays an important part even when speech does take place. Unfortunately, in our examples, we are mostly restricted to the verbal dimension, or rather to what remains when it is transcribed.

7.2 Facework

When we engage in social interaction, we are sensitive to the way others see us. If a man presents himself as a skilled cook and then produces an inedible meal, he may feel embarrassed. He has 'taken a line' which he cannot maintain. Moreover, others may feel embarrassed on his behalf. In such situations, we speak of *losing face*, and if we manage to rectify the situation, we *save face*. One of the conditions for normal interaction is what sociolinguists call *facework*, the process of managing one's own and others' face.

The importance of face and facework in interaction was first noted and developed by Erving Goffman, who contributed many key ideas to sociolinguistics. Face, in this sense, was not an entirely new concept, but it is reasonable to give

Goffman the credit because he developed and systematized the notion. He defines it in the following ways:

> The positive value a person claims for himself by the line others assume he has taken during a personal contact.
>
> (Goffman 1999: 306, orig. 1955)

and in the same article:

> an image of self delineated in terms of approved social attributes.
>
> (ibid.)

Face threatening activity.

The concept is present in everyday language in expressions like *save face, lose face, shamefaced, barefaced* (+ liar, robbery, cheek, etc.).

Protection of face is the responsibility of all participants in an interaction; interactants strive to protect both their own face and also that of the others. However, maintaining face is not normally the purpose of the discourse; rather, it is a condition for the interaction since without it the interaction may break down. Behaviour which protects face is described as tactful or diplomatic, and behaviour which goes too far the other way is tactless, crass, gauche or undiplomatic.

Any action or utterance, however mild, which might conceivably upset the delicate balance of face maintenance is a *face-threatening activity* (FTA). There are many kinds of FTA and they occur frequently.

FTAs in the process of talk management include:

○   starting an unsolicited conversation;
○   challenging an opinion or assertion made by the addressee;
○   interrupting another person's turn;
○   raising a topic known to be unwelcome to the addressee;
○   changing the topic;
○   adversely commenting on or directing the addressee's speech (e.g. Please speak up! Could you please get to the point?);
○   raising taboo topics or uttering taboo words;
○   ending the interaction.

Other verbal FTAs include requests for help, offers of help, 'making a pass' in a sexual sense, rejecting an offer, rejecting a pass. Non-linguistic FTAs include encroaching on another's physical space by, for example, entering someone's home, workshop, office; making accidental physical contact (like the boy in the anecdote at the start of the chapter); upsetting someone's drink; inadvertently or deliberately obstructing access; sitting at the same table; taking the last available seat/biscuit/spoon; failing to recognize someone; burping; and so on.

FTAs may be potentially highly embarrassing or infinitesimally so. An interactant who sees another lose face will feel embarrassment, and an interactant who is made to lose face will be embarrassed or offended. For the discourse analyst one of the most interesting things about FTAs is that they are often verbal and they are usually mitigated by verbal or sometimes paralinguistic and kinesic means (voice pitch, volume, hesitation, posture, gesture, touching, etc.)

Performing an FTA without adequate mitigation may be popularly referred to as *making a gaffe, making a boob, dropping a brick, dropping a clanger, slipping up.* Commenting on such a verbal act, people might say, 'You didn't handle that very well' or 'She could have put that better, perhaps.' People who fail to handle threats to their own face and to conceal their distress may be called *touchy* or *over-sensitive*.

Power and solidarity are clearly central to all of this since they affect the whole nature of the degree to which an act is threatening. Acts which would be threatening when addressing a stranger or a social superior may be deemed unthreatening within the family, to a close friend or to a social inferior, for example, an officer giving an order to a soldier.

As we all know too well, there are occasions when speakers deliberately and maliciously try to cause another to lose face. In aggressive confrontation, contestants may opt for open abuse, a direct attack on the other's face. Even in less extreme situations, participants who take the line of 'plain speaking' (not suffering fools gladly, and so on) may use unredressed FTAs. This can be described as being *blunt* or *forthright* or, more critically, as *rude*.

But even with intentional challenges to face, facework is in play, and the malicious participant may try to undermine the other by surreptitious means. In everyday parlance, such behaviour is described as *spiteful, bitchy, catty*, or *snide*. The tactic here is to appear to conform to politeness constraints, either genuinely or superficially, and to present the FTA in the form of a *dig* or a *back-handed compliment*. The victim can save face by capping the comment with a wittier or more hurtful snide response, by pretending to be amused (the 'good sport' line), by jocularly exposing the FTA ('Ooh, get her!') or simply ignoring it.

Sometimes competitive facework can be a highly ritualized game, as in male peer-group banter, football crowd ritual insults ('You're rubbish and you know you are!'), African American 'dozens', where the participants try to cap each other's insults, often targeted at mothers or relatives, and Prime Minister's Question Time in the British Parliament. Because such exchanges are socially sanctioned as 'games', victims are obliged not to show open resentment, but these interactions sometimes mask real malice. The presence of an audience is obviously important in weighting all FTAs.

We have discussed facework as if it were restricted to spoken interaction, and it is usually discussed in this way, but in fact it is also present in written text, even in formal scientific writing, though we do not discuss that here.

7.3 Hedging

In the context of discussions of scientific or other academic publications, facework most often shows up in the guise of *hedging*. Hedging is a linguistic avoidance of full commitment or precision. It is a vague but useful term covering a range of phenomena. Like the term *face*, the word *hedging* existed in this sense in everyday language before it was taken up as a technical term by discourse analysts. In general usage, it is usually pejorative, but not when it used by language scholars.

Grammatical and lexical realizations vary, and a linguistic expression is not intrinsically a hedge; it can be said to be a hedge only in context. Hedging includes such strategic devices as approximators: *roughly, approximately, sort of, more or less,*

...1 also modality: *may, might, could, should, possibly, probably*. Another
...edging exploits projecting verbs like *think, believe, suppose*:

> ...ink when they entered they were in the growth stage.

We can introduce our own opinions fairly forcefully with a neutral reporting verb
like *say*:

> I say that he was wrong.

or

> What I say is that he was wrong.

but it is more hedged if we combine a modal with the reporting verb to give, for
example:

> I would say both would be customer organizations.

The unhedged proposition would be:

> Both are customer organizations.

The use of *I would say* and the choice of the modal verb *would* (*be*) instead of *are*
make the claim less bold. Like most hedges, it is ostensibly an indicator of uncertainty, but it is as likely as not to be motivated by face considerations. In this case,
the speaker is a student in a business studies seminar,[1] responding to a query by the
tutor, perhaps unsure of the facts, perhaps not wanting to risk full commitment,
but also perhaps exhibiting a degree of deference to the tutor, who has the status of
'knower' in this context and hence has greater power. The student apparently does
not wish to appear to take an 'expert' line.

A related example, also using a reporting verb (*say*), presents the main proposition as an embedded clause:

> All I'm saying is that an individual is just one representative of the market ...

A more explicit example of deferring to the knower is the following:

> I would say Nimbus is external – correct me if – I read this a long time ago –
> I would say it's external and it was developed by Halliday, Dr Halliday and
> he joined Phillips – am I right?

Here the same speaker uses the sequence *I would say*, states the first part of his
answer and then interrupts himself by starting the somewhat formulaic hedge
Correct me if I'm wrong. He then interrupts himself again with an advance non-
formulaic hedge, a disarmer, in the form of the information that he read about it a
long time ago, implicating that he might not have full recollection. He ends with
another indication of deference to the addressee's status as knower in the form of a
request for confirmation. These are all manifestations of what we call politeness.

7.4 Politeness

Starting from Goffman's ideas of face, Brown and Levinson developed an elaborate
model of *politeness*, in a work which proved to be of major importance in pragmatics

Grady's utterance — work on many levels
politeness — hedging, face TA, underlying threats
paralinguistic actions etc Politeness, power and solidarity | **105**

and sociolinguistics. The term FTA is taken from Brown and Levinson (1987) although the idea is present in Goffman. It was based on their earlier research with speakers of Tzeltal, a Mayan language in Mexico (Penelope Brown) and Tamil, a Dravidian language in India (Stephen Levinson), and their status as native speakers of, respectively, American English and British English. The other key sociolinguistic concept which they used was that of the interacting dimensions of power and solidarity (Brown and Gilman 1972). Brown and Levinson show that politeness (in the wide sense in which they and subsequent scholars use the term) can be the motivation for deviating from Grice's maxims, a point which Grice himself had mentioned but not developed (Grice 1975; Chapter 2 in our book).

In the Brown and Levinson model, two types of face are posited: negative and positive. *Negative face* is basically freedom from imposition; *positive face* is the wish to be approved of in certain respects. This distinction gives rise to two kinds of politeness: *negative politeness* and *positive politeness*. These terms are potentially confusing. Negative politeness is their name for social distancing, non-encroachment, deference; in other words, for what immediately springs to most people's minds when they hear the word *politeness*: saying 'please', using people's titles (e.g. Ms McCabe, Dr Al Shabab, Sergeant), using apologetic language, hedging, being indirect, and so on. Positive politeness includes behaviour which might not always be generally thought of as politeness, namely showing solidarity: being 'matey', using first names, indicating common interest, and inclusivity (including the addressee in the social group).

For example, someone asking for a small favour can use negative politeness or positive politeness:

1. Negative politeness: I'm sorry to bother you, Miss, but could you possibly lend me your pen?

2. Positive politeness: Charlie, chuck us a pen, mate.

Sometimes both negative and positive features can be combined:

Do you mind very much if I come in, love?

If a desired action is felt to be too face-threatening, it may be avoided altogether, and in emergencies (or in pretended emergencies) an FTA can be performed without mitigation. A drowning man is socially permitted to shout 'Help!' in preference to 'Excuse me, sir, would it be too much trouble to throw me a lifebelt?' or 'Hey, mate, lend a hand to your old buddy.'

Excessive negative politeness may be intended and/or interpreted as sarcasm, thereby increasing the threat to face. Some superficially negative politeness expressions have become formulaic sarcastic complaints:

Oh dear, I'm sorry I spoke.

Ostensibly an apology, this utterance is frequently used as a (weak) face-saving reaction to a criticism or a negative response.

7.5 Turn-taking

It is self-evident that people engaged in spoken dialogue have to take turns in speaking. About five per cent of speakers' contributions overlap, and sometimes speakers may try to shout each other down, but, if the interaction is not to break down completely or change into a monologue, they must grant each other opportunities to contribute. *one word answer . tacit —*

In formal spoken discourse practices such as public debates, committee meetings, and legal trials, turn-taking is tightly controlled and is in some instances conventionally ordered (as in a religious service) or has its control assigned to a single participant (the chair in a meeting) or a combination of the two (in public debate or legal trial).

In informal conversation or unscripted interviews, it might appear that turn-taking is completely random, but extensive research has shown that the process is subject to various constraints that might be described as rules. The systematic study of turn-taking and related aspects of spoken discourse is called *conversation analysis* (CA). Conversation analysts claim that turn-taking is independent of sociocultural considerations, and, unlike ourselves and ethnographically oriented analysts generally, are not interested in relating talk to social status outside the conversation. Their goals have not been the same as ours to date, and we exploit CA here, as we do other methodologies, in a cherry-picking manner, simply using ideas and techniques that seem useful at the time.

For the most part, turns are short and opportunities for change of speaker are restricted. However, a turn may consist of just a grunt of agreement or sounds indicating participation or comprehension: 'Uh, uh.' While a speaker is taking a turn, she (or he) controls the floor. Also, there are recognizable points of entry for a new turn (transition relevance place: TRP), and to initiate a turn at some other point would be construed as an interruption and therefore as impolite.

Speakers signal the completion of their turn in various ways, for example, by intonation, or a change in pitch and volume, by dragging out the last syllable, by a gesture or change of posture or gaze, or saying something like 'or whatever' or 'you know', by finishing a sentence, or usually by a combination of two or more of these. When there is competition for turns, the person wanting to take a turn looks out (subconsciously or not) for signals that the turn is over, or that it might at least appear to be over.

Grady blank expression

A skilled manipulator of turn-taking in interviews can maintain a turn by avoiding giving the signals of termination. This skill is observable in interviews with politicians, who often prevent the interviewer from posing a new question so that they can complete a political message. When they reach what might look like a TRP, instead of pausing they introduce a conjunction (e.g. 'and so …') before the pause so as to block the opening. Sometimes, there is an explicit appeal to the right to complete a point, which the interviewer may or may not accept.

Political interviews are an example of special cases where long turns are often called for; others include post-event sports interviews and television chat shows. But long turns of this kind can be invited or requested in everyday conversations, when a speaker is invited to recount an experience or a joke, though even here occasional responses are normal.

Turns tend to go in pairs, known as *adjacency pairs*. A greeting expects another greeting in response; a question expects a reply; an offer expects acceptance. A second part which conforms to the expectation is called a *preferred second part*, and it will come as no surprise to you to learn that a second part that fails to fit expectations

is a *dispreferred second pa*   borative
sequence between a tutor

T: .... both these in
S:

     users yes that's rig
T: they're both profes   า a
     step further betwee   ıly
     on (S: yes) of the a

S:
T: and know-how yes

S's first turn echoes and en   onse to
the S contribution 'and knc   ndorses
S's lexical choice by echoir   esent in
T's longish turn and the re   compre-
hension and agreement, which could also have been achieved by a nod or a grunt.
    Dispreferred second parts are FTAs and tend to be hedged:

> I don't know that I would necessarily agree with that – I mean the amount of
> time getting in the car driving somewhere and paying money to wash things,

Sometimes there is an intervening adjacency pair between the first and second part.
This is called an *insertion sequence*. For example:

A: D'you want a beer?

    B: What've you got?

    A: Grolsch 'n mm Bud

B: Grolsch please.

Before completing the offer–acceptance pair, B initiates a new pair by asking a relevant question. A completes this inserted pair, and B then completes the first pair
with an acceptance, the preferred response. Incidentally, the terms *preferred* and
dispreferred are not intended to refer to the state of mind of the participants, but
rather to the normality of the response. It could be that A secretly hopes that B will
refuse the offer of a beer, but, even if we had any way of knowing, that would not
affect our analysis of the acceptance as 'preferred'.

7.6 Topic control: two television news interviews

One of the attributes of power is some degree of control over input to a discourse,
which in the case of face-to-face interaction in some situations includes control
over turn-taking and hence over the content of the discussion, that is, topic control.
    In most modern societies, there is at least lip-service paid to the principle of
equality, but in practice inequalities of power permeate social relations. The
extreme example of an intrinsically unequal institution which does not pretend

otherwise is the military, where rank is institutionally marked and formally recognized, and where, within prescribed limits, a person of higher rank can give unmitigated orders to a person of lower rank. Broadly speaking, this is true also of schools though much less absolutely than in earlier times. In fact, generally, there is considerable inequality of power between adults and children. Of course, relations between different military ranks or between teachers and students are not static, and the use of status-marked features varies according to the nature of the interaction: taking disciplinary action versus chatting in a bar or at a school dance, for example.

Interview 1

Within the boundaries of a media interview, the interviewer has considerably more power than the interviewee and has the right, within limits, to choose topics and turns, although this can be challenged. A major situational factor is the audience. The participants are aware that this is not a private conversation but a performance.

In the following 23 seconds of dialogue (*BBC2 Newsnight*, 9 May 2006), the television broadcaster Jeremy Paxman, in London, is interviewing John Curtin, introduced as 'an animal rights activist', via a television link to a studio in Birmingham. The interview followed a lengthy report on an animal rights letter campaign against the multinational pharmaceutical company GlaxoSmithKline. Also present in the London studio was an interviewee supporting animal testing, but his contribution is not included here.[2]

(P = Paxman; C = Curtin; [= overlap)

P: Mr Curtin, do you accept that er some people are going to find these sort of letters frightening?

C: eehm within the er you've just had a completely hysterical lead em ah piece there that was em I'd say was more in tune with er the *Daily Mail* than a there's a massive level of propaganda against us at [the moment

P: [would you like to address my question?

C: what we're dealing with erm here is [SmithKline

P: [can you answer my question?
         [do you accept

C: [what we're [dealing with he SmithKlineSmithKline

P: [hang on a second here, matey

C: I will answer your question [yeh

P: [please do you accept that many people will find these letters frightening?

C: I can't give you an answer to er some people may do yes.

The interviewer is noted for his aggressive style. On 13 May 1997, he posed the same question twelve (or fourteen) times to the Conservative Home Secretary, Michael Howard, who was using the usual politician's strategies to avoid giving a direct answer. This is widely recognized as the most face-threatening interview in television history.

In the section transcribed, P is determined to maintain his role as topic controller in the face of an interviewee who wants to make his own points. C does not respond to P's opening turn with a preferred response, a yes or no. Instead he complains of the bias of the newsreel report but is unable to complete his turn because P interrupts with a request for him to answer the question. The wording conforms grammatically to politeness norms by opting for interrogative and conditional and wording it as a preference choice for the addressee: *would you like to answer*. This is a conventionally polite indirect speech act, mitigating the FTA in a routine way. As the interview proceeds and C appears not to be conforming, the directive is still conventionally polite but fractionally less hedged: *can you* instead of *would you like*. At last, P drops politeness altogether and shouts a direct order, 'Hang on a second here, matey.' In the circumstances this looks less like positive politeness than aggression, using a familiar address form to signal disrespect. The message might be interpreted as: You have overstepped the mark and I am taking off the kid gloves.

At the beginning, C attempts to use his turns to make his political points, ignoring P's agenda; P insists on his role as manager. His directive to answer the question moves the discourse onto a metadiscoursal plane by referring to his own question. In turn-taking terms he opens an insertion pair. Since C fails to provide a preferred response either to the yes–no question with which P opens or to the insertion opener about answering the question, the discourse appears to be in danger of breaking down. At length, the interviewee produces a preferred response to the insertion sequence: 'I will answer your question yeh.' P puts the opening question again. C first gives a dispreferred response: 'I can't answer that question,' but then repairs it with a preferred response: 'some people may do yes.' The dialogue is briefly back on track.

We have ignored several important dimensions of these exchanges. Kinesics and paralinguistics play a major role, which space prevents us from investigating here. There is a slight mismatch, for example, between P's polite wording and his paralinguistic signals. The rapid timing and intonation of C's eventual preferred response ('some people may do yeh') have the effect of downplaying the importance of the question, and he moves on quickly to his next point (not transcribed here).

At more than one point, the interviewee complains about being interrupted, for example:

> **C:** okay you're not going to let me speak I thought hopefully you will.

He clearly came to the interview situation with his agenda, which did not coincide with that of the interviewer. In spite of the mismatch of power and P's repeated interruptions and objections, he was successful over the whole interview in mentioning three points (not all transcribed here) that were outside P's agenda: the House of Lords debate, a demand for a commission of inquiry into animal experiments, and, most controversially, instructions on how to find attacks on the company in question on the Internet. At this last point, P brings out the big stick:

> **P:** let's just stick to the matter in hand rather than tittle tattle on the
> Internet [shall we
> **C:**   [tittle tattle?

P: (shouting) yes tittle tattle I've not had a chance to check it and nor
         have you

There is a marked contrast between spontaneous and edgy exchanges of this
kind and the much more staid semi-scripted or pre-planned type of interview
where there is no fighting over turns or topics. In the early days of broadcasting,
this second type was the norm, but there is now a clear preference for some
confrontation.

Interview 2

Later in the same programme, Paxman had an entirely separate interview with the
US Ambassador, Robert H. Tuttle; it took place in the American Embassy. This is
a more decorous affair with far fewer overlaps and no shouting or complaints about
not being allowed to speak. Even so, similar power struggles occur.

An important part of the context is that Iran was developing a nuclear industry in
spite of American objections and a potential UN resolution, that Jack Straw had
been removed from the post of Foreign Secretary, the third most senior position in
the British Government, and that he had recently ridiculed the idea of a possible
military strike on Iran.

In answer to an opening question about a hypothetical military strike
against Iran, the ambassador uses the word *diplomacy* three times in the same short
turn:

(A = Ambassador; P = Paxman)

A: I think that the emphasis here is on diplomacy and I think a UN
         resolution would move forward diplomacy put some pressure on the
         Iranians and I think that's what we're looking for is diplomacy not not
         not military

P: do you agree with Jack Straw then that a military attack is inconceivable?

A: I think that the emphasis Jeremy has to be on diplomacy and that's
         where it's been

P: that wasn't my question – is an attack inconceivable?

A: I think the President has made it clear that ah he will not take the military
         option off the table no leader ever takes no responsible leader Jeremy
         ever takes a military option off the table   [but

P: [Our Foreign Secretary our
         last Foreign Secretary did he said it was inconceivable and nuts

A: I think the Prime Minister who runs the government made it clear what
         his position was

P: did the White House complain about Jack Straw?

A: no no no nuh the relationship between the State Department and the
         White House and er Secretary for Secretary Straw was good I had a
         very good relationship with Secretary er Straw

(section omitted)

P: so it would be quite off the wall to suggest that he was removed for being insufficiently amenable to the White House and replaced with someone more pliable like Margaret Beckett? that would be just off the wall?

A: you said it – off the wall

(section omitted)

A: Jeremy, I'm not going to answer that question I'm an optimist I think it'll have to be a diplomatic solution I believe it'll have a diplomatic solution

P: and if it doesn't?

A: Jeremy, it's going to have a diplomatic solution

P: it's going [to –

A: [but no leader and any responsible leader ever takes the other options

P: it's going to have a diplomatic solution

A: I believe that it will have a diplomatic solution I I believe that's why your er Foreign Office and my State Department spent thousands of hours on this very difficult issue.

It is hardly wild speculation to suggest that, like the animal rights campaigner, the ambassador came to the interview with an agenda of his own. This clearly included pressing home the message that the USA was committed to a diplomatic solution. The words *diplomacy* or *diplomatic solution* occur nine times in a short stretch of talk. Only once is P the source, and this is when he repeats the ambassador's utterance verbatim. When he manages to complete this utterance on his second try, he delivers it flatly without question intonation, but a probable inference is that he is querying A's switch from expressing a hope to making an unhedged prediction. A responds by substituting a statement of belief, less committed than the bald prediction but not quite an open self-correction. Earlier, P speaks of *military attack* and *attack*, but A prefers the more euphemistic *military option*. Later, he avoids the word *military* entirely and talks of *other options*.

Status and face

An interview of this kind is a sort of verbal duel. It differs from the open bantering and points-scoring of Prime Minister's Questions in that any one-upmanship involved, if present at all, is covert and is not a primary goal of the speech event. The acknowledged purpose is to inform the television audience of aspects of the USA's relations with Britain, most immediately regarding the possibility of conflict with Iran. The additional goals may well include such varied things as: on one side, eliciting surprising information, catching interviewee off guard, putting on a good show, furthering interviewer's career, and maintaining prestige as an effective and courageous interviewer; and, on the other side, maintaining smooth relations between Britain and the USA, furthering the diplomatic career, maintaining a reputation as a capable ambassador, and so on. Protecting one's own face is more important in these situations than protecting the face of the other participant, but at least a semblance of amiability and politeness is a conventional requirement; this is complicated on the one side, though, by the professional prestige associated with being an aggressive interviewer.

In most settings, it is probable that the US Ambassador has more social clout than even a famous TV anchorman and interviewer, and here the interview takes place on the ambassador's home ground, the American Embassy in London, but within the confines of the interview the greater power is with Paxman; therefore, he can ask face-threatening questions without mitigation.

The ambassador, on the contrary, takes a placatory approach, smiling frequently, speaking with a low pitch, using the addressee's first name from time to time. He makes frequent use of the expressions 'I think' and 'I believe', a type of grammatical metaphor which can replace modal verbs like *may* or *can* and which renders the main proposition as a mental projection and hence less open to challenge. When he delivers the repeated negative in response to P's undiplomatic query as to whether the US had influenced the removal of a senior government minister, A does so not in a rapid emphatic way but in a slow, hushed, reassuring delivery, like someone calming a child.

These are both highly skilled professional communicators and negotiators, and the only time when A is obviously at a loss is later in the interview when P says:

> **P:** you are aware of course that many people in this country consider
>   Tony Blair to be George Bush's poodle.

Here A noticeably hesitates, looking startled, and then, recovering, says with a questioning intonation and a smile:

> **A:** and your question?

P replies: 'I'm asking if you're aware of it', and A then proceeds, a little late but at some length, to refute the criticism of Blair. In context, P's statement is certainly shocking, but his only assertion is that A is aware of something, namely the proposition that many people consider that Blair is Bush's poodle. He is not responsible for the proposition that Blair is Bush's poodle since it is attributed to 'many people in this country' without evaluation. Nevertheless, the tabling of the proposition in any form presents a challenge for Anglo-American diplomacy; hence A's obvious discomfort.

The utterance 'and your question?' is an example of several metatextual comments in this transcript, all involving the word *question*. It is obviously a stalling strategy, an impromptu means of buying a little time to concoct a more face-saving response than 'yes' or 'no'. P's elicitation was couched in declarative form, which provided the ambassador with a loophole. If P had asked: 'Are you aware ….,' this line would not have been open to him. On the other hand, a denial would have been obviously untrue and a simple affirmative would have been undiplomatic.

In response to a question about whether the US would expect British support if an attack on Iran should take place, the ambassador explicitly refuses to answer the question. In an informal friendly chat between equals this would be an unlikely option, and even in fairly formal interviews an explicit refusal is rare, though evasive answers are extremely common. (At a later point in the interview, he observes that it would be inappropriate for him to comment on conversations between the two leaders.)

However, given the diplomatic context and the fact that A has already indicated repeatedly that he wants to keep war off the agenda, it is socially permissible. Even so, he mitigates it marginally by prefacing it with P's first name, a touch of positive politeness.

The first instance of a metatextual contribution is near the beginning where P rejects A's answer by pointing out that it did not answer his question: 'that wasn't my question', and rephrasing the question more baldly:

> is an attack inconceivable?

This is very face-threatening: a dispreferred follow-up to an answer, namely a rejection of it as valid, followed by a more direct version of a question which the addressee has already shown he wishes to avoid answering. Nevertheless, P makes no verbal concessions to politeness. He can get away with this because of the power temporarily conferred on him by the discourse event, the television interview. This is comparable to that of a cross-examining lawyer in a courtroom. So we see that power is to some extent temporarily conferred in accordance with the speech event or practice; it is also negotiable although access is largely controlled. There is the added complication of P's idiosyncratically confrontational interviewing style.

However, social status pertaining to the world outside the immediate context of the interview is not entirely absent. It is hard to imagine even Paxman shouting 'tittle tattle' at the US Ambassador as he did at the animal rights campaigner. When he insists on his question being answered, he does so after allowing the ambassador to complete his turn. On the other hand, he is on record in an interview with Tony Blair as responding to Blair's claim that weapons inspectors 'were put out of Iraq':

> They were not put out of Iraq, Prime Minister, that is just not true. The weapons inspectors left Iraq after being told by the American government that bombs will be dropped on the country.
>
> (*BBC Newsnight*, 6 February 2003)

To this, Blair replied:

> I'm sorry, that is simply not right. What happened …

Notice that here we have a Prime Minister, who has in effect just been accused in public of lying, instinctively apologizing (I'm sorry) for the dispreferred response he is about to utter ('that is simply not right').

7.7 Spoken and written discourse

Scholars discussing language often make generalizations about the differences between spoken and written language as if the two were clearly distinct. In fact, this is not the case. Of course, if we restrict the terms to the channel of delivery, no distinction could be more obvious. But the distinction becomes more problematic when we start to talk of stylistic characteristics, and say, for example, that spoken language is characterized by sentence fragments, false starts, contracted forms and self-corrections. Generalizations of this kind tend to treat 'spoken language' as referring exclusively to spontaneous chat, and 'written language' as referring to formal, careful writing, and exclude such things as hastily scribbled notes, shopping

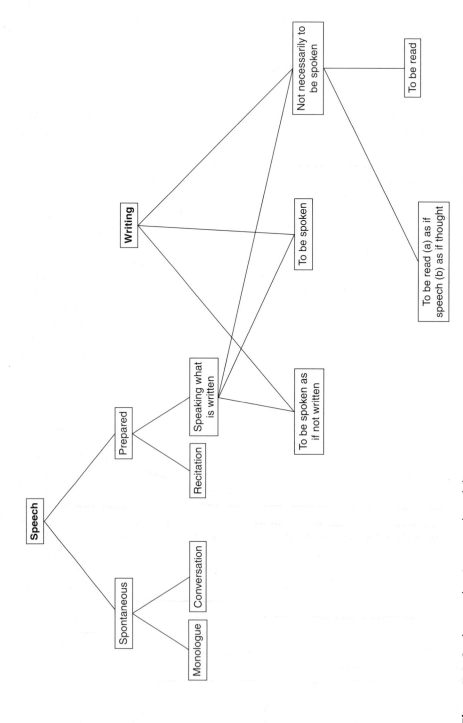

Figure 7.1 Spoken and written modes of discourse
Source: Gregory and Carroll (1976: 47).

lists, some emails, and phone texting. Of course, most of the people who make these generalizations are aware of the complications, but it might be less misleading to speak of spontaneous (as opposed to prepared) speech, and formal or careful writing. The need for even more precise categorization is illustrated in Figure 7.1, taken from Gregory and Carroll (1976).

Political speeches are usually prepared, or, in Gregory and Carroll's terms, written to be spoken as if not written. That is to say, the speech is scripted but is delivered in such a way as to give some resemblance to spontaneous talk. Of course, some political speeches may be entirely spontaneous, and, more frequently, they may be carefully planned but not delivered directly from the script. It is also worth bearing in mind that many political speeches are not written by the person who delivers them but by aides or professional speech writers; sometimes they are the product of group collaboration. Any permutation of preparedness and spontaneity is possible. Another important factor is that the speaker has a monopoly of the floor, with the possible exception of interruption by hecklers, and so although it is a form of face-to-face discourse with the audience as a key participant, it is one-sided in terms of verbal output.

The same is true of many university lectures or papers presented at academic conferences, but whereas a minority of academics may read aloud a written text with no concessions to the features of face-to-face interaction (such as: smiles, eye-contact, direct address), it could be disastrous for a politician to do so. When politicians in a self-styled liberal democracy speak to the public, they need to persuade and to some extent to gain audience approval. This is also true if they are writing, say, a newspaper article, and the two may have much in common, but there are a few characteristics that distinguish the two genres.

7.8 Desperately seeking solidarity

On 18 September 2005, Tony Blair, at the time Member of Parliament for Sedgefield, County Durham, Labour Party Leader and Prime Minister, gave a speech on education to constituents and Labour Party members in his constituency. Tony Blair is a skilled communicator, well-known for his much-parodied use of interpersonal and metatextual features in interviews and public speeches: expressions like 'and, you know ....', 'what I am saying is ....', 'as we know ....'. Our source here is not our own transcript of the televised actual delivery (as in the Paxman interviews), but a download from a government website. Therefore, it is a tidier version, possibly closer to the original script than to the actual delivery. Also, we lack the audience response.

In this speech, the speaker incorporated a number of face-to-face features into what was largely expository propaganda for his government's achievements and his plans for educational and economic change. He was well aware that within the Labour Party, especially among the ordinary membership, there was strong opposition to the policies he was promoting in this speech, some of which had the support of the Conservative Party.

He opens the speech with a brief greeting and welcome:

> Good morning, everyone. It is a great pleasure to welcome you here to my constituency of Sedgefield and to be able to talk to you a little about

education and education policy, but also about some of the important
changes that have been happening in our region.

This starts as phatic communion, establishing a social rapport with the audience before
getting into the serious business. He begins with two purely ritual moves (greeting and
welcome), and then gives a preview of the substance of his talk. Even in this brief
opening sequence, he manages to introduce a note of local solidarity by referring to
'our region'. This is justifiable in the sense that he is the Member of Parliament for that
constituency, but the audience is well aware that he lives in 10 Downing Street and
has a very valuable house in Islington. His next move is to talk about the improved
economy of the region, comparing it favourably with London and the South-East,
mentioning 'economic growth', 'new technologies', 'nanotechnology' and '40,000
more jobs'. This addresses a long-standing and widespread resentment of what many
northerners see as a bias towards London and the South-East in all British governments
and a history of relatively greater affluence in the South-East.

At this point, he makes what might seem a strange digression in a speech about
regional economy and national education policy. He starts talking about football.

Newcastle, as we know, is a thriving and great European city – with a great
football team. OK, we won't go there.

He then recounts an anecdote about how, as a young MP, he provoked a near-riot
in a local primary school classroom by asking the children which team they supported. So we have the flattery of Newcastle's status (in effect, a summing-up of
his previous moves), followed by a compliment to the football team, and then an
in-group joke based on mutual knowledge (common ground) about local football
rivalries. (In fact, Sedgefield is near but not in Newcastle.) 'OK, we won't go there,'
is a currently fashionable idiom. This entire sequence, the reference to football, the
funny story about the children, the colloquialism, has a populist motivation, projecting the 'man of the people' image to which most politicians aspire, often to
ludicrous effect. He concludes the anecdote:

The head teacher said: 'Please, either don't come here again, or when you
do don't talk about football.'

The fact that the school head could order Blair in this way (albeit the younger Blair,
not the PM), and the fact that he tells the story of his own gaffe, further reinforce
the presentation of himself as an unpretentious person at one with the community
and the audience. He uses this strategy of digression and little joke later in the
speech when he again reverts to his earlier days in the area:

Over these past twenty years I have seen this region change, and I have
learnt a lot from these changes. Some of the things that most influenced my
political thinking, both as Member of Parliament, then on the opposition
front bench, then as opposition leader, then as Prime Minister, have
actually happened here in this region. And I remember one of the most
important meetings I ever attended in my life, though at the time it didn't
seem like that, it was in the County Hall, the Durham County Council
building, it will be very familiar to some of you, and in which I once

worked incidentally – you may not know this – in a holiday job in the
Vehicle Licensing Department, I think it was. All I know was that it was
me, at a young age, surrounded by a very large number of young women.
It was a very tough work experience.

The first part of this sequence, as far as '…. familiar to some of you', is an overt statement of Blair's long-standing political service to the region during his impressive
career with a flattering claim crediting the region with being the source of his political wisdom. The digression from 'and in which I worked, incidentally, …' as far as
the end of the extract is another piece of positive politeness, a serious bid for solidarity. This is delivered in a spontaneous style with interpolations and a touch of
vagueness about detail 'I think it was' (surely he must know!), but it is an effective
piece of interaction. It serves once more to remind the audience of how far back his
local connections go. The solidarity markers include: mention of his youthful holiday job which serves to counter his affluent privileged image; the interpersonal
parenthesis 'you may not know this', which is the kind of comment a person might
make to a close acquaintance who knows most things about them; the direct appeal
to common ground with local people in the audience, probably in a majority: 'it will
be very familiar to some of you'; and finally the little joke about being surrounded by
young women being a very tough work experience. This shared local knowledge tactic has been exploited earlier. It tells the audience that they and the speaker have a
background in common; like them he knows where the old coke works was; it says
that he is not addressing some remote audience or speaking to posterity but is rooted
in this location with its distinctive industrial history, now changing for the better:

> Look just up the road here at the new housing estate to be built at
> Fishburn, where the old coke works once was.

All of this leads into a sequence where he recalls a local political figure:

> … Mickey Terrence, who will be known to some of you here, but who had
> been a branch official in the 1926 General Strike, and he was an
> extraordinary man, Mickey Terrence, a wonderful man of principle and
> integrity and extraordinary canniness as well.

Blair's larger goal in this speech is to sell to a region with a strong socialist history an
ideology which many Labour Party members and unaffiliated voters regard as conservative. The political substance of his speech, which we have largely omitted
here, is a highly emotive eulogy of privatization, which he presents as a desirable
and even inevitable solution to economic and educational problems although he
does not offer any substantive arguments. Introducing the figure of the late Mickey
Terrence is part of the solidarity game (local hero, father figure, 'known to some of
you here'), but it has a further purpose, which is to recruit this distinguished (and
conveniently dead) socialist in support of Blair's case for scrapping the last rem-
nants of socialist ideology and instituting a right-wing conservative programme. He
reports that, in this meeting which Blair later recognized as 'one of the most important' in his life, what Terrence said 'essentially', was:

> There is no point in worrying about the demise of the coal industry (some
> text omitted) … what we have got to do in the north-east is to set out our

> stall differently, to decide we have got a different economic future and go
> out there and get it.

Although he attributes these sentiments to the old Party activist, the words are his
own, not Terrence's, and, even if they *were* Terrence's, they could hardly be construed as an endorsement of the policies outlined in the speech, which were
undreamt of at the time. But Blair uses it as such, thereby appealing to solidarity
within the Labour movement with its activist past (the 1926 General Strike), its
socialism, its roots in urban industrialism, and implying that his policies are in keeping with this common ideological heritage. Indeed, he suggests that it was the old
class warrior, Terrence, who gave him the idea.

> And I reflected that if he, with all his background and all his tradition, had
> the courage to make changes, then really we should be prepared to
> embrace that change as well, we within the Labour Party, but also outside
> of it in the wider community.

In his initial description of Terrence, he uses the word *canniness*. *Canny* is a
Geordie word, typically north-eastern, and, though not unknown outside the
north, not obviously at home in Blair's Estuary-tinged Oxford-educated accent; it
is yet another claim to local solidarity.

Throughout this talk, Blair uses the pronoun *we* fifty-four times. He uses it variously to mean, the population of Britain, the government, the Labour Party, the
people of the region and the people in the hall. Sometimes it is not at all clear what
the scope of reference is, and this is strategically sound because it blurs the fact that
his ideological goals and passions may not be those of the audience and the north-
east in general.[3] He does not, as Margaret Thatcher once did, or as he did himself in
the speech to the Women's Institute (cited in Chapter 5, Section 5.4), make the
revealing blunder of using the 'royal we'[4] to refer *unequivocally* to himself, but he
comes close in the following. He might be crediting the government as a whole
with what are widely seen as his policies, but he once includes a key word he likes
to associate with himself: *passionate*.

> That is in a nutshell why we are so passionate and so insistent about public
> service reform ...[5]

> And yes we have some success to our credit ...

> We are establishing skills academies ...

> We have an impressive line-up of companies ...

> We aim to have twelve in place ...

At one point, he makes it clear that he is using *we* in two senses:

> We should be prepared to embrace that change as well, we within the
> Labour Party, but also outside of it in the wider community.

As he approaches the end of the speech, Blair moves out in his geographical references from the constituency and the region to other cities, the nation as a whole,
and the world, but much of his effort has been devoted to an extended bid for solidarity. We have restricted our analysis to this aspect.

Activities

1. Download a political speech and/or an interview from the Internet and try to identify the features mentioned in this chapter.
2. Record a television or radio interview. Try to transcribe a section, marking any overlapping turns. This is a difficult procedure and you should not try too much text at the outset. Think about what information the viewer has that your transcript omits.
3. Try to identify ten face-threatening acts that you are involved in or observe in a normal day. Are they mitigated by politeness strategies? Which?
4. If you want to be daring, try deliberately threatening someone's face without any mitigation. Are there any consequences? You do this at your own risk.

Further study

Political interviews and speeches
See Chilton (2004), Chilton and Schaeffner (1997), and Fairclough (1989 and 1998).

On solidarity, face and politeness
The foundational work on power and solidarity is Brown and Gilman (1972), and Ervin-Tripp (1972). Goffman (1955) is the original essay on face and facework, and the seminal politeness model is Brown and Levinson (1987). Holmes (1995) looks at politeness in relation to gender. Jaworski and Coupland (1999) includes abridged excerpts of the last three.

Spoken discourse and CA
Sinclair and Coulthard (1975) devised a model of analysis (S & C) on Systemic Functional principles applied to classroom discourse. This has since been widely applied. Coulthard 1992a is a collection of papers, mainly exploiting S & C. Basturkmen (2000, 2002) discusses interaction in university seminars. Tsui (1994) incorporates turn-taking and adjacency pairs in her (predominantly S & C) study of casual conversation. Eggins and Slade 1997 is a comprehensive treatment of casual conversation, using a Systemic Functional framework. Chapter 2 includes interesting discussion of both CA and CDA. The major names in CA are Schegloff and Sacks, e.g. 1973, abridged in Jaworski and Coupland (1999). Greatbatch (1998) discusses news interviews and includes a good introduction to CA.

'We' in political discourse
Ward (2004) is an insightful analysis of the role of *we* in trades union negotiations. Faiz Abdullah (2004) discusses the role of *we* (Malay *kita*) in establishing a national ideology.

8 The discourse of prejudice

8.1 Frames and race

In Chapter 1, we introduced the notion of cognitive frames, and we returned to it in Chapters 4 and 5. According to Lakoff (2004), conservatives (right-wing Republicans) in the USA have done a better job than more progressive groups of establishing frames favourable to their views, a fact which Lakoff regrets. His aim is to 'take back public discourse' from the 'conservatives' and hand it to the 'progressives', whom he implicitly identifies with the Democratic Party, but who seem to roughly correspond to what we shall call *liberals* or *left-liberals*.[1]

Cognitive frames are metaphorical constructs (see our Chapter 5). Lakoff identifies the metaphorical model for the nation preferred by American neo-conservatives as a family with a strict father. Since they perceive the USA under a conservative government as the epitome of that model, they can exploit a further metaphor (the metaphor 'the nation is a person') to present the world as a family with the USA as the strict father and other countries as children ('developing nations') who need to be disciplined or punished if they step out of line ('rogue states').

Some racist thinking fits easily into a comparable frame. There are people who consider their own 'race' as superior to others and more mature; these others can be perceived as childlike and hence patronized, or as rebellious and threatening and hence deserving of punishment. The discourses of slavery and colonialism were based on such a metaphorical account, and it survived into post-slavery and in neo-colonial societies.

An equally dominant frame is the 'primitive Africa' frame, which tends to operate in conjunction with the 'evolutionary difference' frame. At the least sophisticated level, that of the extreme right, the 'primitive Africa' frame can be triggered in contexts that have little connection with Africa. The taunt 'Go back to Africa' is still occasionally heard from racists and is likely to be addressed to people who have had no link with Africa for many generations. Though African migrant numbers are significant, the majority of migrants in the early twenty-first century are not from Africa or of African descent.

Racist expressions like 'just down from the trees' are based on the fantasy of an evolutionary scale in which the racist is at the most advanced evolutionary stage and other ethnic and racial groupings are at a more primitive stage of development. In nineteenth-century America, the descendants of the earlier English colonists represented Irish immigrants as apes in jokes and cartoons. These appeared in the prestigious magazine *Harper's Weekly*, among others (Feagin and Feagin 1993: 90–1). In the 1930s, Nazis applied the same analogy to Jews. When you metaphorically take away people's humanity, you prepare the ground for victimization that is more material.

Referring to Chinese immigrants, the American President, Rutherford B. Hayes, wrote in 1879:

> The present Chinese invasion is pernicious and should be discouraged.
> Our experience in dealing with the weaker races – the Negroes and
> Indians – is not encouraging.
>
> (cited in Dicker 2003: 62)

Although it may take a more subtle form, the genetic inferiority argument still surfaces quite frequently on the basis of dubious intelligence tests, in its most devious guise presenting Far Eastern Asians as the top group with whites a close second.

Racists can happily hold conflicting stereotypes simultaneously: immigrants are attacked both for taking up housing and for packing too many people into a small space; they are accused of living off welfare and also of taking up 'our' jobs; they are despised for being poor and resented if they get rich.

In addition to the 'invasion' metaphor used by President Hayes, dominant metaphors still associated with the conservative frames for immigration are:

○ immigration as a destructive force (flooding; swamping; draining resources);
○ the nation as a container of limited capacity (bursting point);
○ nation as family (kith and kin);
○ immigrants as parasites (living off the state; living off our taxes; sponging on social security).

However, the debate is often less strident than this, especially in official circles or at the more respectable end of the media, and, although it may sometimes assume some of the frames mentioned, it takes the form of arguments about numbers and wages and overpopulation. Therefore, the critical analyst needs to look at the details of the arguments.

Different mores?

With the horrors of the Holocaust (the Shoah) still within living memory, modern racist arguments are less likely to depend on biological claims than on notions of cultural hierarchies ('some cultures are more advanced than others'). In the interests of respectability, they may cite not inequality but cultural incompatibility.

The 'culturally different' line of argument does not always state the superiority of 'Our' culture, but it often assumes it. An opinion piece in the left-liberal newspaper, *The Independent*, from an American correspondent, under the headline 'How the Hispanics are changing America', was triggered by a mass strike and demonstrations by immigrant workers in the USA. In spite of its many balanced observations, and, although it is addressed to British readers, it has features of a right-wing scare story. The columnist writes:

> The everyday language [in South Florida] is increasingly Spanish. And so –
> to the discomfort of non-Hispanic Americans – are the mores. One of my
> earliest acquaintances with the new Hispanic face of the United States

came in Southern Florida where – I suddenly became aware – English was barely understood. In a supermarket, I watched as customers paid barely disguised back-handers to the staff behind the delicatessen counter to secure the best cuts of roast chicken at the price of the worst.

(Mary Dejevsky, *The Independent*, 3 May 2006, p. 37)

The comments on the relative status of Spanish and English are important. They relate to a conservative ideological assumption that multilingualism is a problem. This is a key area of contention in the US, as it always has been, though formerly minority languages were ruthlessly suppressed and Spanish is more resilient (see Dicker 2003). But, in this text, the language threat is just an incidental scare. After a concession in the form of a staggering understatement:

The US is hardly a corruption-free zone,

it continues:

But what I witnessed in the Florida supermarket was the sort of petty everyday 'flexibility' that is taken for granted and denotes a whole other way of life.

Spanish-speaking immigrants in the USA are from many countries and many cultures and classes. The suggestion here is that they are generically dishonest in ways unknown to the host culture. This is not a rabidly right-wing article; it mentions, for example, the historical Hispanic ownership of much present US territory, and concludes that 'the onward march of Hispanic America' cannot be reversed. But even as it concedes that the stereotypes of mainstream USA are invalid, it leans on them:

I had tended to view the US through a north-eastern prism, as still imbued with its Puritan origins. So – wishfully – do many Americans.

This is the stereotype of the typical American as 'White Anglo-Saxon Protestant'; it is in the process of being reluctantly relinquished by a woman with a Slavonic name. The statement still carries a presupposition that longer-established Americans are more honest than the newcomers.

8.2 Two reports on immigration

The UK already has a strict immigration policy in operation; hence, reports on this topic often specify 'legal' and 'illegal' immigrants. However, these two groups are often merged in popular and media discussion, making it difficult to evaluate the arguments.

In 2006, an organization called the Institute for Public Policy Research (IPPR), an independent charity, which describes itself as 'the UK's leading progressive think tank', published a report on immigration. This was reported in British newspapers on 31 March 2006. We here consider two of these reports. *The Independent* could be described as a left-leaning liberal progressive paper, well within the mainstream of British politics; the *Daily Mail* is right-wing conservative.

A liberal account

Under a headline 'Immigration: the facts we are never told', *The Independent* filled most of its front page with bullet points from the report. Surprisingly, for those accustomed to seeing such headlines in the British press, all the points given were favourable to immigration and consisted mainly of economic facts, for example:

○ If allowed to live legally, they [illegal immigrants] would be paying more than £1 bn in tax each year.

○ Legal migrants comprise 8.7% of the population, but contribute 10.2% of all taxes. Each immigrant pays an average of £7,203 in tax, compared with £6,861 for non-migrant workers.

(The Independent, 31 March 2006, p. 1)

A more discursive account is given on page 2, alongside a related 'personal interest' item telling separate stories of two illegal immigrants: 'Charles', a Brazilian nursing assistant who worked in food preparation for less than the minimum wage but was arrested and deported; and 'Alfred', a Nigerian who came to study but worked as a cleaner 'in appalling conditions' and disappeared after his employers threatened to report him to the immigration authorities if he continued to complain.

The main report is clearly calculated to give a favourable slant on immigrants. The personal stories offer a view into the painful lot of the illegal immigrant: the human details behind the statistics.

A conservative account

The *Daily Mail* report chose to sideline the IPPR report and focus more on information from 'the respected City forecaster Capital Economics'. It does include IPPR, though it delays its mention, keeps the entries brief and uses it to support its generally negative picture of immigration. The report describes IPPR as 'Labour's favourite think-tank', a description not calculated to endear it to most of the *Daily Mail* readership. IPPR describes itself as an 'independent charity'. Capital Economics is an independent commercial company that charges fees for economic reports and commentaries. 'Our loyalties are quite simply to our clients', they claim on their website. It is not clear from the *Daily Mail*'s account who commissioned Capital's report or whether it was published elsewhere.

The *Daily Mail*'s report is on page 2. The headline is: 'One million: The real number of migrants who arrived last year'. The emphasis in this report is on the large numbers ('One million' in the headline, but 'nearly a million' in the text) and on the fact that these are 'far more than the official figures admit'.

The tone of the report is signalled at the outset by the use of the lexical item *admit* in 'far more than official figures admit'. This presupposes that high immigration figures are valued negatively. We do not admit to good things or even to neutrally valued things; we admit to misdemeanours, crimes, sins; we admit that we are wrong. (See the discussion of *collocation* later in this chapter.)

Facts and figures

Whereas *The Independent* points out: 'Nearly 50% of foreign-born immigrants leave Britain within five years', the *Daily Mail*, with reference to the Capital Economics forecast, says:

Estimating the real scale of immigration last year between 830,000 and 976,000, the report said that around 350,000 were likely to have left the

country. This meant a net increase of more than 500,000 – more than
double the official tally of 223,000.

(Daily Mail, 31 March 2006, p. 2)

These two figures convey opposed messages (one suggesting: Don't panic!, and the
other: Panic!), but the facts are not necessarily in contradiction since the first is
based on a five-year time scale, and the second on figures for last year only.
However, later the *Daily Mail* offers the following calculation:

> The million-a-year migrant estimate puts immigration at a level which
> would transform the economy and the face of British cities. It would push
> the population up to 73 million from the current 60 million within two
> decades so that 21st century immigrants would become one in five of the
> population.

(Mail)

We should not be willing to accept the 'million-a-year' premise; this is an exaggeration even by their own cited figures of '830,000 to 976,000'; 830,000 is well
below a million. Moreover, the fact that 50 per cent of immigrants leave within five
years, reported by *The Independent* but omitted by the *Daily Mail*, would give a
significantly lower total.

The report cites Sir Andrew Green of the MigrationWatch think-tank, an anti-
immigration body, that this estimate is 'intelligent speculation'; he says that the
numbers suggested by Capital Economics are:

> by no means impossible. If they turn out to be even roughly right, the
> consequences for our society could be severe.

(Mail)

To a wary reader, this is a clear admission that the figures could be wildly inaccurate, but one wonders how many readers will find that the words 'consequences'
and 'severe' and 'our society' resonate more powerfully than the implicit doubts
about the figures.

Packaging the information

Both *The Independent* and the *Daily Mail* report the estimated figure of £4.7 billion
for deporting all illegal immigrants, but the force of the information is different in
the two contexts. *The Independent's* bullet point states:

> Deporting them would cost £4.7 bn and leave acute shortages of cleaners,
> care workers, and hotel staff.

The *Daily Mail* says:

> yesterday there were rumours of a government amnesty for half a million
> illegal immigrants after Labour's favourite think tank said the state could
> save £4.7 bn by abandoning the idea of deporting them.

Whereas *The Independent* foregrounds the high cost of repatriation by placing it
in New position in an independent clause, the *Daily Mail* backgrounds it in a

dependent clause within another dependent clause. It is the rumours and the amnesty for half a million immigrants that are foregrounded.

The next paragraph refers to the IPPR's estimate of a potential £1 bn in tax revenue if illegal immigrants were legalized, but, rather than viewing this positively, follows with the paragraph:

> The Home Office – which has given an amnesty to around 100,000 asylum seekers over the past 30 months – declined to deny that it was considering the idea.
>
> (Mail)

Arguably, *rumours* has a slightly negative ring, but, more strikingly, in much the same way as *admit*, the expression *declined to deny* carries with it suggestions of guilt. The implicature is that this is something we might expect the government to deny and that hence it is probably a bad idea. It suggests that the idea is something the government would be embarrassed to admit, but, since the government will not deny it, it might happen. In context, the economic advantages of the idea (legalizing the immigrants) are interpretable not as a case for implementing the idea but rather as evidence that the government might be considering it. The *Daily Mail* does not have to make a case against immigration; it is presupposed; the paper can count on the widespread perception among its readers (and many others) that immigration is a bad thing.

At the end of the *Daily Mail* report, the director of IPPR (already associated in this report with the Labour government) is cited:

> we are not going to deport hundreds of thousands of people; our economy would shrink and we would notice it straightaway in uncleaned offices, dirty streets and unstaffed pubs and clubs.
>
> (Mail)

This is the point that *The Independent* makes twice on its front page, and it might at first appear to provide some balance between the two. But the *Daily Mail* report has already commented on this issue as follows:

> Existing workers, it [Capital] said, are fearful of demanding pay rises because they can easily be replaced by migrants.
>
> (Mail)

This is one of the oldest anti-immigrant claims on record; it rings down the years, and yet it is produced here as if it were a brand-new research finding. The *Daily Mail*, not usually a champion of workers' high pay, now speaks out for Our low-paid workers against Them, the aliens. *The Independent* makes the point that immigrants do necessary work that UK citizens refuse to do, but does not mention the potential effect of keeping down wages, arguably a negative point for left-wing readers.

Two different messages

What we see in these two reports is two accounts of the same issue, published on the same day, both presenting themselves as objective and factually based, but creating different meanings. *The Independent* presents three broad 'narratives' (our wording):

○ immigrants benefit our society economically
○ improving their lot would bring further benefits
○ (less centrally) the present situation is inhumane and people are suffering.

The *Daily Mail* is saying (our wording):

○ we all knew already that there were too many immigrants
○ now we learn that there are more than the government has confessed to
○ it is likely to get even worse.

The economic facts are presented in the *Daily Mail* only to support the claim that the government plans to be 'soft' on immigration.

Both headlines highlight the novelty of the information, suggesting that up to now we have not been told the truth. The *Daily Mail* suggests that we have been given false numbers by telling us that 'one million' is the 'real number of migrants' (their underlining), even though the first word of the report hedges that with the modifier 'nearly' and later gives even lower figures. This seems to be stretching a point even allowing for Grice's maxims, which permit approximation.[2]

When we read beyond the headline, we understand that when *The Independent* talks about 'the facts that we are never told', it is referring to facts which reflect well upon immigration. It presents its report flamboyantly as if it is new, and, for once, this is justified intertextually since, as we have said, most discourse regarding immigration focuses on the negative aspects.

Immigration and ideology

Critical discourse analysts are advised to make their ideological orientation clear (Fairclough, 1989: 5; van Dijk, 1993a: 252), and we can say that the ideologies to which we subscribe determine that, with certain reservations, we welcome the *Independent* article and deplore the *Daily Mail* article.

Nevertheless, although *The Independent* is making a brave attempt to promote a liberal view in pointing out the advantages of encouraging immigration, both articles address the currently dominant perception of immigration as a problem: one reinforcing the view, the other challenging it. Neither presents the existing occupants of the country (Us) as past or potential migrants, who might justifiably be enraged if they were forbidden from taking up a job in some other country, yet many UK citizens have worked abroad for lengthy periods and many more plan to do so in future. And, of course, they *all* have migrant ancestry if we trace back far enough.

So far, there are no newspapers giving voice to the belief that there is a basic human right for people to travel as they wish throughout the world, which, combined with the right to work, would allow the legal free movement of labour. The main thrust of *The Independent*'s argument for relaxing the rules is economic, and their argument is that those already living in the country (We) will benefit from immigration (Them). Of course, this is politically more effective than appealing to moral principles or higher-level considerations, but the fact that this is so is symptomatic of the dominance of anti-immigrant ideologies and a conservative national identity frame.

8.3 Prejudice

We regard racial prejudice as an individual's attitude or set of opinions; these opinions make up and are generated by racist ideology. Individual racists do not necessarily possess identical sets of opinions or attitudes and do not necessarily identify themselves as racists, but their individual sets of attitudes and opinions overlap sufficiently on relevant issues to entitle them to membership.[3]

Prejudice against other social groups is a widespread feature of social life. It is one aspect of group solidarity and is largely inspired by fear: fear of the unfamiliar, fear of difference, fear of competition for wealth, territory and influence, and fear of change. It is a valuable resource in acquiring and maintaining power, and it has been exploited by many an ambitious politician, often with lethal consequences. Prejudice may sometimes have some rational base, sound or unsound, but it can become embedded in ideology, operating at an unconscious as well as a conscious level, and informing what is thought of as 'common-sense'.

Everyone has prejudices, but not about the same issues. In this chapter, we are interested in prejudice based on perceived racial or ethnic difference, but we make brief excursions into comparable phenomena. We exclude from discussion purely personal prejudice against individuals. Hating individuals of a different race does not constitute racism unless you hate them generically; that is, directly or indirectly, *because of* their race. In fact, freedom from racism means that you *can* dislike any individual regardless of race.

Fundamental to prejudice is the simple dichotomy of Us and Them, the Self and the Other. Prejudice of this kind can exist at all sorts of levels, using an enormous range of criteria in order to distinguish the Other from the Self: social class, skin colour, language, nationality, dialect, religion, gender, sexual preference, place of birth, ancestral origins, social customs. People generally think that the ways in which their social group does things are natural and that alien practices are aberrant.

Of course, resistance to alien practices is not static. Societies are in constant flux and one way in which they change is through contact with other societies. The more the interaction, the greater the influence. But a dominant social group may accept and even welcome all kinds of innovations in basic aspects of culture – food, music, and even dress – while maintaining an essentially negative perception of the other culture. In any case, prejudice can exist between social groups that the outsider would be hard pressed to distinguish in terms of language, life-style and economic status.

One outcome of prejudice is the creation of stereotypes. Certain qualities, real or imaginary, are taken as typical of the target category, and there is an underlying assumption that all members of the category conform to this stereotype.

Prejudice is largely inseparable from material discrimination in such areas as employment, promotion, wages, education, relations with the law and political representation or, at the most extreme levels, 'ethnic cleansing' (ridding a geographical area of members of a particular ethnic category) and genocide. However, prejudice and material discrimination are not the same thing.

One argument sometimes raised against legislation on discrimination is that it is impossible to change people's attitudes by passing laws. But the first thing is to attack the material injustice as far as it is feasible to do so and then work towards changing attitudes. In fact, attitudes *do* change as an inevitable result of legal or constitutional change even if it sometimes takes a long time. No one could possibly argue that the official abolition of slavery in the USA by the Thirteenth Amendment to the Constitution in 1865 resulted in anything remotely resembling equality, but it was indisputably a step in the right direction. Resistance to legislation against discrimination is mostly promoted by those groups that fear losing economic and political power.

8.4 Lexical meaning

People often talk about words (lexical items) as if they had fixed and unchanging meanings. In fact, the meanings of words change in many ways. Perhaps the most obvious is that they change over time. A quick look in an etymological dictionary shows just how extreme these changes can be. Also, words may have different denotations in different registers. In specialist medical registers, *abortion* includes the sense of a deliberately induced termination of pregnancy as in general usage, but it also includes the notion of accidental or natural termination, for which the lay term is *miscarriage*. Such differences clearly carry the potential for breakdowns in communication, for misinterpretation and misunderstanding.

Obviously, it would be ridiculous to suggest that word meanings are entirely fluid and that we are free to use any words with any meanings at any time; there has to be some sort of stability. But, reluctant as many people are to accept the fact, change and variation are always present in language, particularly through metaphorical extension (see Chapter 5). To use Halliday's term, words have *meaning potential*, which is realized in text.

Philosophers, linguists and literary critics have sometimes distinguished two kinds of meaning: *denotation* and *connotation*. To simplify, denotation is the narrow meaning, which you might think of as the dictionary meaning: for example, *eagle*: a large diurnal bird of prey, etc. Connotation concerns the emotional charge of the word, its associations; *eagle* may variously connote *grandeur, power, cruelty, tyranny, nature red in tooth and claw*. Some connotations may be personal and idiosyncratic; a person who once shot an eagle might associate the word with feelings of guilt, but many connotations are widespread and conventional. We are interested in the second type.

Connotation becomes important when we consider the lexical choices made by speakers and writers, not least because it is a major factor in manipulating opinion.

A sentiment frequently heard is that one man's terrorist is another man's freedom fighter. In other words, we assign labels to people, things and events according to our bias, in this instance, political bias. The connotations of *terrorist* and *freedom fighter* are crucially different; in the first case negative and in the second positive. To take a somewhat random example, French histories do not describe the people who bravely resisted Nazi occupation in the 1940s as terrorists; nor do British or American or Australian histories of France. But these same accounts might well apply the label to those who perform similar acts in comparable circumstances in different places at different times in history. Obviously, if people have blown up your nearest and dearest, you will not wish to describe them as *freedom fighters*, with all the term's favourable connotations. Many political leaders throughout the world have engaged at earlier stages in freedom fighting/terrorism, but when established in power they denounce 'terrorism', referring not to their own activities in retrospect but rather to similar activities by their enemies. Freedom fighters are people on our side, and terrorists are the enemy.

Co-text, collocation, and concordance

Instead of asking people to say what they associate with a particular word, a procedure fraught with all kinds of difficulties, we can investigate a word's meaning by identifying multiple instances of its occurrence in a large body of texts (a *corpus*) and seeing how it is used, what sort of message is being conveyed, and what other lexical items tend to co-occur.

Thanks to advances in computer science and lexical studies, it is not difficult to examine this aspect of language in considerable detail, especially the co-occurring items, and there is already a huge amount of information available based on this kind of analysis. Words which occur in the vicinity of a target item are known as *collocates* of that item, and the phenomenon of such co-occurrence is called *collocation*. Some aspects of collocation are identifiable intuitively, but computational analysis of a corpus, using a *concordancer* (a software package for locating lexical items and identifying and quantifying collocates), may not only confirm intuitions but also reveal collocational tendencies that are not otherwise suspected. Collocations overlap to some extent with associated ideas, but they do not correspond exactly.

In the English language media, until relatively recently, *fundamentalist* collocated with *Christian, Bible, literal*. Recently, there has been an increase in its collocation with *Islam, Islamic, Muslim, terrorist*. The Christian right in America still describe themselves as *fundamentalists*, but the word is now largely assigned by the Western media to Muslims, and especially to militantly anti-western Muslims. In order to investigate this changing use using corpus analysis one would need at least two corpora, one of which would consist of recent media texts. In some contexts, fundamentalist is almost a synonym for fanatic or terrorist. A word like *bigot* or *extremist* is essentially derogatory, but *fundamentalist* is still usable as a non-pejorative word, though for people with a long-standing antipathy to religious fundamentalism, it is not. Also, many would be unable to escape its recent textually created political collocations.

We could find out a lot about what the lexical item *native* means by seeking out instances of its use in some ready-made corpus. For an overview, we might wish to use a massive corpus from a wide range of sources. A quick search with an internet search engine identified 129 million instances of *native*, and, of these, over 57 million referred to *native Americans*, and 7,730,000 to *native speech* or *native speaker*. Identifying collocates like this is an interesting indicator of how the word is mainly used but, since the online search results include repetitions of the same instance in the same text from different sources, and since it is likely that American postings are more frequent than those from other sources, we cannot draw strong conclusions. To find out what the word means to the *Daily Mail* or any other newspaper, we would need a corpus compiled from that paper over a specified period.

Krishnamurthy (1996) used computational methods to investigate the words *ethnic, tribal* and *racial*. This discussion offers an excellent example of the use of these methods for socially critical purposes. At the end of the present chapter, we offer a brief related activity.

8.5 Lexis and ethnic identity

A great deal of social discourse is devoted to distinguishing the Self from the Other, and ethnic and national labels are one important way in which social groups identify the Other. Sometimes, however, the targeted group – or some sub-group within it – will seize on the discriminatory label and make it their own. More seriously, they may embrace a negative stereotype, as happened with the 'pimp' image in some forms of popular music, but we will not go into this issue.

The term *black* changed from a stigmatized slur to a neutral or highly positive term in the late 1960s when American political activists described themselves as *Black Americans* and came up with slogans like 'Say it loud, I'm Black and I'm proud'; at the same time, political and religious groups called themselves *Black Panthers* and *Black Muslims*. Homosexuals, though currently generally preferring the term *gay*, may sometimes use the previously homophobic term *queer*, perhaps ironically. Establishing their down-to-earth credibility, American entertainers may boast of being *trailer-trash* or *poor white*. Even the taboo word *nigger* is used by many African Americans who might well object to its use by others, which adds another degree of complexity to the vexed question of offensiveness since many people resent this usage by anyone under any circumstances.

Probably all languages have taboo words: words which are socially proscribed and whose utterance can give offence. It may seem an anomaly to have words which are not supposed to be used, but, in fact, it is generally understood that the degree of offence varies according to the context of situation – the speaker, the place where the word is uttered, the person spoken to and anyone who might overhear. Thus, in the nineteenth century, people spoke of 'language that was unsuitable for the drawing room'. Racial terms that are used with intent to offend or that are deemed offensive by their targets acquire taboo qualities. Like sexual and scatological obscenities, they are widely used in certain contexts (for example, bars, some workplaces, football crowds) but are also socially stigmatized.

While tolerance of sexual or scatological taboo words has increased, pejorative terms denoting ethnicity or nationality have become less widely tolerated. There are some similarities between these two broad categories of socially disapproved vocabulary, but there are crucial differences. The motive for restricting the use of the second type is fundamentally different from the more arbitrary and traditional taboos associated with basic biology because it emerges from a demand for respect for others.

Lexical sensitivity

This section is about people's sensitivity to words and how they can react to their use. Given the history of ethnic relations and the emotive force of classificatory labels, it is difficult to discuss issues of 'race' and particularly of terminology without upsetting people. Most people know that terms like *negro, black, coloured*, have been perceived differently by concerned groups at different points in recent history. Indisputably, people have a right to choose what they are called, but sensitivity to terminology can lead to overreaction which may provide ammunition for reactionary attacks on so-called 'political correctness'.

Huck Finn in trouble

An extreme example of this is the frequent banning of the novel *Huckleberry Finn* from some school syllabuses (and sometimes public libraries) in America; reportedly, the fifth most banned book in the USA. The book is a widely recognized literary masterpiece – a valued text, written by an eminent author of liberal views who grew up in the slave-owning southern states. It is arguably one of the most powerful indictments of racial and social inequality in fiction. But it is written in the voice of an illiterate vagrant white child, whose ideological conditioning is brilliantly conveyed and critiqued.

Perhaps some of the people who banned this book would have preferred an enlightened narrator, who explicitly took the stance of the author (Samuel Clemens, better known by his pen name, Mark Twain). Twain was a liberal anti-slavery author, though this book was written in 1864, about 20 years after the effective end of slavery in the USA. For those who have difficulty with irony, or for those who look only at decontextualized extracts, the book can clearly present problems.

At one point, when Huck's travelling companion, the runaway slave, Jim, is captured, Huck confides to the reader that he is guilt-stricken about helping Jim escape ('stealing' him). Suddenly, he is struck by a thought that is the product of the religiosity of the southern states, which Huck has only partially absorbed but which is part and parcel of his own ideology:

> And at last, when it hit me all of a sudden that here was the plain hand of Providence slapping me in the face and letting me know my wickedness was being watched all the time up there in heaven, whilst I was stealing a poor old woman's nigger that hadn't never done me no harm, and now was showing me there's One that's always on the lookout, and ain't agoing to allow no such miserable doings to go only just so fur and no further, I most dropped in my tracks I was so scared.

Eventually, confused by his deep friendship with Jim, he decides to help him escape again, but he does so with the thought:

> All right, then, I'll go to hell .... I shoved the whole thing out of my head and said I would take up wickedness again, which was in my line, being brung up to it.

What Clemens is up to is not hard to detect. He is illustrating the powerful effect of the prevailing ideologies of the southern states in the nineteenth century. He manages to attack not only the evils and contradictions of slavery but also the hypocritical and sanctimonious religion that bolstered up the institution. Huck is an unreliable narrator; we can trust his account of events but not his interpretation of them. However, the author is writing for a reader who can see beyond Huck's perceptions. So Huck does the right thing even though he cannot entirely escape his ideological background and is forced to feel conscience-stricken about it. Arguably, he is able to defy his social conditioning because he is already something of an outsider – illiterate, homeless, despised by the community on whose fringes he survives, and a person who thinks of himself as intrinsically 'bad' – a transgressor.

We tend to think that this book could be a good choice for high school syllabuses in the area which gave rise to it. Apart from its literary merits, it might prove a vehicle for moral analysis and cross-cultural understanding. But it is easy to understand why teachers, administrators and parents might shy away from it.

Although there have been massive social changes since Huck and Jim ran away together, deep inequalities and raw sensitivities remain. We mentioned in Chapter 4 the comments on slavery of the former president of the Southern Baptist Convention ('a much maligned institution'). Clearly, in this context, a text like *Huckleberry Finn* might present major difficulties and would certainly require skilful management.[4]

For some, even if we could set aside all the difficulties we have mentioned, the book would still be ruled out. It is enough that some characters in the novel, notably the second key character, Jim, are referred to repeatedly by the noun *nigger*, which brings us back to the start of this part of our discussion. For many people this is the ultimate taboo word. It should not be uttered in any context – even to discuss it as an issue or to condemn its use. Thus, if they wish to refer to it, they will use some such expressions as *the N-word* or write it as *n******. It seems more than likely, then, that this was a major determinant in the political decisions to exclude the book from school syllabuses.

The main point we are making in this section is that it is dangerous to draw critical conclusions on the basis of the use of specific words, or even longer extracts, isolated from their co-text, socio-historical context and the intention of the author, as far as this is deducible. We all sometimes do this; we do it in this book; but we should do so with caution. We also have to take account of the fact that the social context affects readers' responses to a text, and sometimes even the responses of some who have not actually read it.

8.6 Political correctness

Negative reaction to bigoted language is frequently attacked as 'political correctness', a label which carries connotations of hypersensitivity and authoritarianism. Thus, reactionaries are able to present consideration for the feelings of others, more specifically for groups and individuals already at some disadvantage, as socially undesirable.

Certainly, it is all too easy to over-react to suspected offence, and individuals sometimes deliberately exploit their potential 'victim' status unjustly. Humour is perhaps the easiest type of discourse to misinterpret, and this is especially true of satire, where an author may ostensibly present an argument in order to reveal its absurdity. In the eighteenth century, in *A Modest Proposal*, Jonathan Swift attacked the exploitation of the Irish peasantry in a bitterly satirical pamphlet ostensibly recommending that the English should eat Irish children. Some readers believed him to be actually in favour of cannibalism, and others thought he was writing with frivolous bad taste about a dire situation. As we have seen with Huckleberry Finn, the views of a fictional character or an unreliable narrator are not necessarily the views of the author, and yet the views and wordings of fictional characters are frequently assigned to the author as if they directly expressed his or her opinion.

Our decision in this book to view racially sensitive words as in some sense taboo is borne out by the fact that their exploitation in certain contexts is widely perceived as comic, which is also true for the use of items that violate sexual and scatological taboo.

Much comedy depends on surprise or shock, and breaking taboos is a large part of this. Sexual innuendo has long been a staple of humour, playing around the edges of taboo without going too far. A more raucous form of humour steps over the boundaries and raises a laugh by explicitly breaching the taboo. Shock is often a factor in humour. It has been argued that part of the motivation for humour is to enable us to laugh at the things that we have difficulty in dealing with – death, pain, sex, disability and disappointment.

But humour is often based on cruelty, and jokes made by an oppressive category at the expense of a socially oppressed one seem to have a different motivation. A great deal of current humour is based simply on the principle of defying so-called political correctness. Mocking physical handicap, cultural difference or sexual preference is justified as courageous, 'cutting-edge' comedy. Race, but not immigration, is largely avoided now in television, radio and film, but with a slight ideological shift, this could change.

In a society that generally prizes certain kinds of nonconformity, where the word *rebel* has acquired favourable connotations and *respectable* can be used pejoratively, it is not unusual to represent bigoted and conformist discourse in a positive light as *refreshing, frank, cheeky* or even *daring*. In an interview column for a popular media magazine, the actor Simon Callow is reported as saying of a character he is playing:

> He's the local rebel and he causes trouble. He's a cad, but rather attractively unPC.

> (*Radio Times*, 25 February–3 March 2006, p. 154)

In this way, largely by textual – and more specifically lexical – means, the progressive may be packaged as conservative and the conservative as progressive. Once a label like PC is established with its negative connotations of *officious, hyper-sensitive, unreasonable, smug*, it can be used as an alternative to argument. Racist or other bigoted discourse can be defended as 'defiantly unPC', and, to respond to a critique of racial or other prejudice in text, the accusation that the critic is being PC is frequently used in place of a defence.

So-called political correctness is often attacked by citing its extreme manifestations such as the *Huckleberry Finn* controversy. Expressions like 'race relations bullies' (a Conservative Member of Parliament's speech, cited by van Dijk 1998b: 380–1) attempt to reverse the roles of victim and victimizer. The concern about lexical labelling is also frequently ridiculed with satirical inventions of PC expressions like *follically challenged* for *bald* or *chronologically challenged* for *old*. In fact, so powerful is the desire to discredit social change that many people believe that these are terms seriously advocated by language activists rather than parodies.

Setting 'liberal' limits on protest

Thanks to the maligned PC campaigners, the more offensive terms for ethnic and other minorities are now largely restricted, in print, film and TV, to works of fiction, where, as we have seen, they may be attributed to voices other than the author's and may be defended on grounds of verisimilitude, irony, and so on. Otherwise, they tend to show up in comedy, or in an explicitly overt way to make a political point.

An example of this is the unPC term *poof* for a male homosexual used by a journalist in *The Observer* newspaper. She was defending the BBC against a critical survey by a gay rights group called Stonewall, the gist of the article being that our society has rightly adjusted to the demands of underprivileged groups, and particularly gays, and that for them to demand more is unreasonable. The article was headed:

> Come on, boys, don't whinge: the BBC doesn't deserve Stonewall's attack, which alienates the rest of us.

Incidentally, two weeks later, *The Observer* published a correction to this article that read as follows:

> 'Come on, boys, don't whinge' (Comment, 5 March) was an unfortunate choice of headline over the piece on Stonewall's study of 168 hours of BBC broadcasts. The survey, Tuned Out, was actually researched, written and edited by six women.

The tone of the article is in the vein of 'I'm as liberal as the next person, but ...'. Van Dijk (1993b) calls this discourse strategy *denial*: 'I'm not a racist but ....'. In this text there is no explicit remark of this kind, but, as van Dijk explains, denial can take many forms, and here it is diffuse.

> Nobody pretends it's a perfect world for homosexuals. Or women. Or darker-hued skin. Or children. But just as we don't stick kids up chimneys any more so most of our disenfranchised are better off than they were, with all of us working towards better still – and much of the credit for that belongs to the BBC that doesn't deserve to be beaten up by Stonewall or any other band of truculent poofs.
>
> (Carol Sarler, 'Come on, boys, don't whinge', *The Observer*, 5 March 2006, p. 31. Copyright
> Guardian Newspapers Limited 2006.)

Before this, the author of this piece has tried to indicate her liberal credentials, and so the use of the term *poof* in this context must be intended to shock. The expected reaction (from the heterosexual 'liberal' reader) is a slightly surprised laugh. The author admits that 'our disenfranchised', identified as homosexuals, women, other races and children, may have problems, but immediately hints at the idea that their plight may be as much a thing of the past in this country as the horrors of nineteenth-century child labour. (By including women, she implicitly includes herself, which could be seen as a denial tactic – roughly equivalent to 'Hey, I'm a member of a victimized category myself so I can't be accused of prejudice.') The argument of this text reminds us of J. R. Feagin's generalization about racism in the USA:

> Assuming racial discrimination to be mostly a thing of the past, many whites will assert that African Americans are 'paranoid' about racism and will often give them firm advice: Forget the past and move on because 'slavery happened hundreds of years ago'.
>
> (Feagin 2000: 2)

The newspaper article continues and concludes:

> They need, indeed, to take care. Enough of us, now, are so fed up with guilt and apology that if they don't want to feel the sharp turn of a tide of good will, they should get over themselves, get a sense of humour and get back to us some other time.

(Sarler, 'Come on, boys, don't whinge', p. 31)

Note, incidentally, the use of the triple structure based on the verb *get* in the last sentence; this is a rhetorical device beloved of politicians and is well-known to elicit applause, and even a standing ovation, when delivered on a rostrum.

Self and Other are clearly signalled in this article. 'We' have already been typified as 'the averagely liberal media worker' who is 'guilt-tripped to the gills'; 'They' are

> squawking fundamentalists of all stripes, tying our work and our words into increasingly constraining knots.

The use of the word *poof* (in fact, the whole nominal group *any other band of truculent poofs*) has already reinforced the message that the author's tolerance is being pushed to the limit. In the final paragraph, the criticism and exasperation are replaced with a threat: 'They need to take care.' In effect, *We* have given enough; if *They* ask for more, *They* will be punished. It echoes an earlier threat:

> It [Stonewall] calls it monitoring. I call it pushing its luck.

The nature of the punishment is left unstated. It is hard to imagine what dire penalties this journalist and her fellow-sufferers might impose on these demanding minorities. Both take the form of assertions, but that these statements constitute the speech act *threat* is unmistakable.

There are lively echoes here of Lakoff's *strong father* frame with Stonewall in the naughty children role. If an article of this kind had appeared in a journal of a far-right party or even in a mainstream conservative newspaper, it would not be surprising, but this is *The Observer*, the Sunday sister of *The Guardian*. In Britain, the terms *Guardian readers* and *Observer readers* are journalistic shorthand for left-leaning liberals, the supposed proponents of so-called 'political correctness'.

Activities

1. Read again the brief extracts from the *Observer* article in Section 8.6.

   a. The author implicitly identifies herself with 'the averagely liberal media worker'. On the evidence of the limited text given here, does this seem a valid suggestion? What leads to your decision? If your answer is 'Yes', what does this say about the author's view of the political attitudes of media workers?

   b. What do you think about the expression *darker-hued skin*? How is it linguistically different from the other paralleled items (*homosexuals, women, children*)? How might it have arisen?

   c. Why does the author use the lexical item *beaten up* instead of the more literal – and more obvious – *criticized*?

d. Locate the occurrences in the text of first and third person pronouns and the groups that they occur in (1st person: *we, all of us, enough of us*; 3rd person: *they*.) Is the reference precise or vague? How far does it reflect the notion of Self and Other?

e. What do you understand the adjective *truculent* to mean (at the end of the first paragraph)? How would the impact be different if the author had used the lexical item *argumentative?*

f. Why do you think the author chose the lexical item *band* in 'band of truculent poofs'?

g. The primary target of the article is a gay rights group, but the author includes references to women, children and *darker-hued skin* and, earlier, to *squawking fundamentalists of all types*. How does this affect the scope of the article? What social groups might be suggested by *squawking fundamentalists of all types*? Does the term *fundamentalist* usually connote Self or Other in current journalism? Break down the meaning of *squawking*.

2. Look at the words: *ethnic, racial* and *tribal*.

a. Write down the first five things that come to mind for each of the words:

b. Try the same test on as many people as you can conveniently persuade to do it.

c. Work out your own dictionary definitions for these words.

d. Compare your definitions with those given in a number of dictionaries.

e. Read Krishnamurthy (1996), which gives a detailed account of these words in action. Compare it with your findings.

f. If you have access to the software and a corpus, you might be inspired to try a project similar to Krishnamurthy's with lexical items of your own choice.

Further study

Teun van Dijk has published prolifically on racist discourse. His publications are based on extensive research into written and spoken texts from several countries. A key article, which is succinct and accessible, is van Dijk (1992). Using textual evidence from various sources, notably British newspapers, he shows how commentators on racial issues attempt to absolve themselves of the charge of racism (*denial of racism*) and, using techniques such as *reversal moves*, charge the victims with being the 'true racists' and cast themselves in the victim role (compare the *Observer* journalist in Section 7.8). Van Dijk (1996) has a specific bearing on this chapter in its discussion of racism and the press with analyses of anti-immigrant texts of a more vehement kind than the extracts from the *Daily Mail* which we discussed in this chapter. See also the important text, van Dijk (1998a), especially Chapter 12: 'Identity' and Chapter 28: 'The ideology and discourse of modern racism.' For a more comprehensive treatment of racism in relation to the print media, see van Dijk (1991). Also van Dijk (1998b).

Ruth Wodak has done influential research on racism and prejudice, sometimes in collaboration with van Dijk. Wodak (1996) appears in the same edited collection as one of the van Dijk papers mentioned above. This paper examines racist discourse in Austria and includes an interesting discussion of definitions of the word *racism* and related words.

Also in the same collection is Krishnamurthy (1996), mentioned already. This is a sound example of a computational lexical analysis, investigating the words *ethnic, racial* and *tribal*. (See Activities.)

Paul Chilton is another central figure in critical discourse analysis. Chilton (2004) is mentioned in our Chapter 7. In his Chapter 7, 'Foreigners', he carries out a detailed analysis of two notorious examples of racist discourse: the British MP Enoch Powell's 'Rivers of Blood' speech of 1968, which led to his expulsion from the Conservative Party shadow cabinet, and a recorded conversation among a group of young racists who were later tried and acquitted for the murder of a young black man, Stephen Lawrence. Chilton shows, among other things, how the members of this group use their perceptions of Powell to legitimize their own stance.

Not central to CDA but of interest to students of racism and prejudice, Feagin and Feagin (1993) and Feagin (2000), cited in this chapter and elsewhere, approach the issue of racism through sociology and history. Both books provide a committed critique of racism in the USA, past and present.

Dicker (2003) is a history of languages in the USA: a mine of information about the story of immigration and discrimination, focusing on institutional and individual attitudes to the status of minority languages and English.

9 The discourse of consumerism

9.1 Commerce then and now

When discussing major changes in society in the past half-century or so, there is a tendency to emphasize technological progress, particularly in the fields of computing and communications, with cheap air travel and increased motor transport coming close behind. Another massive social change is the rapid global growth of commercialization and consumerism. Clearly, this is closely bound up with the technological advances which have extended and improved the channels and modes of discourse from slowly diffused word of mouth and print to include instant electronic access, more rapid printing methods and digital photography, providing not only improved means for accessing markets but also new products to sell there.

There is nothing new about commerce, of course. Since early times, it has played a central role in human social development, leading to cross-cultural interaction, the movement of populations, currency, banking, empire, taxation – in fact, most aspects of civilization as we know it. The earliest writing we know of (in Sumer, modern Iraq) is probably financial accounts and tax records. From a European perspective, at various points in history, there have been great leaps forward in commerce, for example, the twelfth-century Venetian introduction of banking[1] and the fifteenth-century European 'discovery' of the New World, motivated by a search for trade routes and profit. The Industrial Revolution and the development of European empires in the eighteenth and nineteenth centuries changed the map of the world. The colonization of India was in large part carried out by the East India Company, a capitalist enterprise, which had its own armies as well as the support of the British Army (the 'king's army').

The long-standing significance of commerce is evident in the idioms and metaphors of languages (see Chapter 5). In English, we speak of *selling an idea*, and if we are not fully convinced, we say *I don't buy it*. A traitor *sells* his country or his comrades, or he just *sells out*; in Spanish too *vender* is literally *sell* but metaphorically *betray*; the same is true of *vendre* in French. Like marketing itself, metaphors of buying and selling are international; a German traitor *verkauft sich* and an English traitor *sells himself*. A soldier who fights to the last bullet *sells* his life *dearly*. Politicians *buy* support with or without money changing hands. With the right manoeuvres a general can *buy* some time for his army. The biologist Stephen J. Gould, writing of a school of biologists, says:

> Thus cladists *buy* potential objectivity at the *price* of ignoring biologically important information.
>
> (Gould 1983: 364)

So, we assert that there is *a price to pay* even where no financial transaction is involved, and we can be *short-changed* when someone cheats us. People *put their wares on display*, or, more surreptitiously, do things *under the counter*. Some people *shop around* for the right school or university or partner. Colourful extrovert individuals are criticized for being *cheap*, and a hurtful comment is described as a *cheap shot*. A foreign office memo on Margaret Thatcher's impending visit to the USA in July 1975 included the following:

> She did not want to be too easily available to reporters and television interviewers. She felt this would cheapen her.
>
> (Declassified British Government archive material, 1973–75)

It is a little surprising that so many of these metaphors have negative connotations.

In his biography of Karl Marx, Francis Wheen (1999: 121) mentions that many of Marx's descriptions of capitalism in the nineteenth century read like predictions of the present time. *The Communist Manifesto* (1873) declared that capitalism had given

> a cosmopolitan character to production and consumption in every country. In place of the old wants, satisfied by the productions of the country, we find new wants, requiring for their satisfaction the products of distant lands and climes.

If these social conditions were evident in the 1870s, how much more obvious are they today? From our present standpoint, the world a century and a half ago was vastly diverse and locally differentiated as compared with the present world of galloping globalization with its multinational companies, richer and more powerful than some nation states, and with Coca-Cola and McDonald's restaurants from Moscow to Montevideo. Even in the past few decades most cultures have changed dramatically because of globalization.

Since the collapse of the Soviet bloc and the conversion of China and Vietnam to capitalism, there are few alternatives to free market capitalism. Groups such as puritanical religious sects or ecological activists may attempt to follow a 'purer' way of life, but the tide of history seems to be against them.

Of course, there are parts of the world where warfare, civil strife, poverty and famine mean that social trends run counter to some of what we have been describing, and perhaps these are an inevitable corollary of our affluence. Even in these environments, though, consumerization[2] is in evidence. Isolated African towns without electricity display Coca-Cola signs. The more tobacco sales decrease in rich countries, the greater the effort to promote cigarettes to the poor. Multinationals buy labour and raw materials cheaply and sell back manufactured products, just as slavers did two hundred years ago, and armaments are manufactured not in the war zones but in wealthier parts of the world. However, in what follows, we limit our discussion to discourse in rich societies generally, but mainly we focus on Britain since that is where we are sitting as we write.

One outcome of the success of modern capitalism has been the consumerization of most societies. In traditional agrarian societies commerce played an important role, of course, but people were not so unrelievedly subjected to pressure to consume ever more by the discursive practices of advertising and other consumerist propaganda, both managed and incidental. Now, there is almost no aspect of human activity that is not extensively commercialized. The ubiquity of television and other electronic media means that from early childhood, individuals are conditioned into a life of consumption.

There is virtually no escape from consumerism, and resistance to unethical mass marketing is immediately accommodated by commercial institutions and made marketable; hence the absorption into mainstream marketing of organic and 'green' commodities and even fair trade practices.

The discursive practice of advertising is one place where the discourse of consumerism is most easily visible, though by no means the only one. Advertising is practised within an environment of consumerist discourse involving the media, government and political parties, popular entertainment and many others. To take an obvious case, glossy magazines carry large quantities of advertising together with articles, reports, reviews and photographs, which are ostensibly not advertisements. However, to a considerable extent these other items are created with specific advertising in mind; in fact, the advertising sometimes appears to be the primary consideration. But even if we ignore this, we can see that consumerism is more generally perpetuated through the co-text because of its concern with fashion, cosmetics, cars, so called life-style issues, wine, food, computers, the body beautiful, furniture and home improvements. Sometimes, we have to look carefully to distinguish an article from an advertisement.

9.2 Advertising

One aim of advertising is to inform, and a lot of advertising is informative without being overtly persuasive. But the main aim of most advertising is to promote the sale of goods or services, which means that it must persuade.

There is almost infinite variety in advertisements, yet we usually recognize them as advertisements immediately, though we would be hard pressed to identify any formal features common to all.

There are few constraints on form since advertisements can come in a multitude of shapes and via different media: print, posters, film, radio, electronic (the Internet, electronic billboards, etc.). Most often, advertisements are multimodal, exploiting both linguistic and pictorial resources. They may involve human or animal actors or animations, recorded in film or sound. They may include simulated or real situations. They can contain hundreds of words, one word or no words at all. Sometimes they do not even mention the thing that they are advertising, but rely on intertextuality and mutual knowledge to make the connection.

Occasionally, an advertisement may be incomprehensible in itself but can be understood retrospectively when later related ads appear. This can be spread over a period of time, and can be in print, on billboards, or in television presentations. A localized example over two pages of a magazine is this: a largely empty page in a magazine carries only two lines of text in small letters:

> This page is voice controlled.
>
> Shout 'TURN' to turn page.

Of course, the page does not turn when the reader shouts. So the reader turns the page by hand and finds a conventional advertisement for a car with the message:

> For real voice control, get into a new Fiesta Freedom.

How advertisements persuade

The advertisement just described is classifiable as a joke of sorts. Discourse analysts and sociolinguists have described jokes in some settings as verbal gifts. Jokes operate as part of the in-group culture of social groups; sharing a joke is a social activity between peers. If the readers of the Fiesta advertisement 'get' the joke and are mildly amused, some rapport has been established. There is often an element of self-esteem in getting a joke, a feeling of self-congratulation. This is a long way from persuading them to buy the car, but it is a step forward. They may have registered the name and can associate it with a small degree of pleasure.

Advertisements heavily exploit intertextuality. They often explicitly imitate familiar genres: television ads often consist of pastiches or parodies of other television programmes (soaps, police serials, quizzes, talent competitions, chat shows) or feature films (gangster, westerns, historical romance, classic art movies; from time to time ads in anglophone countries parody French films, even using French dialogue). In the print media, advertisements sometimes imitate technical manuals, works of art, or newspaper articles. Our reading of them incorporates our familiarity with the real versions.

We do not propose to try to give a comprehensive account of advertising here. Rather we shall focus on some persuasive elements in a number of advertisements, and more especially in one advertisement in detail.

It is a truism of discourse analysis that even texts that are not a product of face-to-face interaction are a kind of dialogue. Writers, broadcasters and other text producers answer hypothetical questions, forestall potential objections, and so on. Writers of children's books accommodate their style and content to the readers' assumed age and answer the questions they might ask. It does not always have to be a conscious process since we have all had a great deal of practice since childhood, making such allowances all the time in our daily social interactions.

Advertisers are usually highly conscious of the target audience. Research and planning precede most creations and placements of ads. Although some advertisements may be targeted at a relatively broad spectrum, most home in on defined social categories, taking account of a number of factors, primarily what they buy and where and how often. The location of the advertising is also important; advertisements need to be placed where the optimal audience will be exposed to them. Targeting an audience is an indispensable part of marketing procedure. We shall now look at one instance of this practice.

Targeting a defined population

A striking characteristic of contemporary affluent societies is the rapid increase in average life expectancy, resulting in a large population of old people. The 50-plus age group constitutes 35 per cent of the British population. Some are poor, but many have significant wealth: 'a collective pot of £175 billion of disposable income, which is greater than any other age group', according to a *Saga Magazine* advertising promotion. This has not gone unnoticed by marketing bodies, and there has been an increase in the production and promotion of goods and services calculated to appeal to older customers.

Saga Magazine is a glossy monthly periodical targeted at the over-fifties. Superficially, it resembles other glossy monthlies such as *Cosmopolitan* or *Marie-Claire*. However, it is not sold in newsagents but is available direct to Saga customers. In magazines of this kind, advertising is not an afterthought, something to fill in a few free pages. It is at least as important as the rest of the material since it is the main source of income. Articles and photographs can be used to back up advertising by dealing with related matters. An editorial plan to cover some topic in a future edition (say, motorboats, arthritis, plastic surgery) may be used as an incentive for companies to place relevant advertisements there.

A corollary of all this is the selling of advertising space, which also needs to be advertised. *Saga Magazine* promotes itself via the Internet to advertisers looking for an affluent market. Under the heading: 'Why advertise with Saga Magazine?' and before listing some of its more prestigious advertisers, it observes that

> Few companies can afford to ignore the phenomenal spending power of this most lucrative audience …

It advertises its monthly readership of 2,678,000 and gives the statistic of 72 per cent of readers in social classes A, B and C1, i.e. roughly the top 50 per cent of the adult population in financial terms, telling the potential client:

> This is an audience without conditioned purchasing habits, in fact, 59% are always prepared to try new products.

It further describes its readership as

> a huge exclusive audience with even higher disposable income than the national average.

Every point made is highly charged with positive appraisal features, in one instance attributed to *Saga Magazine* (*unrivalled*) but mainly applied to the readership (*growing faster, more leisure time, ability and willingness to shop, high percentages, prepared to try new products, even higher disposable income, large sums of money, lucrative, affluent, phenomenal spending power*). Out of eight bullet points, four – possibly five – refer explicitly to the affluence of the readership, which is mentioned again in its instructions on how to access the sales team, and two bullet items are devoted to their willingness to spend. It effectively focuses on the two major points of interest for advertisers: audience size and spending power. Although with its bullet points and brevity, it creates an impression of succinctness, in fact it is repetitive, making the same two points several times in slightly different ways. Its last reference to that audience is to 'Saga's highly-targeted, affluent readership'.

It is interesting to consider what is omitted from the text that might conceivably be expected to be present. There is no indication of the charges for advertising; presumably that information comes at a later stage of the interaction; this event is the initial baited hook. Nor is there any mention of the quality of the magazine, its format, content, number of pages, or mode of distribution. Information of this kind is present on the website, but it is not even touched on in the reasons to advertise that are listed here. This promotion is addressed by one set of professional advertising experts to another, and it signals this in its form and content.

The language is almost entirely impersonal, largely in the third person plural referring to the readers of the magazine or the income category to which they belong. The pronoun *you* occurs only once, in 'If you would like to advertise with Saga.' This reinforces the impression that this is a communication between professionals with no attempt at manipulation.

9.3 Analysis: an advertisement

Turning to *Saga Magazine* itself, it is obvious that the assumed audience is different from the advertisers targeted on the website promotion. Before we come to the advertisement in question, we look at the co-text. In the April 2006 issue, the front cover (not an advertisement) carries a photograph of a beautiful woman, which is customary for magazines of this type. The image is that of French film actor and model, Catherine Deneuve; it is placed above the caption:

> The divine Deneuve
>
> So much more than a flawless face.

The caption plays on the stock expression *more than (just) a pretty face* by substituting for the feeble *pretty* the stronger epithet *flawless*. The other text on the page consists of title and contents.

Although it is a recent photograph, the model appears to be in her thirties, but most readers know that she is much older; in fact, at the time of publication, she was 62 years old. The feature article inside (headed 'Catherine the Great') plays up this contradiction, stressing her enjoyment of being a grandmother and her gardening, and contrasting her image the previous night at a film festival as 'the queen of glamour in a floaty red designer gown' with the moment of the interview:

> Now, with a little pot of peppermint tea … she seems much smaller, dressed simply in nondescript trousers … and flat slip-on shoes.

The accompanying page of photographs of Deneuve earlier in her career would not seem out of place in a magazine targeted at a younger readership, especially Deneuve in a bikini in 1962, but the written text constantly plays with the dichotomy of, on the one hand, the glamorous film-star and 'face of Chanel, YSL, L'Oréal and MAC', and, on the other, a 62-year-old grandmother.

In some advertisements in the magazine, the age group (and gender) targeting is made fully explicit: a two-page cosmetics promotion for a 'mature skincare innovation' called Age Perfect includes the words: 'From age 50, daily mature skincare'.

The left-hand page is a close-up photograph of a pensive, handsome, young-looking woman with the discreet caption:

> Dayle Haddon. 'To stay feeling young, don't let yourself go.'

In terms of face threat, this is a high-risk approach. The command is unmitigated, and there is another in the text on the facing page:

> Fight the appearance of sagging and age spots.

The words *sagging* and *age spots* carry negative appraisal, but they are repeated elsewhere in the ad. Apart from the euphemistic *mature* instead of *old*, only the L'Oréal slogan *Because you're worth* it makes any concession to politeness, and the mitigating effect is lessened by its status as a fixed expression, familiar to many readers.

The strategy here, then, is to be direct, creating a sense of urgency and a lack of alternatives. In Chapter 7, we mentioned that politeness requirements are suspended in emergencies and speakers go 'bald on record', especially when it is in the interest of the addressee: 'Watch out!' or 'Get up, get up! Big snake!' (Brown and Levinson 1987: 95–6):

> In cases of great urgency or desperation, redress would actually decrease the communicated urgency. (ibid.)

The reader can deduce that her own skin condition leaves no space for niceties of expression. The crisis must be averted. Further, although the point is not made explicitly that the advertised product is the means to deal with this emergency, the assumption that the relevance maxim is in operation here triggers the implicature that it is.

Age-group targeting in advertising is not restricted to the old. In a contemporary issue of *Marie-Claire*, a magazine for women of a younger age group, a similar L'Oréal advertisement appears, incorporating a photograph of the model Claudia Schiffer in place of that of Dayle Haddon. Using the same form and lay-out as the parallels in the Saga Age Care advertisement, it incorporates the words: 'From age 30, targeted anti-wrinkle action' and the quaint imperative: 'Fill your wrinkle furrows daily.'

Some advertising in *Saga Magazine* reflects the contradiction of youth-in-age set up by the image of Deneuve on the front cover. There are advertisements for plastic surgery and ads selling youthful appearance or youth-like well-being itself, one of which we shall now look at in some detail.

Not all cosmetics advertisements use the bald-on-record strategy we saw in the L'Oréal promotions. Some take a gentler, more complicated approach.

The back cover of the *Saga Magazine* featuring Catherine Deneuve is a sort of echo of the front cover. It is also largely filled with a photograph of a woman: the actor, film director and singer Jane Birkin, middle-aged but retaining a youthful appearance. Unlike the front cover featuring Deneuve, which is in colour, this three-quarter portrait is in monochrome; it also differs from the front cover in that it is part of an advertisement. Whereas the Deneuve portrait is poised and elegant, the Birkin picture conveys an impression of spontaneity and naturalness.

Deneuve has an open but serious expression, her right forefinger on her almost closed, flawless lips (hinting at discretion perhaps); a gold chain trails from her loosely folded hands, vaguely suggesting a rosary; she appears to be wearing a leopard-skin coat. She looks rich, remote, a triumph of cosmetic art.

In contrast, Birkin is grinning broadly at the camera; we can just make out a laughter line; her arms are bent and raised with her hands plunged into her tousled hair. There is a tiny gap between her incisor teeth, which are otherwise perfect. She is wearing a simple, v-necked top; it may have cost a fortune but the fact is not obvious. The impression is of cheerful well-being and vigour. She is thin and looks healthy, and she could be taken for a woman in her thirties. There is a small caption to the right of the photo: 'Jane Birkin by David Bailey 2005', indicating that it was only one year old at the time of publication, which places her age in the photograph as 58. The British photographer David Bailey was at one time married to Catherine Deneuve. Birkin's career and personal life have been predominantly in France. All three first gained fame in the 'swinging sixties', a period with which many Saga readers can identify. It is apparent that some thought has gone into the placement of the two portraits. If not, the result is remarkably serendipitous.

Near the foot of the page on the right is a small insert with a photo of a small box bearing the logo IMEDEEN with four pills in front of it. This logo is repeated below the insert and is the last item on the page. Superimposed on the model's hair is the headline 'ONCE A BABE ALWAYS A BABE'. The word *once* is in huge capitals extending for the full width of the page; the rest is in smaller capitals. This is in colour, as are the insert photograph, the pills, the logo and the line of text in small font at the top of the page in capitals:

NOW IMEDEEN DEVELOPS PRIME RENEWAL™ TABLETS TO HELP FIRM SKIN FROM WITHIN

Everything else is monochrome.

There are over two hundred words of text on the page, but, apart from the caption attributing the photography, there is no explicit mention of Jane Birkin. However, in accordance with Grice's maxim of relevance, we can read the heading 'Once a babe always a babe' as applying to the woman in the picture. We tentatively gloss *babe* as *sexy young woman*. It is not at the time of publication a term current among the over-fifties in Britain, but it is familiar from television.

The main prose text appears in two columns superimposed across the lower part of the photograph. Using the second person pronoun *you*, it directly addresses the reader:

You walk into a room, heads turn. You like having fun. The odd flirtation.

When students of pragmatics are first exposed to the idea of Grice's maxims (see Section 2.5), they rightly tend to be initially sceptical and raise the issue of deliberate deception. When asked to expand on this, they sometimes mention the domains of advertising and politics. As we hope we have shown, Grice does not suggest that prevaricating, waffling, misleading or outright lying do not occur, but rather that even deliberate deception would not work without an assumption that the maxims are being observed. We have already seen that a major rationale for departing from the maxims is politeness and facework (the protection – or manipulation – of one's own and other people's face: Chapter 7). These play a large part in persuasive language.

A compliment is a verbal gift and can serve as mitigation of a face-threatening act. As we mentioned in Chapter 3, *flattery* is a popular strategy in sales promotion. We choose to call it *flattery* because *flattery* carries connotations of undeservedness, which is not true of *compliment*. Clearly compliments in an advertisement are unlikely to be well founded because the copywriter does not know the recipient as an individual and is in fact addressing a mass audience, albeit simulating face-to-face, one-to-one inter-action. Asking someone to buy something is obviously an FTA, and drawing attention to a person's physical defects is even more threatening. Unless advertisers have opted for the 'bald on record' strategy mentioned earlier, they need to pay attention to mit-igation. Hence, this one starts off with fanciful praise.

The transition from the vivacious image of Jane Birkin to *you* is abrupt and immediate. There is a slight potential ambiguity in that, at first glance, *you* may be addressed to Jane Birkin, but the reader can absorb this while accepting it as relat-ing to herself. Her identity is already being associated with the image.

A form of intertextuality is in play here: many readers over 50 will remember that Birkin was famous in her youth for slightly scandalous records and film appear-ances. She looks as if she could still turn heads. Now the reader is being told that she can do the same. There is a hint – no more – of sexual daring: *having fun* can sug-gest anything from laughter to wild promiscuity; *flirtation* can be relatively innocent or it can lead to other things.

The text has attributed to the reader social power which springs from sexual attrac-tiveness: *you* as Actor walking into a room; *you* (implicated) as Initiator of heads turn-ing (= *you make heads turn*). *You enjoy having fun* is a grammatical metaphor, representing *you* (metaphorically) as Senser enjoying a positive Phenomenon (*having fun*). But *you* is also the implicit Subject of *having fun*; more congruently, it would be *you funning* if such a verb existed – a behavioural process with you as Behaver. *Flirtation* is another grammatical metaphor, a nominalization of the verb *flirt*. Again the addressee (*you*) is implicitly the one performing the behavioural process of *flirt-ing*, the Behaver. In appraisal terms *enjoy* and *fun* are highly positive (Affect). Throughout, the addressee is associated with positive concepts.

The text moves on to introduce the product:

> Now Imedeen turns its attention to the specific skincare needs of vibrant, life-loving, sexy, attractive post-menopausal women.

Introducing the word *post-menopausal* into a non-threatening advertisement of this kind is something of a challenge to the copywriter, and this one deals with it by piling up the positive modifiers before it occurs, offering further indirect flattery. It does not actually assert that the attributes apply to *you*, but the relevance maxim supports the implicature that they do so apply. All the other words are value-laden attributes; *post-menopausal* is a non-evaluative classifier. It could be read as deliberate bathos, a joke (in fact, we laughed when we read it), but, in this context, it is unlikely that this is intended. After so much positive appraisal, the word comes as a cold shock. It sounds clinical and has negative collocations like *hospital* and *osteoporosis*.

Why use the word at all? In a society where sex and youth are commercialized, it is necessary to flatter the potential customer at the same time as reminding her that she is vulnerable. Clearly, *old* is out of the question. It has become a derogatory term and has acquired the status of an insult. (See Chapter 2 for cultural attitudes to age.) *Middle-aged* would rule out the over-sixties. *Elderly* is often used to blunt the edge, but it would exclude the middle-aged and is barely a euphemism now; it does not collate with *sexy* and all the other flattering terms; nor does it suggest flir-tation and having fun, activities already ascribed to the reader. Similar objections could be levelled at *post-menopausal*, but this has the advantage of being a technical term and is not entirely incompatible with being vibrant and life-loving and so on. Moreover, *post-menopausal* covers a wider age range than *elderly* or *middle-aged*. In any case, a slight shock serves the purpose of reminding the reader that, wonderful as she may be, she is still getting on and could use some help. It may even serve to orient her to a *medical treatment* frame. But, as far as face is concerned, this remains a risky strategy, and it is the only point in this advertisement where politeness considerations are suspended. (This kind of pressure is not restricted to advertisements targeted at the aged; instilling insecurity and a sense of personal inadequacy is one of the most important strategies of the cosmetics industry.)

The third move is to introduce the product, Prime Renewal, which is described as:

> a unique supplement designed to target the specific changes that can happen to skin at this time.

The word *supplement* is borrowed from the register of diet; it is a quasi-medical term. Dietary supplements are additions to normal food intake in the form of vitamin pills, minerals and so on. It is difficult to know what is being *added to* in the case of this product: possibly natural skin oils, possibly other treatments, possibly nothing at all. It does not really matter since the term *supplement* assigns the product to a recognized scientific category. In the same sentence the text introduces a problem (*specific changes*) and a solution (the product) and tells us that no other product is like it and that it is highly specialized. The modifier *unique* is positive appraisal (Judgment: Social Esteem).

A common strategy in advertising is to attribute scientific authenticity to the product; for want of a better word, we might call this process *scientification*. Obviously, this is particularly important in health and diet products, but it also plays a major role in the cosmetics field, which in our society shares a fuzzy boundary with the domain of health science. It is in the interests of cosmetics manufacturers to assign maximum scientific status to products: hence the tendency to play up powerful ingredients that are supposed to produce near miraculous effects. This strategy may exploit real scientific facts, which are sometimes relevant and sometimes not; or it may fall back on pseudo-science. Advertisements in *Marie-Claire* include expressions like:

- silicone enriched formula
- collagen biospheres
- thermo control technology
- hydration booster
- corrective serum
- mild microdermabrasion.

One series of hair care products advertised bears the trademarks *Miraculous Repair*, *Miraculous Recovery* and *Miraculous Rehydration* with their echoes of the fabled miracle cure.

In the Imedeen advertisement, the science kicks in as soon as the problem has been introduced. In parenthesis, an example of the 'specific changes' is given:

> Less collagen, for a start.

The reader may not know what collagen is, but she may suspect that the lack of it calls for action. Later the text mentions

> unique ingredients, including the Imedeen Biomarine Complex™.

These are

> supported by soya isoflavines, and the new patented Vitea™ Protection Complex

In case the reader is curious as to what these are, the text explains that they are *powerful antioxidants* and include:

> extracts of white tea, tomato and grapeseed, plus vitamins C & E, zinc and camomile

These appeal to the current enthusiasm for natural health remedies; it is a truth universally acknowledged that if something is natural, it must be good for you. But to keep those committed to mainstream science on board, two consecutive sentences place (*scientific*) *tests* in thematic position: *As scientific tests show*, and *Tests also show*.

It would be easy to miss the modality, but a careful examination reveals that no identifiable promises are made about improving skin condition. Scientific tests show that regular dosage over three to six months *may significantly improve* skin firmness and density. The fact that it *may* do this leaves open the pragmatic possibility that it may not.

'Tests also show' various listed improvements: 'reduction in the *visibility* of age spots, lines and wrinkles, and skin on hands and cleavage *looked* smoother' (our italics). Does this mean that the defects were still there but less noticeable? Or was this a purely subjective perception of participants in the test? Anyway, it falls short of a rash promise that the same treatment will solve the prospective customer's problems. Nor are we told about the nature of the tests, the procedures, the number of subjects in the trials, or whether they ruled out other variables that might affect the results. In fact, the sorts of questions that scientists would ask about clinical tests are not addressed at all. This could be motivated by economy of space or by a lack of credibility in the nature of the tests.

Twice the reader is told that the product is *designed* to help, but this is not to claim that it does help. The second time this happens is at the end when, after all the science, the last three sentences directly address the reader again with an implicated promise but not one that would be legally binding:

> Imedeen Prime Renewal is designed to help you look good as you always have. Not just for the age you are now. But for ages to come.

At a higher intertextual level, this advertisement draws on the huge body of commercial promotions which exploit the cognitive frame of age as a treatable ailment, and it adds to that body of text, helping to reinforce the frame.

9.4 Medical science and vested interests

Societies often need to publicize health matters. Sometimes these are public health issues: vaccination campaigns, malaria eradication, AIDS treatment and prevention, contraception, public hygiene, and so on. In such cases, advertising can play a crucial role in disseminating information and persuading people to take the necessary action. In some countries, this is mainly the preserve of public bodies and non-governmental agencies, but it may also engage large corporate interests, often to good effect.

At other times, however, these interests are far from beneficial, as when pharmaceutical companies dump medicines on poor societies, or promote, to people without adequate hygiene provision and with little understanding of infection, the belief that powdered milk is a better baby-food than breast milk.

Drug companies have a vested interest in disease, as do many others, for example, insurance companies, researchers, medical practitioners, therapists, and the news media.

What doctors call a 'constellation of symptoms' does not count as a disease until the symptoms are shown to have something medically significant in common and are assigned a label. Over time, society groups symptoms differently and invents new labels. What is perceived as a single disease at one time in history may be more than one at another; and what one age regards as unrelated conditions may later be classed as a single ailment. Women no longer suffer 'attacks of the vapours' and now nobody is described as having 'a delicate constitution', but we suffer from diseases unheard of two hundred years ago. (And often, of course, discrepancies remain between specialist and non-specialist perceptions and labels.)

The identification of some set of conditions as a named disease is established through texts such as research reports in specialist journals, conference papers, drugs promotions to medical practitioners, general advertising, press releases and media follow-up. Thus, human physical disorders that were previously only vaguely identified are reconceptualized as treatable illnesses.

Medicalization: creating diseases

No doubt most research is carried out with integrity, but a medical expert writes:

> It is also increasingly recognized that even the most rigorous randomized clinical trials and epidemiological studies follow a narrative course that is highly constrained by the political, cultural and ideological context in which they are planned and undertaken and that the published paper that describes a major research study tells a limited, partisan and reconstructed story, however much the researchers have struggled for ice-cold impartiality.
>
> (Greenhalgh 1998: 250)

Still worse, the identification of an illness could be made with ulterior motives, or the scale and distribution of a recognized condition could be deliberately exaggerated. It has been claimed that this does, in fact, happen frequently, and the process has been pejoratively called *disease mongering* and *medicalization*. The management of medicalization is in large part the management of discourse.

Sex has been in part a commercial issue since early times, but it is a truism that in affluent capitalist society it has been incorporated into commerce on a massive scale. The medical and pharmaceutical industries have not neglected this marketing opportunity.

One area that critics of disease mongering have attacked is that of so-called female sexual dysfunction. This has been critiqued by Tiefer (2006). Part of the argument goes roughly like this (our wording):

> The massive profits resulting from the sale of Viagra and similar drugs to men have led to a search for something comparable to sell to women. But first, they need an illness to treat. What was previously regarded as a psychosexual or sociosexual condition is now moved into the medical domain as female sexual dysfunction, FSD, a physiological ailment for which there must be a cure, preferably one involving drugs. Although there may be genuine problems, it is in the interests of disease mongers to magnify the nature and extent of the problem and to increase anxiety among women.

Whatever the pros and cons of the FSD debate, this is clearly a discourse issue. Tiefer (a medical psychiatrist with relevant professional experience) shows how, largely through texts, various phenomena are drawn together, conceptualized as a unitary concept and labelled as an illness. Tiefer regards the concept of FSD as reductionist and dangerous.

Other American researchers have drawn attention to ADHD (attention deficit hyperactivity disorder), where children who in the past were described as *extremely naughty* are now prescribed regular medication, mainly the drug Ritalin. Not only researchers, children and the media are involved as social actors here, but also parents, teachers, school heads, education authorities, and general practitioners[3] (see Further study). Again, one outcome is increased profits for pharmaceutical companies.

These issues are not straightforward. Sometimes individuals or classes of individuals may be penalized for the fact that their health problems are *not* socially recognized and labelled. Large vested interests may militate against, as well as for, reification of physical or mental malfunctions as respectable diseases. Disputes of this kind are power struggles between different factions, usually unequally matched in terms of social power. Insurance companies and employers may go to great lengths to discredit attempts to assign a label which would acknowledge medical credibility and possibly result in the right to demand compensation. Even when a label *is* assigned, they may challenge its validity, as has happened in the past with the disputed ailments repetitive strain injury (RSI) and chronic fatigue syndrome (CFS). This last is a poorly understood 'spectrum disorder', not a unitary condition, and the official criteria for diagnosis are different in the USA and Britain. Its diagnosis as myalgic encephalopathy (ME) implies an identifiable physiological cause.

We earlier included the news media in the list of categories of people with a vested interest in such issues. This may seem a strange claim, and it is true that their interest is less direct than that of researchers or drug producers. There is the issue of direct pharmaceutical advertising as a source of income for much of the media, but even setting that aside, the media are key players in the discourse of disease and its management, largely because of their insatiable need for attention-grabbing stories. This too is an economic matter since stories sell newspapers or increase audiences for television; in turn, funding and advertising revenues increase.

Given that health problems affect all human beings at some time in their lives, any development in diagnosis or treatment is indisputably a legitimate topic for the attention of the media. The trouble is that what makes the best kind of story is either a crisis or a breakthrough. We frequently hear of killer bugs or new strains of disease, and they disappear from the news as fast as they arrived, but unfortunately the diseases sometimes prove to be as serious as the publicity suggested, as in the case of AIDS.

Even better than a scare story is a miracle cure. The *breakthrough* is a crucial concept to many interest groups. Most scientific research is incomprehensible to the majority of the population, and the whole practice of research is perceived differently by researchers and the general public. The media view tends to coincide with that of the non-scientist, which sees scientific research as narrowly utilitarian in its motivation and usually culminating in a 'Eureka!' moment. This perception is reinforced by feature films, documentaries and popularized accounts in the press and elsewhere, in popular scientific histories, for example.

Researchers have an interest in promoting the idea of the breakthrough since it is a way of getting their work into the media. This is not just for personal prestige but is crucial in maintaining funding for the research team or university taking the credit; it also serves to help the research field in general. In a huge and amorphous field like cancer research, for example, it is necessary to keep cancer research itself in the public eye, ensuring the continued flow of funds from institutional and charitable sources and keeping the public contributing to cancer charities. As is so often the case, discourse is bound up with money.

The conventions that govern the discourse of scientific research within peer groups are different from those that obtain in wider contexts. Research reports and academic articles conform to fairly constrained schemata and, for a variety of reasons, claims tend to be couched cautiously with considerable hedging. This is not so true of the news media. Nor is it necessarily true of press releases or more popular accounts produced by the same scientists.

Because journalists are usually under pressure to come up with stories quickly and frequently, the temptation to accept press releases at face value must be considerable. Lakoff (2004) makes this point about the media receiving political feeds from think-tanks, but it applies equally to scientific information.

Even extensive coverage in a television or radio programme cannot deal with the complexities of these issues in anything but a relatively superficial way, and this is more true of a newspaper report, but these media have considerable influence on public perceptions of disease. The pressure on the journalist or the programme maker is always to produce a simple, coherent story with a clear outcome. Thus, although some dissident voices may be admitted because a little conflict may boost the entertainment quotient, the desire for a comprehensible narrative and a decisive conclusion frequently overrides other considerations. In other words, the nature of media discourse about medical matters is in large part driven by purely internal discourse considerations, namely, the need for a well-constructed story. This is because, although the genre of television documentaries has a considerable interest in informing its audiences, it is even more concerned with entertaining them and leaving them satisfied. We often hear of more fastidious researchers who have contributed to documentaries complaining that their work and their words have been misrepresented and oversimplified. The documentary makers argue that they have

Social practice	Genres	Participants
medical research	research reports, specialist journal articles	scientists, research subjects
news reporting	press releases, news reports, popular articles	journalists, scientists
TV/radio documentary making	science documentary	film/radio programme makers, scientists, sufferers
pharmaceutical marketing	press releases, leaflets, advertisements	marketing staff, journalists, NHS personnel

Table 9.1 Agents in creating a disease

been scrupulous, and probably in most cases they have, but their understanding of the discourse is different.

Of course, the media are almost as happy to discredit medicalization and miracle cures as to publicize them. In Bad Science, a regular feature in *The Guardian*, the journalist Ben Goldacre entertainingly informed the readership of various abuses of good faith in these fields. In one article he ridicules the *Daily Mail* for its sudden announcement about drug companies 'inventing diseases' when it frequently presents credulous accounts of questionable diseases itself. He cites 'Night Eating Syndrome' with a 30 per cent cure of all symptoms by a drug manufactured by the pharmaceutical company Pfizer, results based on what he implies is superficial research. His main point, though, is that it is pointless to blame the drug companies and the media since we are all complicit in this kind of deception.

> We have collectively got to a point where distress and discomfort are only legitimate when they have an objective biomedical diagnosis, and we are all players in that game.
>
> (Ben Goldacre, *The Guardian*, 15 April 2006, p. 13)

Thus, we see that various social practices identified with various genres and with more than one social group of agents play a part in the discourse processes that go to 'creating a disease' or resisting its creation. These are partially summarized in Table 9.1.

9.5 The consumerization of education

CDA practitioners have recently drawn attention to what we shall call the consumerization of education (also known as *marketization*; also *the entrepreneurial university*, see Further study). Since the era of Margaret Thatcher in the 1980s, British hospitals, schools and universities have been pressured to operate like commercial companies, competing with each other for business and interacting with their patients or students in ways previously seen as more appropriate to supermarkets, department stores or manufacturing industries. Later governments have perpetuated this policy and significant structural changes have taken place. Inseparable from this is the discourse of the social practices concerned, and critical discourse analysts have examined relevant texts (see Further study).

Behind the consumerization process lie the discourses of economics. Radically different economic theories emerged from different ideologies, or served to create different ideologies. The ideology of the free market promotes the belief that few external constraints on commerce are necessary because market forces will always work to the benefit of the economy.

One Conservative government innovation in the 1980s was permitting schools to sell soft drinks, confectionery and fast food to children and commercializing school meals. This step has subsequently been widely condemned as significantly detrimental to the health of the child population with increased obesity and a reinforcement of bad dietary habits. Incidentally, the disputed disease ADHD, mentioned earlier, is tied into this discourse. The school as a literal market place of attractive but unhealthy goods could be cynically viewed as a metaphor for the consumerization of society in general.

Perhaps the most concrete manifestation of the expansion of commercialism in education is the proliferation of business studies, a relatively new construct, but now one of the most flourishing aspects of university activity. Business, once perceived as the antithesis of academe, is now at its heart, reconstructed as academic practice with the genres appropriate to it: lectures, essays, seminars, projects, examination papers, research reports, dissertations and theses. It could be argued that rather than offering an example of the encroachment of commerce into educational territory, this is just the opposite: the universities grabbing another opportunity to extend their power and influence and to make money. But either account is compatible with the view that education is increasingly involved in commercial practices.

More interesting to the analyst are the changes in the way that universities present themselves and in the institutional practices that continue to develop in the social restructuring of higher education. Fairclough (1992) referred to some of these trends as the 'colonization of discourse by promotion', and Owen (2004), while questioning the term *colonization*, suggests that this process has gone even further since 1992.

As humanities professors who once boasted of their innumeracy become increasingly familiar with spreadsheets and drop into their everyday talk enterprise words like *synergy* and *productivity*, universities are required to make every effort not only to recreate themselves as businesses but also to be seen to be doing so. The linguistic changes evident in promotional genres (advertisements, website information, brochures) are not merely cosmetic; they permeate university life because they are symptomatic of genuine structural changes – revolutionary changes, perhaps.

A key word in the consumerization process is *customer*, common now to shops, buses and railways, hospitals and universities. Fifty years ago, and even more recently, patients and students were not referred to as *customers* except as a joke. Universities were not widely perceived as businesses; courses and degrees were not perceived as commodities for sale. Even where fees were payable, the relationship between the academic and the student was not construed as comparable to that between a shopkeeper and a shopper.

A certain stigma still attaches to the notion of *selling* degrees. We have already mentioned that traditionally the word *sell* carries negative connotations, and in the context of academic qualifications, it is still suspect. A powerful notion remains that the issuing of degrees and diplomas as a marketing transaction is not quite respectable or right. Everyone believes that there are unscrupulous self-styled 'universities' in other parts of the world which offer qualifications virtually over the counter in exchange for a fee and with little effort from the buyer. From time to time, public discourse reflects the suspicion that something similar may sometimes occur in recognized institutions nearer home. There is always a ready audience for media stories of declining standards in education because a stock belief of adherents to conservative educational ideology is that modern educational practices are bad and standards are slipping. Hence, 'easy degrees to increase fees' makes an attractively scandalous news item.

This risk notwithstanding, universities have adopted the metaphorical frame of education as commerce, and the dangers are countered by elaborate evaluation procedures, which purport to assess rigorously the quality of the goods on sale.[4] Incidentally, quality assessment has produced one spin-off which runs right through the education system from primary schools to universities, namely the league table. This is a sports metaphor, of course.

An example of university marketing

Promotional material for business courses from one university actually includes the word *shop* in its self-description in the form of a stock metaphor (*one-stop shop*), currently used in hospitals and elsewhere. A website document that simulates business publicity material advertises its Regional Enterprise and Development office (RED). Under the heading 'What We Do', it informs the reader that:

> RED provides a one-stop-shop for all business development needs and offers a range of services including [a list follows].

In answer to its own question 'What is RED?', it tells us that RED

> is the business gateway to the University of Derby. Its aim is to transform your people and develop your business.

On a separate page, a photograph of a young woman holding a framed certificate accompanies a news report headed:

> RED team member receives Excellence Award

The university issued

> over fifty awards to recognize excellence above and beyond the call of duty.

The Awards were celebrated 'with pomp and ceremony'. We learn more of the winner's commendable behaviour that led to her receiving the 'Excellent Customer Service Award'.

This entire text is strongly reminiscent of the American business practice of selecting an employee of the month. The self-conscious and self-congratulating language is also typical of corporate promotions (*pomp and ceremony; prestigious recognition; even more grand than last year's*).

This is a promotion for a business-related sector of the university, and so we might think that other studies would strike a less commercial note. But on another page we find that favourite of the supermarket, the bargain offer with its typical exclamation mark:

> Why not think about a fast-track degree?
>
> You could achieve your qualification in just two years!

The next heading rhetorically asks the stock question of a self-centred and commercial culture:

> What's in it for me?

In the initial RED page, none of the following key words of the traditional university appear: *study, student, course, examination*. We do find the word *learning*, but it is modified by the adjective *bespoke*, which usually collocates with tailoring (here: *bespoke work-based learning*); it also occurs in the form *E-learning*. We also find *business, enterprise, enterprises, services, wealth, market*, and there is an illustrated reference to Bosch Atco/Qualcast, a company which manufactures and markets lawnmowers and has benefited from RED's services.

Similar texts are produced by universities of all kinds, new and old, glass and red-brick and stone. Granted that universities were once unreasonably embedded in arcane and inefficient practices and perhaps insufficiently answerable for what they offered their students, we should ask whether the current trends are to the general benefit of universities themselves or society at large. CDA can help.

Activities

1. This chapter may be thought to err on the pessimistic side. Try to think of any organizations that may resist consumerism. Look at the texts they produce. You might look at consumer protection organizations like *Which?* or ethical practice pressure groups like Fair Trade or Tourism Concern. Consider how far each should be seen as a force for resisting consumerism and how far they are part of the trend.

2. Select advertisements in a magazine of your choice, and investigate the following questions:

    a. To what extent does the non-promotional material in the magazine interrelate with the advertisements?

    b. Are the advertisements targeted at any specific population (age-group, income-group, sub-culture, special interest group)? How is this reflected in (1) the goods advertised? (2) the advertisements themselves?

    c. Can you identify any cognitive frames or metaphors that the advertisements exploit? Any examples of facework and politeness phenomena?

3. Find examples of promotions for diseases and cures on the Internet, on television or in the press. How do they convince their audiences? Do the criticisms of activists like Tiefer seem justified?

4. Compare texts about medical matters written for doctors (e.g. in professional journals like *The Lancet* or professional medical reference books) with texts on medical matters produced for the public. How do they differ? What reasons can you offer for the differences?

5. Look for evidence of consumerization in the discourse of schools or universities or in discourse about education emanating from official bodies via the media. What key words can you identify? Look for cognitive metaphors or frames such as 'school is a marketplace' or 'education is a commodity'.

Further study

New capitalism

See Fairclough (2004) for an article on what is for Fairclough the main target for CDA: global capitalism. It includes analysis of a written text by Tony Blair.

Advertising

Cook (1992) takes a favourable approach to advertising. One interesting insight is the importance of the *ludic function*, the playfulness that he rightly claims is central to much discourse but is generally neglected. Cook (1994) is about literature, but Chapter 6 analyses a perfume advertisement using stylistics and schema theory, treating the advertisement as an aesthetic object. Myers (1998) gives an introduction to the complex worlds of advertising, analysing the social practices involved in the production, transmission and interpretation of adverts, taking into account not only the prospective purchasers but also the clients and agents involved.

Medicalization

Payer (1992). As the title suggests (see bibliography), this is a campaigning book by an activist. This may be the original use of the term *disease mongering*. Phillips (2006) is an activist essay, one of a set of articles on 'disease mongering' available in this on-line medical journal issue. It deals with 'attention deficit hyperactivity disorder'. The author claims that US teachers are recruited as 'disease spotters' and 'sickness brokers' and encouraged to direct parents to pharmaceutical remedies. We discussed Tiefer (2006) in the chapter. See also others in the same issue of *PloS Medicine*.

For less critical accounts of popular versus technical medical discourse (from a functional grammar perspective), zealots might wish to look at Nwogu and Bloor (1991) and Francis and Kramer-Dahl (1991, 1999). Strictly for functional grammar enthusiasts.

Myers (1990) is a study, not of medical but of biology discourse, contrasting genres which are targeted at fellow specialists and those which address the scientific community in general (or an even wider audience). Myers shows that scientific concepts are created through text, and he painstakingly tracks down all the texts involved in one such creation. Myers (1989) is a related article, dealing with professional politeness.

Education

Gerlinde Mautner's (2005) article on the entrepreneurial university is underpinned by a computational corpus study of the words *entrepreneur* and *enterprise* and their variants. She considers texts from opponents as well as advocates of entrepreneurialism, and includes some striking data. Owen (2004) critically and wittily reflects on an advertisement for a senior university post. Fairclough (1992) is an early work on this topic.

10 Discourse and the law

All persons are equal before the law and are entitled without any discrimination to the equal protection of the law. In this respect, the law shall prohibit any discrimination on any ground such as race, colour, sex, language, religion, political or other opinion, national or social origin, property, birth or other status.

(UN International Covenant on Civil and Political Rights)

10.1 Equality before the law

The principle of equality before the law is proclaimed in numerous institutional documents throughout the world, both national and international. It is a principle against which few would wish to argue, but its implications are not as clear as they might at first appear. It is not inconceivable that the law itself might impose or bolster up inequalities. If the law is set up in such a way as to favour, say, the interests of landlords at the expense of tenants, or vice versa, can we still say that landlords and tenants are equal before the law? In accordance with the principle, the law could be implemented without discrimination as to person but without giving a fair result in terms of natural justice (if such a concept can be said to have any meaning).

A simple example of the anomalies built into the notion of equality is the issue of punishment for an offence. A standard fine for a given offence seems fair and equal treatment, but for a rich person the payment of such a fine is trivial whereas for a poor person it could mean serious sacrifice. Two months in prison is negligible for some people; for others, it might be deeply disturbing and have far-reaching consequences. Courts often have some leeway and take these matters into consideration, but obviously gross discrepancies remain.

The founding fathers of the American Revolution came up with one of the best statements of citizen rights ever produced, the Declaration of Independence, 1776, insisting 'that all men are created equal' and have a God-given right to 'life, liberty and the pursuit of happiness', but these high-principled men were slave-owners, whose wealth was based on the unpaid labour of people whom they could buy and sell and separate from their children without redress. Native Americans were also implicitly excluded from the category of 'men', being referred to in this historic document as 'merciless Indian savages', whom the British king had set loose against the colonists. In accordance with the male supremacist ideology of the era, women were excluded from these 'unalienable rights', and, though this does not figure in the Declaration, in all states some white men were excluded from many rights on the grounds of lacking property.

Property was a big issue with the founding fathers. The phrase 'the pursuit of *happiness*' originally read 'the pursuit of *property*', and a substantial part of the founding fathers' property was slaves. Thomas Jefferson, who was the primary composer of the Declaration of Independence (1776), had numerous children by one of his slaves, a fact which was kept secret until relatively recently. Washington also had large numbers of slaves. In fact, there was initially an anti-slavery clause in the early documentation of the American Revolution, but it was removed because of vested interests. What were they thinking about their slaves' right to liberty and the pursuit of happiness when they drafted it and signed it?

The Bill of Rights of 1789 guaranteed to 'the people' the right not to be deprived of life or liberty without due process of law. Slaves were not emancipated until 1865, and the subsequent history of unequal trials of whites for the murder of African Americans and vice versa, particularly in the South, is widely acknowledged.

These are wide-ranging issues that call for critical analysis. However, we shall restrict our discussion to some problems of implementation of equal justice within the courtroom insofar as discourse analysis and related studies can shed any light on them.

10.2 Disadvantage in court

The law is a game played out in discourses. This could be said of most social practices, but with the law it is particularly explicit and obvious. Texts and words are the stuff of legal procedures: written texts such as statutes, contracts, letters, wills, official documents of all kinds, police reports, signed confessions and spoken texts such as swearing in, spoken evidence delivered in court, examination and cross-examination, pleas, and verdicts.

To most people outside the legal professions, the law court is an alien environment and its discourse practices and its use of language are unfamiliar and confusing. However even-handed the people who administrate it may try to be, only those professionally involved can be at home in a court of law, and everyone else is at a disadvantage. The means of countering this is to employ the services of professionals to act on the lay person's behalf, and this immediately introduces a degree of inequality in that legal processes tend to be lengthy and expensive, and the richer one is, the better one's legal representation is likely to be.

Lawyers are skilled manipulators of language and know precisely what counts as evidence and what kind of utterance from the people they are cross-examining can lead the court to accept or doubt their evidence. They are accustomed to the register of courtroom discourse and able to exploit its nuances. They are experienced in breaking down any confidence that a lay person might retain in the unfamiliar and threatening environment of the court. The non-lawyer lacks these advantages and must struggle to survive.

But although we are all at a disadvantage compared with the professional, the degree of disadvantage varies enormously for the social groups and categories that make up the lay population. Even if we set aside such key considerations as conscious or unconscious racial, ethnic and class prejudice, which may well be contributory factors to the disproportionately high conviction rates for certain categories of people accused of crimes, the administration of justice is made difficult by some intrinsic problems for particular categories. Among the problems that can arise are those associated with variations in the following areas:

- ○ maturity
- ○ education
- ○ dialect
- ○ native-speaker competence
- ○ culture.

In discussing language, ideology and power, Jay Lemke (1995: 14) speaks of

> the dominance of rich over poor, middle-aged over children and the elderly, men over women, one race over others, straights over gays, bosses over workers, teachers over students.

This dominance is reflected in the administration of the law, but we shall look at just a few examples.

Children

Children of all ages are often required to give evidence in trials, and they are often at a grave disadvantage. This is particularly likely to be a problem in the case of children who are the victims of crimes or who are charged with crimes. In many instances, children are now allowed to give evidence via a video-link rather than in a full court hearing, but, although this change was a great improvement, it by no means removes the mismatch between lawyer and child. For example, child witnesses under cross-examination are apt to agree with leading questions or statements like 'So you must have been thinking …', and such questions are permitted in English courts from defending lawyers. (Ben Mills, personal communication.)

Brennan (1994) reports an Australian experiment which, as a measure of understanding, required children from 5 to 15 years to repeat the sense of actual questions originally posed by child counsellors, teachers, and lawyers. (All the data following in this section is from Brennan.) The children across the age spectrum had no problems with the counsellor questions, and they grasped about 80 per cent of the teacher questions, but they grasped only 60 per cent of the randomly selected lawyer questions. The researchers also selected a set of questions which they suspected might cause problems, and the children understood only 15 per cent of these. These results are deeply worrying, especially if we bear in mind that these children in the experiment were operating under much less stressful conditions than the actual children in court.

When we look at some of the questions, we can see just how unfair legal practices can be. The following question was put to an 8-year-old:

> December last year, and was that a weekend or a weekday?

The lawyer asked this during the year following the event in question. In our considerable experience of 8-year-olds, they have hazy notions of which day events happened on only a week ago. Not surprisingly, the child answered, 'I can't remember,' and the lawyer continued:

> Cannot remember. Were the circumstances much the same then as they were on this last occasion you can remember?

The initial question is not an easy one and the addressee is an 8-year-old child in intimidating circumstances being questioned by a stranger. But the lawyer triumphantly repeats for the benefit of the court, 'Cannot remember.' A defence lawyer has an obligation to defend his or her client as effectively as possible. The repetition of 'I can't remember' or 'I don't know' by a witness can establish an impression of unreliability, and it is not difficult for a lawyer, a skilled manipulator of language, to elicit such answers repeatedly by astute questioning. The follow-up question is again a highly inappropriate one to pose to an 8-year-old child. In fact, it seems calculated to confuse anyone. But if that question seems unfair, what about this one to a 10-year-old?

> And did your mother ever say to you that if somebody asks you the questions I am asking you, you should say that we didn't say what was going to be said?

This question is so convoluted with its multiple clause complexes and projections that, unless the lawyer is an imbecile, which is unlikely, he could only be trying to bewilder the child.

Another example reported by Brennan required a 7-year-old victim to say 'how long until the next time' with reference to two acts of abuse. This is patently ludicrous in that it demands the kind of precision about time scales that no 7-year-old could be expected to have in any circumstances; and the circumstances here concern traumatic experiences that must have been deeply distressing for the child. As Brennan says of these courtroom procedures in general, the child is being 'abused again'.

Interpretations and misunderstandings

Roger Shuy (1993) tells many interesting stories about cases in which he was involved as a forensic linguist in American courts. One of these is the story of a man who by a series of misunderstandings was found guilty of involvement in a murder. While he was away, his car was used in the murder by an acquaintance who had frequent access to it, and later, when he found out about the murder, he destroyed the car. In fear for his life, he approached the police and admitted that his car had been used but denied that he had known in advance that it would be used for the murder. He incidentally admitted minor drug dealing. Subsequently, in the man's absence from court, a policeman falsely reported to the court that the man had admitted prior knowledge. From then on frequent references to his 'admission' were understood differently by the man as admission of less serious crimes and by the court as evidence of involvement in the murder.

The situation was made worse by the fact that under questioning the man's account of events was somewhat confused. Shuy attributes this to the man's limited education and lack of oral skill in keeping the time frames separate, thereby confusing his account of what he knew before the murder and what he deduced later. The outcome was that a man who entered the case as a witness, and believed for most of the time that this was still the situation, ended convicted as a participant in a murder.

It is self-evident that communication problems can be caused by dialect variation or an imperfect grasp of the dominant language. In certain areas of Britain, lexical items carry different semantic scope or even distinctly different meanings, for example, regional *while* for standard *until*, *only* for *except*, *borrow* for *lend*, *lend* for *borrow*. In some areas, *come*, *run*, can be simple past tense, *fall* can be a transitive verb. By their nature, misapprehensions about the meaning of utterances usually go unnoticed. The examples of misunderstandings that we have are just the tiny proportion that comes to light.

One of the most notorious examples of an ambiguous utterance in a major trial came up in the case of the trial of Derek Bentley in 1952 (Coulthard 2006b). Bentley was 19 when his 16-year-old accomplice, Craig, fatally shot a policeman during an abortive robbery. Because Craig was under age, he could not be executed for murder, but, although there was no suggestion that Bentley killed the policeman himself, he was found guilty and executed. A key point in the police evidence was the allegation that Bentley said to Craig, 'Let him have it, Chris', which was interpreted as an idiomatic instruction to shoot the policeman. Bentley denied that he had said this at all. The obvious interpretation is that, even if it was uttered, it could have been meant as a direct instruction to hand over the gun, which the policeman had in fact previously demanded. However, the court did not choose this interpretation.

This was not the only linguistico-pragmatics debate in the case. The 'confession' signed by Bentley, who was said to be of low intelligence, stated that, earlier in the evening, he 'did not know he [Craig] was going to use the gun'. In directing the jury, the judge said that this proved that Bentley knew about the gun earlier; otherwise he would have said 'a gun'; in other words, the use of the definite article presupposed that the speaker knew about the gun at the time being talked about. (We shall return to this later with reference to further arguments.) This is an interesting example of the ways in which language can be interpreted differently in court from elsewhere. Although there is some logic in the judge's argument, you do not need a professional linguist to point out that pragmatically, once we take the existence of an item as given, we can refer to it retrospectively using a definite determiner even when talking about a time before we knew of it. If I say, for example, 'I did not know when I was five years old that I would one day drive this car', it does not presuppose that this car existed when I was five and that I knew of its existence.

One of the authors of the present book once served on a jury where the defendant in an assault case claimed that his beer glass had accidentally smashed when the victim (a bouncer in a bar) had tried to 'nut' him (strike him in the face with his head). He said, 'I was drinking beer at the time.' The judge carefully and repeatedly pointed out to the jury that if this was true, the glass must have been touching his face and he would have been injured; therefore, the judge argued, he was lying. But anyone who speaks English knows that 'I was drinking beer at the time' could also pragmatically describe a situation where the glass was not at the speaker's lips, or even in his hand. Compare:

> I was drinking beer at the time, but I had left my glass on the bar.

(constructed)

Australian ethnographers, anthropologists, lawyers and linguists have drawn attention to the serious disadvantages suffered by Aboriginal (i.e. indigenous) Australians[1] as a result of the mismatch between standard Australian English and varieties of Aboriginal English. The astonishing statistic that 'Aboriginal people are jailed at twenty times the rate of non-Aboriginal Australians' (*The Australian*, 29 June 1989, cited in Eades 1994) calls for some kind of explanation. One hypothetical explanation could be that Aboriginal Australians commit more crimes proportionally than the rest of the population; another could be racism on the part of the police and/or the courts. Both these factors may be present, but there is convincing evidence that language and, more particularly, sociocultural aspects of discourse play a major role. According to Eades, the features of Aboriginal English that can cause difficulties include lack of gendered pronouns (*he* for male or female). However, far more important than lexical and grammatical variation in trials involving Aboriginal Australians is the issue of interactive style and discourse practices.

Socio-cultural variation

According to Eades (1994, 2002) and Walsh (1994), typical Aboriginal styles of interaction are profoundly different from those of non-Aboriginal Australians and even further removed from the discourses of the court.

Walsh argues that all conversational style involves different permutations of two dimensions: (a) continuous/non-continuous and (b) dyadic/non-dyadic. To simplify grossly, white Australians tend to have non-continuous and dyadic style and Aboriginal Australians continuous and non-dyadic. That is (Walsh says) non-Aboriginal conversations are clearly defined as having a beginning and an end and typically involve two people talking face-to-face, whereas Aboriginal Australians' conversations tend to be vaguely defined with a high tolerance of silence and involve a group where talk is not directed to any individual. Speakers do not necessarily face each other or stand close. Obviously, this has consequences in courtrooms where non-continuous dyadic discourse is obligatory.

Eades (1994, 2002) argues that socio-cultural differences are so great that cultural interpreters should be provided for Aboriginal people in court. Some of the differences she mentions are related to the features that Walsh describes: eye contact is avoided, being seen as aggressive, but this is viewed by the court as a symptom of guilt – shiftiness. Direct confrontation and rebuttal, which are the essence of court processes, are alien to Aboriginal people, whose culture values agreement. Therefore, Aboriginal people accused of a crime often prefer to admit guilt rather than suffer the trauma of disagreeing and openly arguing. Innocent bystanders have been known to admit guilt when questioned even though they did not know what they were admitting. Aboriginal discourse is indirect and oblique, and it is bad manners to ask direct questions; the strategy is rather to elicit information indirectly.

In response to what Aboriginal Australians perceive as an inappropriate question, they may answer 'I don't know' or 'I don't remember', which, as we have already mentioned, in a law court tends to be interpreted as evasiveness and possibly a sign of guilt. Eades lists numerous further examples of cultural differences that seriously disadvantage this category of Australians. One of the most important is what Eades (2002) calls 'gratuitous concurrence', the tendency to politely agree with any proposition put to them; hence, not only suspects but also witnesses can be induced to provide apparent support for police charges.

As we have said, the rituals and conventions of the court are baffling to the uninitiated. Eades (1994) mentions a case where members of an Aboriginal group involved in a legal process were required to answer individually the same set of questions presented serially to each individual, which seemed bizarre to them. In fact, it seems bizarre to anyone who has no familiarity with legal discourse processes.

In a trial in Ghanzi, Botswana, in the 1970s, a Gikwe ('Bushman') crime victim, who had been tortured with an electric cattle prod by an Afrikaner farmer, was asked if he could see in the courtroom the person who assaulted him. This is a standard practice in trials of this kind. The trial involved a small community where everyone knew everyone else involved by name. The witness simply said, 'It was Lampie.' Again he was asked if he could see the man in the courtroom, and again he gave the same answer. The lawyer asked him to point to the man who had abused him, and again he said, 'It was Lampie.' It was a long time before he was persuaded to point out the man that he and everyone present knew as Lampie. (Liz Wiley, personal communication.)

Women victims

For some years now, there have been complaints of the treatment of rape victims by the police when the crime is reported and by the courts when it goes to trial. Indeed, since filmed interactions in police stations were televised some years ago, attracting a public outcry, it seems that police procedures have been reformed. Since it is in the interests of the defence of an accused rapist to discredit the victim's account, strategies may include attempts to cast doubts on her complicity in the event (consent), her morals, her honesty, and so on. For this reason, many women have been reluctant to press charges. Also, since rape is a difficult charge to prove, the record of successful prosecutions is not high.

A British Home Office study of rape trials (Office of Criminal Justice Reform 2006) reported that legislation to prevent lawyers from publicly questioning rape victims about their sexual history was not working because the rules were frequently 'ignored or avoided'. The authors claimed that judges and lawyers were often ignorant of correct procedures; moreover defence lawyers deliberately manipulated, ignored or evaded the rules in order to damage the image of the victim. Indeed, the rate of conviction in rape cases was shown to be consistently falling; in 2004, only 5.6 per cent of reported cases were successful.

Debora de Carvalho Figueiredo (2004) has argued that British courts operate with a notion of a prototypical rape, which they see as 'real' rape, and those events which do not fit the prototype are perceived as less serious. By studying a corpus of published court decisions on appeals, reported appellate decisions (RADs), she identified two key words: *appalling* and *ordeal*. The presence of these words in the RAD indicates that the court classifies the crime as serious and calls for a 'harsh' sentence, ten or fifteen years, or 'life', which in Britain almost never involves imprisonment literally for life. Their absence usually signals a much lighter sentence. Related words used in the reports include: *terrible*, *grave*, *despicable*, *horrendous*, *terrifying* and *very serious*. The prototypical features of the crime include, among others, the age of the victim (young or old) and the perpetrator being a stranger, especially if breaking into the home occurs. The crime is aggravated by violence or threats with a weapon.

Carvalho Figueiredo gives examples of extremely violent rapes where, because the victim and rapist were married or had previously lived together, a light sentence was imposed or an initially 'heavy' sentence was reduced by 40 per cent. The only exceptions to this and the use of the words *appalling* and *ordeal* apply when the wife is presented as prototypically feminine and virtuous. The labelling and categorization of the rape in relation to the prototype, she says, determine the sentence and sometimes even lead to excusing the crime entirely. She argues that this is a gendered position on rape.

10.3 Speech acts in court

Court cases frequently centre on whether or not a certain speech act has taken place. If speech acts were always explicit performatives like 'I hereby promise to pay you $5,000', judicial procedures would be more straightforward, but speech acts in general, and criminal speech acts in particular, are usually less direct. The speech acts that tend to attract attention in court are threatening, offering bribes, accepting bribes, admitting guilt, and since people usually perform such speech acts indirectly, there is often considerable scope for legal debate.

In English law, disputes about whether an utterance counted as a serious threat date back a long time. An instance cited from 1669 is the following:

> Turberville and Savage exchanged quarrelsome words. Turberville laid his hand on his sword and said, 'If it were not assize time, I would not take such language from you.' These words showed that Turberville's menacing gesture was pure bravado; so far from being a threat, the words were a reassurance. But Savage thrust at Turberville and put out his eye. Turberville sued for damages for assault; Savage pleaded self-defence because he feared an attack. It was held that Turberville had not opened the hostilities, because his words showed no present intention to do violence. Consequently, Savage was not entitled to claim that he acted in self-defence.
>
> (G. Williams, 1983, *Textbook of Criminal Law*, London: Stevens: 174–5)

An utterance such as 'I will not take such language from you', accompanied by the act of grasping a sword, might reasonably be interpreted as a threat, although it is a long way from a performative threat such as 'I hereby threaten to kill you' (which is hardly plausible English at any time in history) or from 'I swear I'll kill you' or 'I'm going to kill you.' However, the court decided that the possibility of interpreting it as a threat was ruled out by Turberville's use of modality (not 'I will not' but 'I would not') coupled with the counterfactual condition set out in the dependent clause: 'if it were not assize time' (but it was assize time). The only basis for any sort of defence for Saville seems to be Turberville's handling of the sword, but the verbal part of this painful interaction was held by the court to have cancelled out any threat there.

A curious feature of American law is that there is a specific crime of threatening the life of the president. It is a crime to threaten anyone's life, but the president has a separate law. A quick glance over presidential history helps to explain this fact. Trials for this crime of threatening seem to have focused on whether or not the utterance was a *threat* made in earnest or some other speech act such as a *jest*. Verdicts showed considerable discrepancies in interpreting these issues; for example, a lower court would find a defendant guilty even though he was thousands of miles away from the president and included a counterfactual conditional; and an appeal court would say that the utterance was clearly a jest (Danet *et al.* 1980). Speech act theorists would say that such threats are infelicitous because the conditions to implement them are clearly not met.

Another speech act issue that has been debated in court is whether the determining factor in defining an utterance as a threat, defamation, and so on is the speaker's intended meaning (illocutionary force) or the take-up by listeners (perlocutionary effect) (Hancher 1981). The courts do not usually deal in this terminology (unless a forensic linguist becomes involved), but the discussion and judgments clearly address these issues. Also, since no one can be objectively sure of the intentions of a speaker or the understanding of a hearer, the question arises of what is a plausible intention behind an utterance or a likely understanding of it. Decisions made in court do not always coincide with the views of Austin, Searle and other academic toilers in this field, but they are closely related.

10.4 Forensic linguistics

In presenting a case, lawyers are permitted to bring in scientific experts to testify. There is a long history of medical, psychiatric and other scientific specialists playing important roles in court cases. In recent years, there has been an increase in the part played by linguists in this arena. According to Malcolm Coulthard, forensic linguistics began with the publication of Svartvik's (1968) analysis of the confessions of Timothy Evans, a young man executed for the murder of his wife and baby, a crime later proved to be committed by the serial killer, Christie, Evans' landlord. Too late to help the unfortunate Evans, Svartvik analysed the confession statements submitted to the court and revealed that the crucial passages were stylistically different from the rest of the text, suggesting different authorship, presumably one or more police officers.

In the United States, according to his own account (Shuy 1993), Roger Shuy became a forensic linguist by accident when he happened to sit next to a lawyer on a plane and found out that he was engaged on a case involving tape-recorded conversations, a field in which Shuy was an expert. Since then, he has gone on to give expert evidence in many trials. We have already mentioned some of his work.

A large proportion of forensic linguistics has focused on the processing of indistinct tape-recordings, identification of regional accents, voice recognition, and other issues which are not germane to discourse analysis in the sense in which we are using it. Graphology, the study of handwriting, has also played its part, but we will restrict our account to a few aspects of work involving discourse analysis in its narrower sense.

Linguistic analysis can sometimes be decisive at a basic level. In a case in Australia, a man murdered his wife and typed a fake six-page suicide note, which he did not sign (Eagleson 1994). By comparing this note with previous items written by the husband and the murdered wife, the suicide letter was shown to match the husband's and not the wife's writing in terms of specific misspellings, punctuation and capitalization, morphology (verb forms), non-standard syntax and lexis. The man was caught because he was less literate than his wife and because he foolishly composed such a long letter, providing data for analysis.

10.5 Identical utterances

In Britain, Shuy's counterpart is Malcolm Coulthard, whose extensive courtroom experience has included the posthumous appeal of Derek Bentley, already mentioned, many years after the original trial and execution. He was also involved in the appeal of the Bridgewater Four, four men found guilty of murdering a newsboy, who had stumbled on a robbery in progress. The appeal court found them not guilty after they had served some years in prison. Falsified confessions were at the centre of both these cases, as Coulthard demonstrated.

In discussing the Bentley case earlier, we mentioned the issue of Bentley's use of the definite article in 'I didn't know he was going to use the gun,' which the judge suggested proved that Bentley was lying. We argued that this was not the case, even on the basis of the evidence available. But Coulthard's analysis goes further and shows that the confession was not, as the police claimed, a free statement made by the accused but a statement concocted from an interrogation.

Two key texts in the Bridgewater case were a police transcript of an interview and a confession signed by Molloy, one of the accused, which was claimed to have been taken down verbatim from his own account, given some time after the interview.

Coulthard showed that the confession could not have been delivered spontaneously because it featured many examples of direct repetition of strings of words from the interview transcript. Computational analysis of texts has shown that people do not reproduce identical wording, and empirical tests have shown that they are incapable of reproducing even a relatively short string of words exactly. We all think that we can remember exactly what was said in a past interaction, and indeed until recently court cases have tended to proceed on this assumption, but it is fallacious. The two texts in question had so many identical strings of words that they could not have been produced independently of each other. There were also stylistic oddities in the texts suggesting that (1) the confession had been put together on the basis of the interrogation document; and (2) some of the utterances attributed to Molloy were more likely to have been composed by the police. Many of the statements appeared more natural as answers to questions. In the Bentley case, too, the point about the use of the definite article in connection with the gun is easily explained if it was in fact an answer to a police question about the gun.

Sentences as complicated as the following appeared in both interrogation transcripts and Molloy's signed confession:

> I had been drinking and cannot remember the exact time (that) I was there but whilst I was upstairs I heard someone downstairs say be careful someone is coming.

In fact, Coulthard found that every word occurring in one of the two documents in question occurred in the other. Until recently, identity of utterance has been taken as a sign of authenticity; these frame-ups have come to light only since linguists using corpus evidence have proved that it does not occur without intervention.

Policespeak

Another indicator of police malpractice in the production of evidence that came up in both the trials mentioned was the style of the language presented in the transcripts, purporting to be an unedited version of what the defendants had said. One characteristic feature of police written report register is the use of the adjunct *then*. This tends to appear between the Subject and the verb: *I then proceeded to caution the defendant*, a rare structure in (non-police) spoken English. In the Bentley case, there were numerous examples of this structure. The word *then* occurred 11 times in 588 words, i.e. once in 53.4 words. In a search of the Cobuild spoken English corpus, the word occurred once in every five hundred words. In the police's own evidence, *then* occurred on an average of one in 78 words. This strongly suggests a police involvement in the construction of the text presented as Bentley's own words. Fox (1993) contrasts these two styles as *policespeak* and *normalspeak* (after *Newspeak*, the invented language in George Orwell's novel *1984*, compare Paul Chilton's *Nukespeak*).

Another characteristic of police reports is a concern for accurate identification of objects and hence a degree of descriptive detail that would appear strange in other genres. An even more notorious case was that of the Birmingham Six, jailed in 1974 for two IRA bombings and released on appeal 16 years later. The confession of one of the accused repeatedly used the expression *white plastic carrier bags* (Coulthard 1992b). The crime was alleged to have involved the placement of bombs in such bags. The man accused claimed later under cross-examination that the suggestion of using these expressions came from the police. It is not typical of normal spoken discourse to produce nominal groups with such identical detail on repeated occasions, or even once. Grice's maxim of Quantity requires us to give as much information as required by the circumstances. Having once identified an item as *a white plastic bag*, we normally refer to it – if at all – as just *the bag*. Even the first mention would be likely to refer simply to *a bag* or at most *a plastic bag* or *a carrier bag*. But in the police report genre such details are important and hence frequent, and the police wished to have them in the confession because they would help to incriminate the suspects. In the event, they eventually helped to demonstrate that the confession was not fully authentic.

English courts now require recordings as well as transcripts of interviews and confessions.

10.6 Lexical density

One method of analysis exploited by Coulthard (2006b) is *lexical density*, a technique devised by the SFL scholar Jean Ure (1971) and considerably developed for computer use by Michael Stubbs (1996). This is a quantifiable measure which has been shown to differ significantly across different registers. Originally devised as a means for investigating what constitutes register variation, it can be useful in distinguishing a written composition from an authentic transcript of spoken discourse. Although there are some theoretical and practical problems, this is a relatively simple procedure, which we will outline, leaving out the complications. Consider the following sentence:

> In return for a progressively diminishing financial subsidy, the British exercised stringent fiscal control over the country.

By the simplest criterion of classing a word as a string of letters between two spaces or between a space and a punctuation mark, there are 17 words here. According to traditional criteria, the words can be divided into two types: function words and content words, or, as we shall say, grammatical and lexical. To put it at its simplest, the first kind of word has a meaning best defined in terms of its grammatical function in a clause and the second has a 'dictionary' meaning, describable in terms of semantic features or its potential for referring to phenomena in worlds real or imaginary. According to these criteria, we get the following two groupings:

Grammatical: *in, for, a, the, over, the* (6 words)

Lexical: *return, progressively, diminishing, financial, subsidy, British, exercised, stringent, fiscal, control, country* (11 words)

Note that we are counting by token and not by type; that is, the same word used twice counts as two words. Lexical density is a measure of the percentage of the total words in a text that are 'lexical' (in this special sense). To find lexical density as a percentage figure, we divide the number of lexical words by the total number and multiply by 100. This is presented formulaically:

$$\frac{\text{Lexical words}}{\text{Total no. of words}} \times 100 = \text{Lexical density}$$

For the given sentence, the lexical density is $11 \div 17 = 0.647 \times 100 = 64.7\%$. Of course, except for illustrative purposes, applying this formula to a single sentence would be pointless, but it can be informative when applied to longer texts of a hundred words and more. Written language tends to have a higher proportion of 'lexical' words to total text than spontaneous spoken language has. To put it another way, formal written texts tend to be much denser than informal spoken texts; other things being equal, denser texts tend to be harder to process than less dense ones, though, obviously, there are many other variables that affect comprehensibility.

In terms of word classes (parts of speech), the breakdown of lexical and grammatical words is typically:

- lexical word: noun (*book, bigotry, absence*), lexical verb (*hit, went, gone, writing*), adjective (*swift, oblique*), numeral (*four, fourth*), lexical adverb (*quickly, fast*)
- grammatical word: pronoun (*he, who, whose, mine*), auxiliary verb (*will, must, can, be, have*), preposition (*on, by, under*), conjunction (*and, while*), grammatical adverb (*very, quite, soon, however*), determiner (*the, a, these, some*).

Coulthard demonstrates that part of a terrorist suspect's supposed spoken confession, which he denied having made, had a high lexical density of 83 per cent (or 8.3 in Coulthard's formulation). Coupled with the high use of nominalizations and extensive use of embedded and dependent clauses (see Appendix), this provided evidence of fabrication, which the police later partly admitted.

None of the examples we have given here would in itself be deemed conclusive evidence in a court of law. The example we cited of the semi-literate suicide note (Eagleson 1994) is perhaps the most conclusive, especially to the non-linguist, but even there the husband was already a suspect and there was other evidence against him. In supporting a case for the defence or the prosecution, it is useful if the forensic linguist can provide more than one measure which bears out claims regarding authorship, and this is the usual practice in such disputes. Not all forensic linguistics in the discourse field works with computational analysis, but advances in corpus linguistics underpin much of it. Everyone working in forensic applications and in corpus work generally says that there is still a long way to go, and it is a currently flourishing field of research.

Activities

1. Carvalho Figueiredo describes 'prototype rape' decisions as 'gendered', i.e. a product of male bias. Do you think this is justified?

2. Compare two contrasting texts, e.g. in two genres, or transcribed speech and pre-pared speech, for any of the following: lexical density; average sentence length in words; sentence complexity (average number of clauses per sentence).

3. Legal disputes sometimes revolve around the readability or ease of comprehension of texts, e.g. insurance forms, instructions to juries, etc. Think of ways of measuring the difficulty of such texts.

Further study

Forensics and courtroom interaction

Work by Malcolm Coulthard is a major source for our chapter. He is the central figure in forensic linguistics in Britain, founder of *The International Journal of Speech, Language and the Law*, formerly *Forensic Linguistics*. Useful readings include: Coulthard (2006a, 2006b, 1996, 1995, 1994b, 1992b), and Coulthard and Johnson (in preparation).

Janet Cotterill is active in forensic linguistics and corpora. Cotterill (2002) is an edited collection of papers by researchers in language and law. See also Cotterill (2003) and Cotterill and Ife (2005).

Gibbons (ed.) (1994) is a fascinating collection on which we have leaned heavily in this chapter. Heffer (2005) is a corpus study of lawyer communication with juries.

Shuy (1993) is the second edition of Shuy's entertaining account of legal cases that have used his forensic expertise.

Woolls (2003), 'Better tools for the trade and how to use them': a self-explanatory title once you know that the trade is forensic linguistics.

Corpus linguistics (not dealing with law)

Stubbs (2004) makes a powerful case for corpus linguistics as the way forward for CDA, and outlines basic principles for 'a substantial cumulative research programme' (ibid.: 268). Koller and Mautner (2004) provide a practical introduction to how computer-generated concordances can help in the critical analysis of texts. This short article gives clear examples which are related to CDA issues.

Stubbs (1996) is a key text on corpus linguistics and includes a detailed study of lexical density and shows how it can be applied to large texts.

Glossary

Adjacency pair: in CA, two related and adjacent turns from different speakers

Affect: in the Appraisal framework, a category relating to emotive attitude (liking, enjoy, upset, etc.)

Appraisal: a taxonomic framework (Martin and White 2005) for analysing attitude and stance of speakers and writers as manifested in speech and writing

Appreciation: in APPRAISAL, relating to aesthetic evaluation (*impress, gorgeous, elegant, ugly,* etc.)

Backgrounding: placing information in a non-prominent position, e.g. by expressing it in a dependent or embedded clause

CA: see CONVERSATION ANALYSIS

Collocation: the statistical tendency for a pair of lexical items to co-occur in a text

Complex Theme: see THEME

Connotation: an additional meaning associated with an expression or lexical item though not strictly part of the narrow meaning (see DENOTATION), e.g. *precocious* denotes 'early developing' but when applied to children it seems to have for many people a negative connotation, a suggestion of an irritating or offensive cleverness

Conversation analysis (CA): an ethnomethodological approach to the analysis of spoken interaction (Schegloff and Sacks 1973), involving, e.g., the study of taking TURNS, ADJACENCY PAIRS

Corpus: a body of linguistic data collected for purposes of analysis, nowadays usually in electronic form; corpora are normally made up of samples of naturally occurring language, i.e. authentic spoken or written text

Co-text: text accompanying any piece of text the analyst is currently focusing on

Denotation: the meaning (in a narrow sense) carried by a word, as opposed to CONNOTATION

Discourse community: a social group linked by genres which members use in common, e.g. medical researchers who use such journals as *The Lancet*, people who participate in the same Internet discussion group, a fan club

Dispreferred second (part), also **dispreferred response:** in CA, the opposite of a PREFERRED SECOND; a 'marked' second part in an adjacency pair, e.g. a rejection in response to a proposal

Domain: the socially recognized context in which discourse occurs, e.g. education, religion, law, commerce, courtroom

Dyadic: one-to-one (interaction)

Embedded: a clause which functions as a part of, or the whole of, a lower rank unit such as a nominal group (NG) is said to be embedded, e.g. in *schools that select by income or by ability,* the underlined clause is embedded in an NG, modifying the

head noun *schools*; in *This is <u>what you need</u>*, the underlined clause functions as Complement in a clause, a role typically taken by an NG

Ethnographic: (as relating to language and communication) pertaining to an approach that regards social setting and culture as central

Ethnomethodological: pertaining to a sociological approach that focuses on local and moment-by-moment management of interaction

Exclusion: the 'playing-down' of information: (1) totally: by SUPPRESSION, e.g. omitting the agent (Actor or Initiator); (2) partially: by BACKGROUNDING

Face: self-image, the ability to maintain a line that one has taken; 'the want to be unimpeded and the want to be approved of in some respects' (Brown and Levinson 1987)

Face-threatening act (FTA): an action or utterance that has the potential to negatively affect FACE

Facework: protection or manipulation of one's own or others' FACE; POLITENESS

Foregrounding: placing information in a prominent position, e.g. by presenting it in an independent clause or as NEW within a clause. See BACKGROUNDING

Forensic linguistics: strictly, linguistics contributing to evidence in court; loosely, linguistics applied to legal matters

Frame, also **cognitive frame:** a cognitive schema in terms of which we perceive and classify phenomena; a unit in an ideology

FTA: see FACE-THREATENING ACT

Genre: socially recognized text type, e.g. business letter, novel, political speech, political interview

Given: a function in Systemic Functional clause analysis (contrasting with NEW): information presented as taken for granted in context; usually conflates with THEME, e.g. *He didn't!* In spoken mode, usually signalled by intonation. With stress on *didn't*, *he* is Given and *didn't* is New. If *he* is stressed, e.g. as an answer to 'Who didn't prepare this?', then *he* is New

Grammatical metaphor: non-congruent expression, e.g. a noun in place of a verb to express a process (see NOMINALIZATION); an adjective in place of a modal verb, e.g. X *may solve* Y (congruent): *a probable solution* (grammatical metaphor)

Grice's maxims: a set of sub-principles (proposed by Paul Grice) that make up the Co-operative Principle explaining co-operative communication: Quantity (degree of detail or generality), Quality (truth), Relation (relevance) and Manner (clarity)

Hedging: avoiding full commitment or exactness in making an assertion, e.g. by signalling approximation (*roughly, about, more or less*), by using modality (*may, possibly*) or by utterances like 'If I'm not mistaken …'

Ideational: in SYSTEMIC FUNCTIONAL LINGUISTICS, one of three METAFUNCTIONS, the other two being INTERPERSONAL and TEXTUAL. Roughly corresponds to semantic meaning, the representational dimension of language

Ideology: set of beliefs and attitudes, consciously or unconsciously held by a social group

Illocutionary act: see SPEECH ACT

Implicature: (more specifically **conversational implicature**, though, confusingly, not always restricted to conversation), what is suggested or hinted at but not explicitly stated, see SPEECH ACT

Insertion sequence: in CA, a sequence of conversation turns intervening between the first and second parts of an ADJACENCY PAIR

Interactant: a participant in an interaction, e.g. an interviewer or interviewee, anyone engaged in conversation, shopkeeper or customer in sales transaction, teacher and students in a lesson

Interpersonal: in SFL, one of the three METAFUNCTIONS, the others being IDEATIONAL and TEXTUAL. The interpersonal metafunction includes such phenomena as nouns in direct address; words like *please* and *thank you*, greetings; also modality (modal verbs like *may*, *could*, and modal adverbs like *probably, certainly*); expressions of frequency and regularity and such functions as Subject, Complement, and the options of declarative, interrogative and imperative

Intertextuality: a concept associated with Mikhail Bakhtin and Julia Kristeva that plays an important role in much modern discourse analysis: (1) the interrelationship of all texts; the meaning of a text is in part inherent in the extent to which it resembles or contrasts with other texts; and (2) the exploitation in a text of elements from another text or of direct or oblique references to another text; or another part of the same text, e.g. quotation, reported speech, semi-quotation or 'echoing' of another text, paraphrase, stylistic parody

Judgement: in the Appraisal framework, a category relating to approval or disapproval concerning truthfulness, tenacity, etc.

Kinesics: semiotic physical phenomena accompanying speech: hand movements, raised eyebrows, frown, leaning forward, etc.; excludes meaningless tics and twitches; some analysts include PROXEMICS

Lexical density: the proportion of lexical (i.e. content) words to total words in a text, usually expressed as a percentage

Metafunctions: in SYSTEMIC FUNCTIONAL LINGUISTICS: the three metafunctions are IDEATIONAL, INTERPERSONAL and TEXTUAL

Metaphor: identifying one thing with a different thing to suggest partial similarity, e.g. *Kevin is a real powerhouse* does not mean that Kevin is constructed of brick and contains machinery but (probably) that he resembles a powerhouse in that he has a great deal of energy

Multimodal discourse: interaction involving more than one mode of communication, e.g. sound and pictorial image (in film and TV), oral speech and writing or image projection (in a lecture or classroom)

Mutual knowledge, also **shared knowledge**: knowledge held in common by participants in an instance of discourse

New: see GIVEN

Nominalization: a verbal process expressed as a noun, e.g. instead of *the inspection team investigated*, a writer may choose *the investigation* (involving SUPPRESSION of the information about the Actor) or *the investigation by the inspection team* (which retains the information)

Paralinguistics: non-verbal semiotic phenomena involved in spoken interaction such as pitch, stress, timing, pauses; some analysts include KINESICS, but it excludes non-semiotic phenomena like tics, stammering, blinking

Participant: (1) the individual taking part in a given discourse, e.g. the doctor and the patient are participants in a medical consultation (also anyone else present and involved); (see INTERACTANT); (2) in SFL, one of a set of semantic roles, e.g. Actor,

Senser. Clauses are analysed in terms of the IDEATIONAL METAFUNCTION as consisting of *process*, *participant* and *circumstance*

Pejorative: pertaining to a word that carries negative CONNOTATIONS, e.g. *dictator, agitator, crony, mob, dreary, sly, harsh, evasive, dawdle*

Performative: a verbal expression, the utterance of which implements a social act, e.g. *I now pronounce you man and wife, I promise to be there, I refuse, I accept, I agree, I apologize.* See SPEECH ACT THEORY and ILLOCUTIONARY ACTS

Phatic communion: discourse in the service of maintaining social relations, e.g. greetings, comments on the weather, empty chit-chat

Phonology: (the study of) the SEMIOTIC sound system of a language

Politeness: action taken in the process of FACEWORK to mitigate FACE-THREATENING ACTIVITIES

Pragmatics: (the study of) meaning in context, involving such concerns as deixis (how items are spatially and temporally identified in a specific instance, e.g. the reference of *here* and *now* depends on when and where it is uttered); also how meanings can be implicated rather than explicitly stated (see IMPLICATURE); how we choose the appropriate interpretation when confronted with ambiguity or sarcasm; what counts as a promise, a threat, a command, etc. Sometimes defined more formally as: 'the relations between signs and their users'. SPEECH ACT theory played an important part in the development of pragmatics. See also GRICE'S MAXIMS

Preferred second (part), also **preferred response:** in CA, the normal expected second part of an ADJACENCY PAIR, e.g. acceptance is the preferred response to a proposal

Presupposition: what a speaker takes for granted, i.e. assumes as given but does not necessarily make explicit; roughly, an assumption

Process: in SFL, semantic phenomena such as *doing, happening, feeling, saying, thinking*, etc., typically expressed as a verb. See PARTICIPANT (2)

Proxemics: physical positioning in a speech event, e.g. distance from other interactants, seating arrangements, etc.

Rheme: that part of the clause that is not the THEME. Typically carries the NEW information in the clause, but there are exceptions

Rhetoric: organization of spoken or written discourse for coherence and effective communication

Semantics: (the study of) 'meaning' in a narrow sense (often contrasted with SYNTAX and PRAGMATICS but sometimes including aspects of the latter); sometimes defined more formally as: the relations between signs and their referents (or between linguistic forms and concepts)

Semiotic: symbolic, conveying meaning

SFL: see SYSTEMIC FUNCTIONAL LINGUISTICS

Solidarity: the quality that binds social groups; togetherness, the possession of shared interests and desires

Speech act: also ILLOCUTION(ARY ACT) The act implemented by an utterance, e.g. ordering, requesting, promising, threatening, congratulating, insulting, asserting. May be direct or indirect, e.g. the utterance of 'It's hot in here' might be an indirect *directive* (a *request* to open the door or turn down the heating). On another occasion the same sentence might be simply a direct *representative* act (specifically, an *assertion* about the temperature)

Speech act theory: an approach to pragmatic meaning established by the philosophers Austin and (later) Searle, involving PERFORMATIVES and ILLOCUTION

Speech community: a vague term indicating a social group linked by a common language, dialect, etc.

Speech function: similar to SPEECH ACT

Stance: the position taken by a speaker or writer regarding the matters expressed; sometimes referred to as speaker stance or authorial stance

Stereotype: a standardized, oversimplified image of a gender, social category, class or group, e.g. one gender stereotype attributes to women an inability to read maps

Suppression: omission of information; a more drastic form of EXCLUSION than BACKGROUNDING

Syntax: (the study of) the grammatical patterns of clause structure and clause combinations; more formally defined as 'the relations between signs'

Systemic Functional Linguistics (SFL): a linguistic approach initiated by M. A. K. Halliday based on earlier work by J. R. Firth (1890–1960), which regards meaning, social interaction and text as central to linguistic studies and declares a preference for data from actual spoken or written language rather than invented sentences

Textual: (1) in a general sense, relating to text; (2) in SFL one of the three META-FUNCTIONS, the others being INTERPERSONAL and IDEATIONAL. Concerned with the ways in which clauses are inter-related in text by cohesion and, within the clause and between clauses, in terms of the way elements are packaged for GIVEN and NEW, THEME, etc.

Theme: in SFL, the starting point or 'peg' in the clause as message. Usually, the initial element in a clause, expressing the GIVEN part of the message. A complex Theme has more than one part, e.g. In fact, Nelly, he did marry her. The underlined section forms a complex Theme consisting of *in fact* (textual Theme), *Nelly* (interpersonal Theme) and *he* (ideational Theme). The RHEME is *did marry her*

Turn: an unbroken stretch of speech of indeterminate length produced by a single participant in a verbal interaction. A turn may also be realized by a gesture, e.g. a nod of agreement or a paralinguistic sound, e.g. a grunt, a groan. In a live email chat group, it may take the form of typing, converted into electronic impulses

Utterance: a vague term for a unit of actual spoken or written language from a single source; the term makes no assumptions about grammatical structure or rhetorical purpose

Notes

Chapter 1

1. Most of the work of Robert de Beaugrande is now available freely on the internet at www.beaugrande.com but see also his article (2004).
2. Research now indicates that this prescriptive use of 'he', 'him' and 'his' was promoted by male grammarians in the eighteenth century. A detailed account is given by Bodine (1975) and is further discussed in Cameron (1985, 1990).
3. The term *participant* is used differently in clause analysis (see Grammar Appendix). We meet this use later in the book.
4. The discussion of the meaning of words in cricket, used as an example of a frame in Section 1.3, is based on Austin (1961) and is also discussed in Lakoff (1987: 21).

Chapter 2

1. Some linguists have claimed that the structure of language can best be studied without reference to contextual meaning. Chomsky, for example, set out to study 'language as an instrument or tool, attempting to describe its structure with no explicit reference to how this instrument is put to use' (1957: 103). This proved to be an interesting project but one that, in itself, brought us no nearer to an understanding of meaning in discourse. Even Chomsky admitted that 'To understand a sentence we must know much more than the analysis of the sentence on each linguistic level. We must know the reference and meaning of the morphemes or words of which it is composed; naturally, grammar cannot be expected to be of much help here.' (By 'grammar', Chomsky means *formal grammar*.) In this book, we use *functional grammar*, which is essentially directed at meaning, not the formal model of grammar devised by Chomsky and his associates.
2. 'Coloured' was an official term under the Apartheid regime in South Africa to mean people of mixed race. Marion Morel wrote a monthly column in a magazine written for non-whites. This story was written in the 1950s and re-published in Hughes (1961).
3. Fairclough (2003: 55–61) classifies assumptions into three types and he illustrates the links between these assumptions and Grice's conversational maxims:
   ○ existential assumptions: assumptions about what exists;
   ○ propositional assumptions: assumptions about what is or can be or will be the case;

○ value assumptions: assumptions about what is good or desirable.

4. Sperber and Wilson (1986) argued that all Grice's maxims could be explained by a more general principle of 'relevance', but we will not pursue this theory here.

Chapter 3

1. There are exceptions, of course, to the ways in which reviews are written. Reviewers may digress from actual reviewing to other matters, such as their own life experiences, their obsessions or desires. In such cases, the use of personal pronouns is frequent. This appears, at present, to be a characteristic of television reviews, where writers appear more like chatty journalists than experts. An additional characteristic of this style is the use of slang and colloquialisms, as in this example from a negative review of a television play:

> The fact that Paul didn't seem to ever bother working made his achievements all the more baffling, particularly as this was meant to be the front of the eighties, a time when I recall the country was still wreathed in economic mire. But let us not get bogged down by such piffling distractions.

> (From Kathryn Flett's review of Poliakoff's
> *Friends and Crocodiles*, in *The Observer*, 22 January 2006)

2. It is, of course, quite possible that the firm of brokers might be able to assist the reader with tax planning, but we have no evidence of this from the letter itself. The matter of charges is complex. Some companies of this type charge a fee, which is usually based on a proportion of the amount of tax saved; other companies advise the client to make certain investments (for example, in tax-free savings) and then charge commission to the bank they refer them to. In either case, the client pays, directly or indirectly.

Chapter 4

1. A detailed discussion of this position can be found in Iedema *et al.* (1994) in the section 'Appraisal and Journalistic Discourse'. A version of this is also available on the web.

2. The works referred to in the example are G. Gustafson and K. Harris (1990), 'Women's responses to young infants' cries', *Developmental Psychology*, 26: 144–52 and G. Gustafson, J. Green and J. Cleland (1994), 'Robustness of individual identity in the cries of human infants', *Developmental Psychobiology*, 27: 1–9.

Chapter 5

1. The quoted words are taken from the Introduction to the Penguin translation of Aristotle's *The Art of Rhetoric* trans. by H.C. Lawson-Tancred (1991).

2. Incidentally, Aristotle, like many present-day politicians and newspaper editors, did not usually show much respect for audiences. To give just two sample quotations:

We are concerned with just those things about which we deliberate … and with audiences of limited intellectual scope and limited capacity to follow an extended chain of reasoning…

(*The Art of Rhetoric,* 1.2)

Maxims give great assistance to speeches, for one thing through the stupidity of the listeners; for they are delighted if someone in generalizing should arrive at opinions that they hold in the particular case.

(*The Art of Rhetoric,* 2.21)

3. *The Art of Rhetoric,* 3.1.
4. See Paul Chilton (1985, 1996 and 2004, particularly Part 3).
5. Introductory section of James Baldwin's (1965) *The Fire Next Time,* Harmondsworth: Penguin Books, 1970.

Chapter 6

1. The word *multiracial* is normally used in Britain and Australia to refer to communities or regions where people of more than one 'race' or ethnic identity live together. It may also be applied to particular groups, as in *multiracial community*. In the USA, it appears to be used to describe individuals of more than one racial origin (see US Census data – www.census.gov).
2. These figures are taken from UN (2005), Table 6: Women in Parliament.

Chapter 7

1. We are grateful to Dr Helen Basturkmen, Auckland University, for this and other samples of spoken discourse data in this chapter.
2. In discussing this text, we mix conversation analysis, sociolinguistics, grammar and pragmatics in a way that purists would find distasteful.
3. '*We* intrinsically creates an opposition and exclusion, but this externalized entity may not be fixed throughout an utterance … The fuzziness of this linkage is used by politicians at times to manipulate texts and disguise agency' (Ward 2004).
4. Thatcher announced to the media, 'We are a grandmother', using a linguistic option traditionally restricted to monarchs.
5. The word 'reform' has an interesting history. Most dictionaries explain the word as equivalent to 'improvement', with the noun 'improvement', by extension, meaning a change for the better. In recent years, however, especially in the discourse of public policy, it has become clear that one person's reforms are another person's retrograde steps.

Chapter 8

1. Mostly, we use the terms *conservative* and *(left-)liberal* rather loosely to refer to a general ideological orientation, especially with regard to race. The terms do

not denote political parties although there may be some overlap with political party labels. Marxists, anarchists and others might be appalled to be included under the *left-liberal* tag, and we apologize. We also use the terms *right-wing* and *left-wing* fairly loosely as synonyms respectively for *conservative* and *left-liberal*. Explicitly racist or fascistic groups or parties are referred to as *far right* or *ultra-right*.

2. The Quantity maxim and also Relevance permit approximation. We know that the expression 'a million' does not mean exactly 'a million', and we assume that it is not relevant to go into fine details, or that the fine details are not known. But in the instance discussed here the approximation is excessive.

3. We are influenced here by van Dijk (1998) though we may not have reflected his views successfully.

4. Furthermore, we have to concede that, in the interests of brevity, we have ignored some more difficult features of the book.

Chapter 9

1. This is a simplistic and also Eurocentric way of referring to the origins of banking. The Chinese seem to have had paper currency and banking practices in fourteenth century BC. Something like banking occurred under the Roman Empire.

2. Our rebarbative term *consumerization* means the process of increasing individuals' perceptions of themselves as consumers and extending the discourses of consumerism into more and more social practices.

3. In Britain, only a specialist (e.g. a child psychiatrist) may make such prescriptions.

4. Greatrix (2006) argues that the quality assessment procedures are inappropriate adaptations of industrial practice and reduce trust in universities.

Chapter 10

1. We have tried to have tried to follow Eades' terminology here. Many thanks to several Australian correspondents and others who advised us on the delicacies of these labels. Apologies if we have got it wrong.

Grammar appendix

Some basic concepts in Systemic Functional Grammar

1 Clause structure and functions

In Systemic Functional Grammar (SFG), clauses are viewed from three perspectives: interpersonal, ideational and textual. These are called *metafunctions*.

1.1 Interpersonal metafunction

The interpersonal metafunction self-evidently involves such phenomena as nouns and pronouns in direct address (vocatives), greetings (phatic communion), and modality, i.e. signalling degree of commitment or personal attitude to a proposition: *may*, *might*, *could*, *probably*, *certainly*, *fortunately*, *surprisingly*.

Less obviously, it also concerns the traditional syntactic categories of subject, object, etc. These are most easily defined in narrowly grammatical terms, e.g. Subject is the element with which (in principle) the Finite agrees in person and number or which is reflected as a pronoun in a question tag:

The experiment was aborted, wasn't it?

The experiment: singular; tag-pronoun: *it*

The experiments were aborted, weren't they?

experiments: plural; tag-pronoun: *they*

The categories are Subject, Finite, Predicator, Complement and Adjunct (SFPCA).

The mood options of declarative, interrogative and imperative are also part of the interpersonal metafunction, being typically realized through differing sequences of S and F:

declarative:	S^F	**He was** playing *an elaborate game.*
interrogative:	F^S	**Was he** *playing an elaborate game?*
imperative:	no S	**Play** *an elaborate game.*

1.2 Ideational metafunction

The ideational metafunction corresponds closely to what is traditionally called semantics or content. It is about 'happenings' or 'goings-on': who does what, to whom, for whom, when, how and why, etc. It is the representation of real or imaginary worlds.

Material process

In a *material process*, where some physical action occurs, the person who performs the action is called the Actor, the person or thing undergoing the action is the Goal, the person 'benefiting' is the Beneficiary. The Actor may be the grammatical Subject or may have some other interpersonal role. In the first clause below (from a history of Ethiopia), *Tewodros* is Subject and Actor; in the second (constructed by us), *Tewodros* is not Subject but is still Actor.

> Tewodros improvised a rather crude explosive.

> A rather crude explosive was improvised by Tewodros.

In the first sentence, *a rather crude explosive* is Complement (direct object), but, in the second sentence, it is Subject. In ideational terms, it is Goal in both. The point is that the syntactic arrangement changes but the real-world roles remain the same. Subject is a syntactic function and Actor is a semantic function, roughly speaking. The grammatical difference between the two derives from the voice system: the option of active or passive. The first (with Actor as Subject) is active; and the second (with Goal as Subject) is passive. If we wished to leave *Tewodros* out of the picture for any reason, the second option would be a good one because we could omit the final phrase to give:

> A rather crude explosive was improvised.

An action may be performed by one participant (Actor) but caused, instigated or initiated by another (Initiator):

> The Council (Initiator) made them (Actor) destroy it (Goal).

Relational process

The typical relational process has the pattern: X is Y. The typical verbs are copular verbs: *be, seem, appear, become, sound, look* (as in *You look ill*, but not in *Look at that!*) or verbs of possession: *have, own, possess*. There are two kinds of relational process: identifying and attributing.

Identifying can be a bit complicated:

> Tracy is the clever one.

The question: *Which one is the clever one?* asks us to identify the clever one. In the response *Tracy is the clever one*, Tracy is Identifier and *the clever one* is Identified. In the same wording answering the hypothetical question *Which one is Tracy?*, the roles are reversed: *Tracy* is Identified and *the clever one* is Identifier. In speech, the intonation would be different.

Attribution is a little easier. In the clause:

> He was a self-made man

Note: *he* is Carrier, and *a self-made man* is Attribute. In the clause:

> The response of the clergy was medieval

Note: *the response of the clergy* is Carrier, and *medieval* is Attribute.

> This challenge had two elements

Note: *this challenge* is the Carrier, and *two elements* is the Attribute.

Mental process

Mental process includes not only narrowly mental events like understanding, knowing, thinking, remembering, imagining; but also emotional or affective ones such as loving, hating, fearing, admiring, despising; and sensory ones such as feeling, hearing, seeing. The two key participants are *Senser* and *Phenomenon*.

In *I remember April*, the Subject *I* is Senser and the Complement (direct object) is *April*.

In the clause:

> Change for the sake of change would never appeal to any Conservative,

the Phenomenon is the Subject: *change for the sake of change*; and the Senser *any Conservative* is part of an Adjunct. We could very roughly paraphrase it as follows, retaining the same ideational roles but making the Senser into the Subject:

> A conservative (Senser) would never like change for the sake of change (Phenomenon).

Other processes

The *behavioural process* involves a *Behaver*:

> She (Behaver) stood in the rain.

> I (Behaver) slept late.

Verbal process involves *Sayer, Receiver* and *Quoted* or *Reported*. Also *Verbiage* and *Target*.

> She (Sayer) said, 'I'm ready.' (Quoted).

> She (Sayer) said that she was ready (Reported).

> Galileo (Sayer) told him (Receiver) the truth (Verbiage).

> The report (Sayer) criticized the emperor (Target).

Existential process involves *Existent*.

> There were six people (Existent) on the committee.

Note: Outside SFL, the term *actor* is sometimes used to refer to a number of participant roles: Actor, Initiator, Behaver, etc.

1.3 Textual metafunction

Clauses consist of Theme and Rheme. The Theme has been described as 'the starting point' or 'the peg on which the message is hung'. (This is a technical term and does not mean the same thing as *theme* in the sense of main topic or subject matter, nor in the sense in which it is used in formal grammar, Theta theory, etc.) In English, Theme is usually the first element in the clause. In simple sentences, it most typically conflates with the Subject, but often it does not.

In all the examples so far, the Subject is also the Theme. For example:

> Tewodros improvised a rather crude explosive.

> A rather crude explosive was improvised by Tewodros.

In the first example, *Tewodros* is Theme, and, in the second, *a rather crude explosive* is Theme. The rest of the clause is the Rheme, but in the following examples, something other than the Subject is the Theme:

In south-western Wallaga	a ruler named Jote Tullu	emerged
Adjunct	Subject	Finite/Predicator
Theme	Rheme	

At the apex of the political pyramid	was	the king
Complement	Finite	Subject
Theme	Rheme	

This discipline	he	instilled	into his troops
Complement (direct object)	Subject	F/P	Adjunct
Theme	Rheme		

2 Nominal groups

A *nominal group* (NG) is a grammatical unit with a noun as its Head; the Head is the key grammatical word in the group. (The terms *noun group* and, in other grammars, *noun phrase* are used in the same sense.) In addition to its Head, an NG may contain one or more Modifiers. Modifiers may be determiners (*the, that, these*, etc.), numerals (*four, fourth*), adjectives (*red, clever, political*), verb participles (*broken, running*), nouns (*bus* in *bus station, Labour* in *Labour Party*), prepositional phrases or embedded clauses (the last two are usually post-modifiers, placed after the Head). (Note that a noun is not re-classified as an adjective just because it functions as Modifier, as in some traditional grammars.)

Modifiers have various ideational functions, e.g. determiners are Deictic (having a 'pointing' function, saying 'which one I'm talking about'); *this* versus *that*, etc. Possessive pronouns (traditionally sometimes classed as adjectives) *my, his, their* are also Deictic, as are possessive nouns: *Cameron's, America's*.

An important distinction is between Epithet and Classifier. For example, in the NG:

venal and rapacious political leaders

the Head is *leaders*. *Venal* and *rapacious* are Epithets; they refer to characteristics or qualities of the Head that we might call accidental or incidental; they describe. But *political* is a Classifier. It narrows the class of leaders to the sub-category of *political leaders* as opposed to, say, *religious leaders* or *military leaders*.

The decontextualized expression *a civil engineer* is ambiguous. It could be:

❍ an engineer concerned with construction, concrete, load-bearing capacities, etc.; that is, a *civil engineer* as opposed to a *mechanical engineer* or any other class of engineer

❍ an engineer who is polite and well-mannered.

The first *civil* is a Classifier; the second *civil* is an Epithet. In the obvious meaning of the expression *civil war*, as in the English, American or Spanish Civil War, *civil* is a Classifier. In *a vicious war*, *vicious* is an Epithet. In *bloodthirsty*, *long-lasting*, *destructive civil wars*, all the Modifiers except *civil* are Epithets. Classifier stays close to the Head.

3 Embedded clauses

When a clause is used as a modifier of a noun or in place of an NG (e.g. as Subject of a clause), it is said to be embedded. For example (Subject underlined; embedded clause double-bracketed):

The first boundary ||that was to be delimited|| was the shortest

The clause *that was to be delimited* modifies the Head noun *boundary*. So we have a fairly long NG as Subject:

the first boundary that was to be delimited

In the next sentence, a clause [[*what both sides share*]] functions as the whole Subject:

||What both sides share|| is a dogmatic belief.

4 Clause complex

Two or more clauses can combine together to form a *clause complex*. Such combinations can be *paratactic*, where clauses are linked on an equal footing, or *hypotactic*, where one clause is bound to another on an unequal basis.

Paratactic linking typically involves *linking conjunctions* (traditionally, co-ordinating conjunctions): *and, but, or*. For example:

It wasn't worth fighting, and nothing could really change.

Hypotactic complexes have one clause (*dependent clause*) depending on another (*dominant clause*):

Even though we have had a very bad experience, || we are still continuing to diversify.

Here the dependent clause is placed before the dominant clause. With a thematic shift, the order of the clauses could be reversed so that the dominant clause comes first:

We are still continuing to diversify || even though we have had a very bad experience.

Clauses can be finite or nonfinite (in contrast to some traditional grammars). Both types can be dependent. In the example above, the dependent clause is finite, i.e. it contains a finite verb (*have*), F in the SFPCA structure. In the following example, the dependent clause is non-finite. This is a clause with a verb participle in the P role and no Finite. Dependent clauses are often initiated by a binding conjunction (subordinating conjunction) such as *when, while, until, unless, because*, but this is not always so, as we see here:

> He also provided transport service, || carrying the goods of the governor.

In the interests of brevity and simplicity, we have restricted our examples, but clause complexes often contain many clauses.

5 Grammatical metaphor

To put it very crudely, we generally think of people and things as being represented by nouns and pronouns, and we think of processes (*acting, feeling, saying,* etc.) as being expressed by verbs. When this happens, the representation is described as *congruent*:

Congruent: Birds fly. Planes fly. Insects fly.

Non-congruent: The flight of birds; the flight of planes; the flight of insects.

Representing the activity of flying as a noun *flight* in this way, we treat it, in a sense, as an entity, a 'thing'. This opens up new cognitive and grammatical possibilities. We can still include the Actor (in the *of*-phrase), but if we wish, we can leave out the Actor altogether, for example, to allow for the abstraction *flight*.

If we want to talk about the process of destroying without mentioning the destroyer, one way of doing it is to use the noun *destruction*. We may not know who was responsible, we may not consider it important, we may have mentioned it already, we may wish to conceal the fact, we may have grammatical or rhetorical needs, but, whatever the reason, we may opt for, say, *the destruction of Dresden*, which can function as a Subject, Complement, part of an Adjunct and so on. It also permits us to think of it as a 'fact' rather than a process. If we retain the Actor as a by-agent phrase (*by the British Airforce*), the information is present but less foregrounded than making it Subject in an active clause (*the British Airforce destroyed Dresden*).

This non-congruent option is called a *grammatical metaphor*. This particular example is an instance of *nominalization*, a noun 'in place of' a verb. It is so called because instead of a partial replacement of one semantic concept for another (e.g. 'journey' for 'life'), we have one grammatical form instead of another. There is no value judgement involved here; grammatical metaphors are no better or worse than congruent structures; they are just another linguistic resource.

For a more complicated example, consider the two fragments which follow:

> The main complaints about the police are of general harassment …

> When people complain about the police, they most often complain that the police generally harass them.

You will not be surprised to learn that the first is an actual quotation from a published text and the second is our clumsy attempt at a paraphrase. Complaining is a verbal process performed by actors that we will call Sayers; the typical grammatical option for expressing verbal processes is a verb: *say, ask, tell*, or in this case *complain*. So the second version is the congruent one; it also happens to be clumsier.

A fuller version of the original reads as follows:

> The main complaints against the police are of general harassment, refusal to act when a complaint about a crime is made, unreasonable searching and questioning.

This contains the following propositions:

> X complains against the police
>
> that the police harass X
>
> that the police refuse to act
>
> > when X complains about a crime
>
> that the police search X unreasonably
>
> that the police question X

By nominalizing the process of 'complaining' as a noun (*complaint*), we can make it the Subject and Theme of a clause; we also presuppose the truth of the proposition that someone complains. It enables us to leave out the Sayer; there is no indication here of who does the complaining. The same is true for the subsequent nominalizations: *harassment, refusal, complaint*, and the 'verbal-nouns' (gerunds): *searching* and *questioning*; we can omit Sayer or Actor.

In the next example, two grammatical metaphors feed the construction of a traditional metaphor, whereby *negatively affect* becomes *hit*.

> The rising cost of steel has hit the construction of off-shore wind turbines …

A rough breakdown of the meaning of the two nominalizations is:

> the rising cost of steel : steel keeps costing more
> the construction of off-shore wind turbines : X construct off-shore wind turbines.

The first is an abstraction, but rendering it as a nominal group in this way makes it eligible as Subject of *has hit*, a verb normally expressing a material process with an Actor. In addition, it allows *the construction of off-shore wind turbines* to have information focus (New) at the end of the Rheme of the clause. No literal action of hitting takes place in the real world, but the concept is conveyed more vividly than by more congruent and literal means.

There is no value judgement involved here: congruent structures are no better or worse than grammatical metaphors. As with traditional metaphor, it is impossible to get to the end of grammatical metaphor. We can say only that a given structure is more or less congruent than another, and sometimes even to say that is difficult. However, the concept does shed some light on what is happening in a text. For example, it helps to explain the relative lexical density of academic texts as opposed to popularizations or prepared text as opposed to spontaneous speech.

Within CDA, deconstruction of grammatical metaphor can be used to reveal how meanings are manipulated.

For further clarification, see Bloor and Bloor (2004) or for a more advanced account Halliday and Matthiessen (2004).

References

Adams, P., Heaton, B. and Howarth, P. (eds) 1991, *Socio-Cultural Issues in English for Academic Purposes*, London: Modern English Publications and the British Council.

Allan, S. 1998, 'News from nowhere: televisual news discourse and the construction of hegemony', in A. Bell and P. Garrett (eds), *Approaches to Media Discourse*, Oxford: Blackwell.

Angelil-Carter, S. 2002, *Stolen Language? Plagiarism in Writing*, London: Longman.

Aristotle 1991, *The Art of Rhetoric*, trans. H. C. Lawson-Tancred, London: Penguin Books.

Austin, J. L. 1961, *Philosophical Papers*, Oxford: Oxford University Press.

Austin, J. L. 1962, *How to Do Things with Words*, Oxford: Oxford University Press.

Bakhtin, M. 1981, *The Dialogical Imagination*, Austin, TX: University of Texas Press.

Bakhtin, M. 1986, *Speech Genres and Other Late Essays*, Austin, TX: University of Texas Press.

Baldwin, J. 1965, *The Fire Next Time*, London: Penguin.

Basturkmen, H. 2000, 'The organization of discussion in university settings', *Text*, 20: 249–69.

Basturkmen, H. 2002, 'Negotiating meaning in seminar type discussion and EAP', *English for Specific Purposes*, 21: 233–42.

Beaugrande, R. de 2004, 'Critical discourse analysis from the perspective of ecologism', *Critical Discourse Studies*, 1: 113–41.

Beaugrande, R. de and Dressler, W. 1981, *Introduction to Text Linguistics*, London: Longman.

Bell, A. and Garrett, P. (eds) 1998, *Approaches to Media Discourse*, Oxford: Blackwell.

Biber, D. and Conrad, S. 2004, 'Corpus-based comparisons of registers', in C. Coffin, A. Hewings and K. O'Halloran (eds), *Applying English Grammar: Functional and Corpus Approaches*, London: Hodder Arnold.

Blackledge, A. 2006, 'The racialization of language in British political discourse', *Critical Discourse Studies*, 3: 61–80.

Blommaert, J. 2005, *Discourse*, Cambridge: Cambridge University Press.

Bloor, M. 1996, 'Academic writing in computer science: a comparison of genres', in E. Ventola and A. Mauranen (eds), *Academic Writing: Intercultural and Textual Issues*, Amsterdam: John Benjamins.

Bloor, M. 1998, 'Lexical and grammatical choices in innovative language use in computer science', in A. Sanchez-Macarro and R. Carter (eds), *Linguistic Choice across Genres*, Amsterdam: John Benjamins.

Bloor, M. and Bloor, T. 1991, 'Cultural expectations and sociopragmatic failure', in P. Adams, B. Heaton, and P. Howarth (eds), *Socio-cultural Issues in English for Academic Purposes*, London: Modern English Publications and The British Council.

Bloor, M. and Bloor, T. 2001, 'There'll be some changes made: predicting future events in academic and business genres', in M. Hewings (ed.), *Academic Writing in Context*, Birmingham: Birmingham University Press.

Bloor, T. 1996, 'Three hypothetical strategies in philosophical writing', in E. Ventola and A. Mauranen (eds), *Academic Writing: Intercultural and Textual Issues*, Amsterdam: John Benjamins.

Bloor, T. 1998, 'Conditional expressions: meanings and realizations across two genres', in A. Sanchez-Macarro and R. Carter (eds), *Linguistic Choice across Genres*, Amsterdam: John Benjamins.

Bloor, T. and Bloor, M. 2004, *The Functional Analysis of English*, 2nd edn, London: Arnold. New York: Cambridge University Press.

Bodine, A. 1975, 'Androcentrism in prescriptive grammar: singular "they", sex-indefinite "he", and "he and she"', *Language in Society*, 4, Cambridge: Cambridge University Press.

Bolinger, D. and Sears, D. 1981, *Aspects of Language*, 3rd edn, New York and London: Harcourt Brace Jovanovich, Inc.

Bosveld, K., Connolly, H. and Rendall, M. S. 2006, *A Guide to Comparing 1991 and 2001 Census Ethnic Group Data*, UK Government Website: www.statistic.gov.uk

Bourdieu, P. 1991, *Language and Symbolic Power* (ed. J. B. Thompson) Cambridge: Polity Press and Blackwell.

Bourdieu, P. and Wacquant, L. 1992, *An Invitation to Reflexive Sociology*, London and Chicago: Polity Press and University of Chicago Press.

Brennan, M. 1994, 'Cross-examining children in criminal courts: child welfare under attack', in J. Gibbons (ed.), *Language and the Law*, Harlow: Longman.

Brody, H. 1998, Introduction, in T. Greenhalgh and B. Hurwitz, *Narrative Based Medicine*, London: BMA Books.

Brown, P. and Levinson, S. 1987, *Politeness: Some Universals in Language Use*, Cambridge: Cambridge University Press.

Brown, R. and Gilman, A. 1972, 'The pronouns of power and solidarity', in P. P. Giglioli (ed.), *Language and Social Context*, London: Penguin.

Caldas-Coulthard, C. R. and Coulthard, R. M. 1996, *Texts and Practices: Readings in Critical Discourse Analysis*, London and New York: Routledge.

Cameron, D. 1985, *Feminism and Linguistic Theory*, Basingstoke: Macmillan.

Cameron, D. (ed.) 1990, *The Feminist Critique of Language*, London and New York: Routledge.

Carvalho Figueiredo, D. 2004, 'Representations of rape in the discourse of legal decisions', in L. Young and C. Harrison (eds), *Systemic Functional Linguistics and Critical Discourse Analysis*, London and New York: Continuum.

Cheshire, J. and Trudgill, P. 1998, *The Sociolinguistics Reader*, vol. 2, London: Arnold.

Chilton, P. 1985, *Language and the Nuclear Arms Debate: Nukespeak Today*, London: Frances Pinter.

Chilton, P. 1996, *Security Metaphors: Cold War Discourse from Containment to Common European Home*, London: Peter Lang.

Chilton, P. 2004, *Analysing Political Discourse: Theory and Practice*, London: Routledge.

Chilton, P. and Schaeffner, C. 1997, 'Discourse and politics', in T. van Dijk (ed.), *Discourse as Social Interaction*, London: Sage.

Chomsky, N. 1957, *Syntactic Structures*, The Hague: Mouton.

Chouliaraki, L. and Fairclough, N. 1999, *Discourse in Late Modernity*, Edinburgh: Edinburgh University Press.

Coates, J. 1986, *Women, Men and Language*, London and New York: Longman.

Coffin, C., Hewings, A. and O'Halloran, K. 2004, *Applying English Grammar: Functional and Corpus Approaches*, London: Hodder Arnold.

Cook, G. 1992, *The Discourse of Advertising*, London: Routledge.

Cook, G. 1994, *Discourse and Literature*, Oxford: Oxford University Press.

Cotterill, J. (ed.) 2002, *Language in the Legal Process*, Houndmills: Palgrave Macmillan.

Cotterill, J. 2003, *Language and Power in Court: A Linguistic Analysis of the O.J. Simpson Trial*, Houndmills: Palgrave Macmillan.

Cotterill, J. and Ife, A. (eds) 2005, *Language across Boundaries*, Houndmills: Palgrave Macmillan.

Coulthard, R. M. 1977, *An Introduction to Discourse Analysis*, Harlow: Longman.

Coulthard, R. M. (ed.) 1992a, *Advances in Spoken Discourse Analysis*, London: Routledge.

Coulthard, R. M. 1992b, 'Forensic discourse analysis', in R. M. Coulthard (ed.), *Advances in Spoken Discourse Analysis*, London: Routledge.

Coulthard, R. M. (ed.) 1994a, *Advances in Written Text Analysis*, London: Routledge.

Coulthard, R. M. 1994b, 'Powerful evidence for the defence; an exercise in forensic discourse analysis', in J. Gibbons (ed.), *Language and the Law*, Harlow: Longman.

Coulthard, R. M. 1995, 'Questioning statements: forensic applications of linguistics', (Inaugural lecture) Birmingham: ELR (University of Birmingham).

Coulthard, R. M. 1996, 'The official version: audience manipulation in police records of interviews with suspects', in R. M. Coulthard and C. R. Caldas-Coulthard (eds), *Texts and Practices: Readings in Critical Discourse Analysis*, London: Routledge.

Coulthard, R. M. 2004, 'Author identification, idiolect and linguistic uniqueness', *Applied Linguistics*, 25: 431–3.

Coulthard, R. M. 2006a, 'And then ….: Language description and author attribution', (Sinclair lecture) Birmingham: ELR (Birmingham University).

Coulthard, R. M. 2006b, 'Some forensic applications of descriptive linguistics', *Revista Veredas de Estudos Linguisticos*, vol. 9. Also appears in Spanish as 'Algunas applicaciones forenses de la lingüistica descriptiva', in T. Turrell (ed.), *Lingüistica forense, lengua y derecho*, Barcelona: Edicions a Peticío.

Coulthard, R. M. and Johnson, A. (in preparation), *Introducing Forensic Linguistics*, London: Routledge.

Crystal, D. 1987, *The Cambridge Encyclopedia of Language*, Cambridge: Cambridge University Press.

Danet, B., Hoffman, K. and Kermish, N. C. 1981, 'Threats to the president: an analysis of the linguistic issues', *Journal of Media, Law and Practice*, 1: 180–90.

Davis, A. 1971, *If They Come in the Morning: Voices of Resistance*, London: Orbach and Chambers.

Dicker, S. 2003, *Languages in America: A Pluralist View*, 2nd edn, Cleveden: Multilingual Matters.

Duranti, A. 1988, 'Ethnography of speaking: towards a linguistics of the praxis', in F. J. Newmeyer (ed.), *Language: The Socio-cultural Context* (The Cambridge Linguistics Survey, vol. IV), Cambridge: Cambridge University Press.

Eades, D. 1994, 'A case of communicative clash: Aboriginal English and the legal system', in J. Gibbons (ed.), *Language and the Law*, Harlow: Longman.

Eades, D. 2002, 'Evidence given in unequivocal terms: gaining consent of Aboriginal young people in court', in J. Cotterill (ed.), *Language in the Legal Process*, Houndmills: Palgrave Macmillan.

Eagleson, R. 1994, 'Forensic analysis of personal written texts', in J. Gibbons (ed.), *Language and the Law*, London: Longman.

Eggins, S. and Slade, D. 1997, *Analysing Casual Conversation*, London: Cassell.

Ervin-Tripp, S. M. 1972, 'Sociolinguistic rules of address', in J. B. Pride and J. Holmes (eds), *Sociolinguistics*, London: Pelican.

Fairclough, N. 1989, *Language and Power*, London: Longman.

Fairclough, N. 1992, 'Marketization of public discourse', *Discourse and Society*, 4: 133–62.

Fairclough, N. 1995, *Critical Discourse Analysis: The Critical Study of Language*, London: Longman.

Fairclough, N. 1998, 'Political discourse in the media: an analytic framework', in A. Bell and P. Garrett (eds), *Approaches to Media Discourse*, Oxford: Blackwell.

Fairclough, N. 1999, 'Linguistic and intertextual analysis within discourse analysis', in A. Jaworski and N. Coupland (eds), *The Discourse Reader*, London and New York: Routledge.

Fairclough, N. 2003, *Analysing Discourse: Textual Analysis for Social Research*, London and New York: Routledge.

Fairclough, N. 2004, 'Critical discourse analysis in the new capitalism', in L. Young and C. Harrison (eds), *Systemic Functional Linguistics and Critical Discourse Analysis: Studies in Social Change*, London: Continuum.

Fairclough, N. and Wodak, R. 1997, 'Critical Discourse Analysis', in T. van Dijk (ed.), *Discourse as Social Interaction: Discourse Studies, 2*, London: Sage.

Faiz S. Abdullah 2004, 'Prolegomena to a discursive model of Malaysian national identity', in L. Young and C. Harrison (eds), *Systemic Functional Linguistics and Critical Discourse Analysis: Studies in Social Change*, London: Continuum.

Fanon, F. 1970, *Black Skin White Masks*, trans. C. L. Markmann, London: Paladin (originally published 1952 by Editions de Seuil, Paris).

Feagin, J. R. 2000, *Racist America: Roots, Current Realities and Future Reparations*, London: Routledge.

Feagin, J. R. and Feagin, C. B. 1993, *Racial and Ethnic Relations*, 4th edn, Englewood Cliffs, New Jersey: Prentice Hall.

Firth, J. R., 1937/1964, *Tongues of Men*, London: Longman.

Foucault, M. 1978, 'The incitement to discourse', in A. Jaworski and N. Coupland (eds) 1999, *The Discourse Reader*, London and New York: Routledge. Excerpt from *The History of Sexuality: An Introduction*, trans. R. Huxley, 1978, London: Penguin.

Foucault, M. 1984, 'The Order of Discourse', in M. Shapiro (ed.), *Language and Politics*, Oxford: Basil Blackwell.

Fowler, R. 1991, *Language in the News: Discourse and Ideology in the British Press*, London: Routledge.

Fowler, R., Hodge, B., Kress, G. and Trew, T. 1979, *Language and Control*, London: Routledge & Kegan Paul.

Fox, G. 1993, 'A comparison of "policespeak" and "normalspeak": a preliminary study', in J. M. Sinclair, M. P. Hoey and G. Fox (eds), *Techniques of Description: A Festschrift for Malcolm Coulthard*, London: Routledge.

Francis, G. and Kramer-Dahl, A. 1991, 'From clinical report to clinical story: two ways of writing about a medical case', in E. Ventola (ed.), *Functional and Systemic Linguistics: Approaches and Uses*, Berlin and New York: Mouton de Gruyter.

Gee, J. 1999, *An Introduction to Discourse Analysis: Theory and Method*, London and New York: Routledge.

Gibbons, J. (ed.) 1994, *Language and the Law*, London and New York: Longman.

Giglioli, P. P. (ed.) 1972, *Language and Social Context*, London: Penguin.

Gledhill, C. 2000, *Collocations in Science Writing*, Tübingen: Gunter Narr Verlag.

Goffman, E. 1955, 'On face-work: an analysis of ritual elements in social inter-action', *Psychiatry*, 18: 213–31. Edited excerpt in A. Jaworski and N. Coupland (eds), 1999, *The Discourse Reader*, London and New York: Routledge.

Greatbatch, D. 1998, 'Conversation analysis: neutralism in British news interviews', in A. Bell and P. Garrett (eds), *Approaches to Media Discourse*, Oxford: Blackwell.

Greatrix, P. 2006, *Dangerous Medicine: Problems with Assuring Quality and Standards in UK Higher Education*, Coventry: University of Warwick Press.

Greenhalgh, T. 1998, 'Narrative based medicine in an evidence based trial', in T. Greenhalgh and B. Hurwitz (eds), *Narrative Based Medicine*, London: BMJ Books.

Greenhalgh, T. and Hurwitz, B. (eds) 1998, *Narrative Based Medicine*, London: BMJ Books.

Gregory, M. and Carroll, S. 1976, *Language and Situation: Language Varieties and their Social Contexts*, London and Boston: Routledge & Kegan Paul.

Grice, H. P. 1975, 'Logic and conversation', in P. Cole and J. L. Morgan (eds), *Syntax and Semantics*, vol. 3: *Speech Acts*, New York: Academic Press. Abridged in A. Jaworski and N. Coupland (eds) 1999, *The Discourse Reader*, London and New York: Routledge.

Halliday, M. A. K. 1978, *Language as Social Semiotic*, London: Edward Arnold.

Halliday, M. A. K. 1993, 'The construction of knowledge and value in the grammar of scientific discourse', in M. A. K. Halliday and J. R. Martin, *Writing Science*, London: The Falmer Press.

Halliday, M. A. K. and Martin, J. R. 1993, *Writing Science: Literacy and Discursive Power*, London and Washington, DC: The Falmer Press.

Halliday, M. A. K. and Matthiessen, C. M. 1999, *Construing Experience through Meaning*, London and New York: Continuum.

Halliday, M. A. K. and Matthiessen, C. M. 2004, *An Introduction to Functional Grammar*, 4th edn, London: Arnold.

Hancher, M. 1981, 'Speech acts and the law', in R. Shuy and A. Shnukal (eds), *Language Use and the Uses of Language*, Georgetown, DC: Georgetown University Press.

Harris, R. and Rampton, B. (eds) 2003, *The Language, Ethnicity and Race Reader*, London and New York: Routledge.

Hasan, R. 1996, *Ways of Saying: Ways of Meaning*, edited by C. Cloran, D. Butt and G. Williams, London: Continuum.

Heffer, C. 2005, *The Language of Jury Trial: A Corpus Aided Analysis of Legal-Lay Discourse*, Houndmills: Palgrave Macmillan.

Henderson, W., Dudley-Evans, T. and Backhouse, R. (eds) 1993, *Economics and Language*, London and New York: Routledge.

Hewings, M. (ed.) 2001, *Academic Writing in Context*, Birmingham: Birmingham University Press.

Holmes, J. 1995, *Women, Men and Politeness*, London: Longman. Excerpt in A. Jaworski and N. Coupland (eds), 1999, *The Discourse Reader*, London and New York: Routledge.

Hughes, L. (ed.) 1961, *An African Treasury*, New York: Pyramid Books.

Hunston, S. and Thompson, G. (eds) 2000, *Evaluation in Text: Authorial Stance and the Construction of Discourse*, Oxford: Oxford University Press.

Iedema, R., Feez, S. and White, P. 1994, *Media Literacy*, Sydney: Disadvantaged Schools Programme, NSW Department of Schools Education.

Ivanič, R. 1998, *Writing and Identity*, Amsterdam: John Benjamins.

Jäger, S. 2001, 'Discourse and knowledge: theoretical and methodological aspects of a critical discourse and dispositive analysis', in R. Wodak and M. Meyer, *Methods of Critical Discourse Analysis*, London: Sage, pp. 32–62.

Jaworski, A. and Coupland, N. (eds) 1999, *The Discourse Reader*, London and New York: Routledge.

Johnson, S. and Meinhof, U. H. 1997, *Language and Masculinity*, Oxford: Blackwell.

Kelly, T., Richards, L. and Nesi, H. 2003, *EASE: Essential Academic Skills in English: Listening to Lectures*, Coventry: University of Warwick.

Kelly, T., Richards, L. and Nesi, H. 2004, *EASE: Essential Academic Skills in English: Seminar Skills*, Coventry: University of Warwick.

Kertzer, D. I. and Arel, D. (eds) 2001, *Census and Identity*, Cambridge: Cambridge University Press.

Koller, V. and Mautner, G. 2004, 'Computer applications in critical discourse analysis', in C. Coffin, A. Hewings and K. O'Halloran (eds), *Applying English Grammar: Functional and Corpus Approaches*, London: Hodder Arnold.

Kramarae, C., Schulz, M. and O'Barr, W. M. (eds) 1984, *Language and Power*, Beverley Hills, CA: Sage.

Kress, G. 1989, *Linguistic Processes in Sociocultural Practice*, Oxford: Oxford University Press.

Kress, G. 1994, 'Text and grammar and explanation', in U. Meinhof and K. Richardson (eds), *Text, Discourse and Context*, London and New York: Longman.

Kress, G. and van Leeuwen, T. 1996, *Reading Images: The Grammar of Visual Design*, London: Routledge.

Krishnamurthy, R. 1996, 'Ethnic, racial and tribal: the language of racism?', in C. R. Caldas-Coulthard and M. Coulthard (eds), *Texts and Practices: Readings in Critical Discourse Analysis*, London and New York: Routledge.

Kristeva, J. 1981, *Desire in Language: A Semiotic Approach to Literature and Art*, Oxford: Basil Blackwell.

Labov, W. 1972, *Language in the Inner City*, Philadelphia, PA: University of Pennsylvania Press.

Lakoff, G. 1987, *Women, Fire and Dangerous Things: What Categories Reveal about the Mind*, Chicago: The University of Chicago Press.

Lakoff, G. 2004, *Don't Think of an Elephant!* White River Junction, VT: Chelsea Green Publishing.

Lakoff, G. and Johnson, M. 1980, *Metaphors We Live By*, Chicago: University of Chicago Press.

Law, J. (ed.) 1995, '*Brewer's Cinema: A Phrase and Fable Dictionary*, London: Cassell.

Lawson-Tancred, H. C. 1991, 'Introduction', in Aristotle, *The Art of Rhetoric*, London: Penguin Books.

Lazar, M. (ed.) 2005, *Feminist Critical Discourse Analysis: Gender, Power and Ideology in Discourse*, Houndmills: Palgrave Macmillan.

Lemke, J. L. 1995, *Textual Politics: Discourse and Social Dynamics*, Bristol, PA: Taylor & Francis.

Levinson, S. C. 1983, *Pragmatics*, Cambridge: Cambridge University Press.

Martin, J. R. and White, P. R. 2005, *The Language of Evaluation: Appraisal in English*, Houndmills: Palgrave Macmillan.

Mautner, G. 2005, 'The entrepreneurial university: a discursive profile of a higher education buzzword', *Critical Discourse Studies*, 2: 95–120.

Meinhof, U. H. and Richardson, K. (eds) 1994, *Text, Discourse and Context: Representations of Poverty in Britain*, London and New York: Longman.

Mey, J. L. 1993, *Pragmatics: An Introduction*, Oxford: Blackwell.

Mills, S. (ed.) 1995, *Language and Gender*, London and New York: Longman.

Myers, G. 1989, 'The pragmatics of politeness in scientific articles', *Applied Linguistics*, 10: 1–35.

Myers, G. 1990, *Writing Biology: Texts in the Social Construction of Scientific Knowledge*, Madison, WI: University of Wisconsin Press.

Myers, G. 1998, *Ad World: Brands, Media, Audiences*, London: Arnold.

Nesi, H. and Thompson, P. 2002, *The Corpus of British Academic Spoken English (BASE)*, University of Warwick and University of Reading.

Newmeyer, F. J. (ed.) 1988, *Language: The Socio-cultural Context* (The Cambridge Linguistics Survey, vol. IV), Cambridge: Cambridge University Press.

Nwogu, K. and Bloor, T. 1991, 'Thematic progression in professional and popular medical texts', in E. Ventola (ed.), *Functional and Systemic Linguistics: Approaches and Uses*, Berlin and New York: Mouton de Gruyter.

Office of Criminal Justice Reform, 2006, *Convicting Rapists and Protecting Victims*, London: Home Office. www.homeoffice.gov.uk

Owen, C. 2004, 'University recruitment: advertisements and textual shelf-life', *Critical Discourse Studies*, 1: 153–7.

Parekh, B. 2000, *Rethinking Multiculturalism*, London: Macmillan.

Payer, L. 1992, *Disease Mongers: How Doctors, Drug Companies and Insurers Are Making You Feel Sick*, New York: Wiley and Sons.

Phillips, C. B. 2006, 'Medicine goes to school: teachers as sickness brokers for ADHD', *PloS Medicine*, 3/2: e182. Online free access journal: www.plosmedicine.org

Pride, J. B. and Holmes, J. (eds) 1972, *Sociolinguistics: Selected Readings*, London: Penguin.

Roudiez, L. 1981, 'Introduction', in J. Kristeva, *Desire in Language: A Semiotic Approach to Literature and Art*, Oxford: Basil Blackwell.

Sanchez-Macarro, A. and Carter, R. (eds) 1998, *Linguistic Choice across Genres*, Amsterdam: John Benjamins.

Schegloff, E. A. and Sacks, H. 1973, 'Opening up closings', *Semiotica*, 7: 289–327. Abridged in A. Jaworski and N. Coupland (eds) 1999, *The Discourse Reader*, London and New York: Routledge.

Scollon, R. 2001, 'Action and text: towards an integrated understanding of the place of text in social (inter)action, mediated discourse analysis and the problem of social action', in R. Wodak and M. Meyer (eds), *Methods of Critical Discourse Analysis*, London: Sage Publications.

Sealey, A. and Carter, B. 2004, *Applied Linguistics as Social Science*, London and New York: Continuum.

Searle, J. T. 1971, 'What is a speech act?' in J. R. Searle (ed.), *The Philosophy of Language*, Oxford: Oxford University Press, pp. 39–53.

Shapiro, M. (ed.) 1984, *Language and Politics*, Oxford: Basil Blackwell.

Shuy, R. W. 1993, *Language Crimes: The Use and Abuse of Language Evidence in the Courtroom*, Cambridge, MA: Blackwell.

Sinclair, J. and Coulthard, R. M. 1975, *Towards an Analysis of Discourse*, Oxford: Oxford University Press.

Sinclair, J. M., Hoey, M. P. and Fox, G. (eds) 1993, *Techniques of Description: A Festschrift for Malcolm Coulthard*, London: Routledge.

Sperber, D. and Wilson, D. 1986, *Relevance: Communication and Cognition*, Cambridge, MA: Harvard University Press.

Stauffer, R. C., Abrams, J. and Pikulski, A. 1978, *Diagnosis, Correction and Prevention of Reading Disabilities*, New York: Harper & Row.

Stubbs, M. 1996, *Text and Corpus Analysis: Computer Assisted Studies of Language and Culture*, Oxford: Blackwell.

Stubbs, M. 2004, 'Human and inhuman geography: a comparative analysis of two long texts and a corpus', in C. Coffin, A. Hewings and K. O'Halloran (eds), *Applying English Grammar: Functional and Corpus Approaches*, London: Hodder Arnold.

Sunderland, J. (ed.) 1994, *Exploring Gender*, London: Prentice Hall.

Swales, J. M. 1990, *Genre Analysis: English in Academic and Research Settings*, Cambridge: Cambridge University Press.

Tannen, D. (ed.) 1993, *Gender and Conversational Interaction*, New York: Oxford University Press.

Thompson, G. 2004, *Introducing Functional Grammar*, 2nd edn, London: Arnold.

Tiefer, L. 2006, 'Female sexual dysfunction: a case study of disease mongering and activist resistance', *PLoS Medicine*, 3/2: e178. Online free access journal. www.plosmedicine.org

Toolan, M. J. 1991, *Narrative: A Critical Linguistic Introduction*, London and New York: Routledge.

Toolan, M. J. (ed.) 2002, *Critical Discourse Analysis: Critical Concepts in Linguistics*, New York: Routledge.

Tsui, A. 1994, *English Conversation*, Oxford: Oxford University Press.

United Nations Department of Economic and Social Affairs, 2005, *Statistics and Indicators on Women and Men*, New York: United Nations.

United Nations International Covenant on Civil and Political Rights, Geneva: Office of the U.N. High Commissioner for Human Rights. www.ohchr.org

United States Government 2000, *Statement on Ethnic and Racial Classification Used in Census 2000 and Beyond*, Washington, DC: US Census Bureau. www.census.gov/

Ure, J. 1971, 'Lexical density and register differentiation', in G. Perren and J. Trim (eds), *Applications of Linguistics*, Cambridge: Cambridge University Press.

van Dijk, T. A. 1991, *Racism and the Press*, London: Routledge.

van Dijk, T. A. 1992, 'Discourse and the denial of racism', *Discourse and Society*, 3: 87–118. Excerpt in A. Jaworski and N. Coupland (eds) 1999, *The Discourse Reader*, London and New York: Routledge.

van Dijk, T. A. 1993a, 'Principles of critical discourse analysis', *Discourse and Society*, 4: 249–83. Reprinted in J. Cheshire and J. Trudgill (eds) 1998, *The Sociolinguistics Reader*, vol. 2, London: Arnold.

van Dijk, T. A. 1993b, *Elite Discourse and Racism*, Newbury Park, CA: Sage.

van Dijk, T. A. 1996, 'Discourse, power and access', in C. R. Caldas-Coulthard and M. Coulthard (eds), *Texts and Practices: Readings in Critical Discourse Analysis*, London: Routledge.

van Dijk, T. A. (ed.) 1997a, *Discourse Studies: A Multidisciplinary Introduction*, vol. 1: *Discourse as Structure and Process*, London: Sage.

van Dijk, T. A. (ed.) 1997b, *Discourse Studies: A Multidisciplinary Introduction*, vol. 2: *Discourse as Social Interaction*, London: Sage.

van Dijk, T. A. 1998a, *Ideology: A Multidisciplinary Approach*, London: Sage.

van Dijk, T. A. 1998b, 'Opinions and ideologies in the press', in A. Bell and P. Garrett (eds), *Approaches to Media Discourse*, Oxford: Blackwell.

van Dijk, T. A. 1998c, 'Principles of critical discourse analysis', in J. Cheshire and P. Trudgill (eds), *The Sociolinguistics Reader* 2. *Gender and Discourse*, London: Arnold.

van Leeuwen, T. 2004, *Social Semiotics*, London: Routledge.

van Leeuwen, T. 2005, *Introduction to Social Semiotics*, London: Routledge.

Ventola, E. (ed.) 1991, *Functional and Systemic Linguistics: Approaches and Uses*, Berlin and New York: Mouton de Gruyter.

Ventola, E. and Mauranen, A. (eds) 1996, *Academic Writing: Intercultural and Textual Issues*, Amsterdam: John Benjamins.

Walsh, M. 1994, 'Interactional styles in the courtroom: an example from northern Australia', in J. Gibbons (ed.), *Language and the Law*, Harlow: Longman.

Ward, M. 2004, 'We have the power – or do we? Pronouns of power and solidarity in a union context', in L. Young and C. Harrison (eds), *Systemic Functional Linguistics and Critical Discourse Analysis: Studies in Social Change*, London: Continuum.

Weiss, G. and Wodak, R. (eds) 2003, *Critical Discourse Analysis: Theory and Interdisciplinarity*, Houndmills: Palgrave Macmillan.

Wharton, S. 2005, 'Invisible females, incapable males: gender construction in children's reading schemes', *Language in Education*, 19(3).

Wheen, F. 1999, *Karl Marx*, London: Fourth Estate.

White, P. 2004, 'Subjectivity, evaluation and point of view in media discourse', in C. Coffin, A. Hewings and K. O'Halloran (eds), *Applying English Grammar*, London: Hodder Arnold.

Wodak, R. 1989, *Language, Power and Ideology: Studies in Political Discourse*, Amsterdam: John Benjamins.

Wodak, R. 1996, 'The genesis of racist discourse in Austria since 1989', in M. Coulthard and C. R. Caldas-Coulthard (eds), *Texts and Practices*, London: Routledge.

Wodak, R. (ed.) 1997, *Gender and Discourse*, London: Sage.

Wodak, R., de Cilia, R., Reisigl, M. and Liebhart, K. 1999, *The Discursive Construction of National Identity*, Edinburgh: Edinburgh University Press.

Wodak, R. and Meyer, M. (eds) 2001, *Methods of Critical Discourse Analysis*, London: Sage.

Woolls, D. 2003, 'Better tools for the trade and how to use them', *Journal of Speech, Language and Law*, 10: 102–12.

Young, L. and Harrison, C. (eds) 2004, *Systemic Functional Linguistics and Critical Discourse Analysis: Studies in Social Change*, London and New York: Continuum.

Index